MW00878889

Also from Alice Nguyen Swann

(as Nguyen Le Dung) *Le Poème du Vietnam*, Genève, Suisse: Editions Perret-Gentil, 1972—a runner up second after the winner of the Literary Prize for Asia in 1973 (ADELF)

(as Nguyen Le Dung) Le Chemin de la Vie, Ottawa, Canada: Bhakti Press, 1977

My
Journey from
Saigon
to
Ottawa

ALICE SWANN

WESTBOW
PRESS®
A DIVISION OF THOMAS NELSON
& ZONDERVAN

Copyright © 2018 Alice Swann.

All rights reserved. No part of this book may be used or reproduced by any means, graphic, electronic, or mechanical, including photocopying, recording, taping or by any information storage retrieval system without the written permission of the author except in the case of brief quotations embodied in critical articles and reviews.

This book is a work of non-fiction. Unless otherwise noted, the author and the publisher make no explicit guarantees as to the accuracy of the information contained in this book and in some cases, names of people and places have been altered to protect their privacy.

WestBow Press books may be ordered through booksellers or by contacting:

WestBow Press
A Division of Thomas Nelson & Zondervan
1663 Liberty Drive
Bloomington, IN 47403
www.westbowpress.com
1 (866) 928-1240

Because of the dynamic nature of the Internet, any web addresses or links contained in this book may have changed since publication and may no longer be valid. The views expressed in this work are solely those of the author and do not necessarily reflect the views of the publisher, and the publisher hereby disclaims any responsibility for them.

Any people depicted in stock imagery provided by Getty Images are models, and such images are being used for illustrative purposes only.
Certain stock imagery © Getty Images.

ISBN: 978-1-9736-3493-5 (sc)
ISBN: 978-1-9736-3492-8 (hc)
ISBN: 978-1-9736-3494-2 (e)

Library of Congress Control Number: 2018908661

Print information available on the last page.

WestBow Press rev. date: 07/30/2018

To Julian, Christopher,
Sophie, Quentin, and Baptiste

Contents

Foreword

Alice Swann succeeds in capturing the attention of the reader, from the beginning of this tale, by describing the very complex nature of Vietnam's history, customs, family structure, and culture.

But this is a woman who has lived a full life on three continents and made her mark wherever she set foot. Her description of her life in Europe is detailed and tantalizing. In particular I found her relationship with her godfather both deep and warm. It was he who urged her to serve her country, by working for the Embassy of Vietnam, which in turn exposed her to so many interesting characters, including her first lover. There, her self-assurance came through despite her young age and her Oriental background. But life becomes complicated halfway through, when she gets pregnant by Jean Paul, all because of her ignorance about contraception. But the love story is a tender and exciting segment of the book. The adoption of her daughter is a well described but difficult chapter in her life.

She ends up in Canada, where she also makes her mark, and where she interacts with famous women who help the Vietnamese refugees settle. Among these are the mayor of Ottawa, Marion Dewar, and the minister of foreign affairs, Flora McDonald.

She herself becomes a Canadian citizen in 1978 and shortly after that gets married to Julian Swann, who invites her out to dinner and proposes to her at the end of it! How many women can tell a story like that? This is a tender, tumultuous, and tantalizing tale that should make interesting reading.

Qais Ghanem, Author, retired physician
www.qaisghanem.ca

Preface

I always had felt the deep desire to write about my unusual journey from Saigon to Ottawa, which occurred during the first thirty-four years of my existence.

My story is a story of faith, as I converted to Roman Catholicism on December 8, 1962, in Belgium.

A witness of Vietnam history—thanks to my family, whose many members and friends were part of that history—I served the Republic of Vietnam, but my diplomatic position was cut short by the political and military events happening in Saigon in 1975.

I was also the first Vietnamese girl to represent the Republic of Vietnam at a magnificent mass celebrated by Pope Paul VI in the Basilica St. Peter on December 8, 1966, in honor of the Catholic Missions in China, Korea, Japan, and Vietnam.

My journey had unexpected crossroads, honors, sorrows, and love stories. I narrated how my journey had begun and what had happened, which made it feel like an incredible tale.

Acknowledgments

I wish to express my thanks to my husband, Julian Swann; my sister-in-law, Bridgid Swann Dunn; my godmother, Claire de Bethune; Tove, widow of ambassador Le Van Loi; my brother Maurice and his spouse Bich Van; my brother Henri; my sisters Anna and Annie; my cousin Therese Thu Huong; Val Coates; Jo-Anne Dillon; my daughter Sophie Scaillet, my son Christopher Swann; other friends and other family members for their support and encouragements.

I wish especially to thank Dr. Qais Ghanem for writing the foreword.

My Journey Begins in Saigon

Remembrance of things past
—Marcel Proust

I was born on November 3, 1941, in Saigon, South Vietnam.

Three centuries ago, Saigon was only a small fishing village bordering a river. The name "Saigon" came from a Cambodian word that means "kapok tree forest." Conquered by the French in 1861, this village developed quickly and became a major harbor and a city influenced by French elegance, with spacious boulevards and colonial-style villas. I remember the French luxury stores on Charner Avenue and Catinat Street, eating ice cream "*Chez Bodard,*" and strolling with my sister Annie in front of elegant hotels like the Continental Palace, the Majestic, and the Caravelle, which were full of foreign journalists and tourists sitting outdoors, enjoying their drinks. Saigon was called "the Paris of the Orient" and "The Pearl of the Far East."

In the nineteenth century, the French took over South Vietnam because they had modern warships and mighty gunpowder. The Vietnamese were mostly an agricultural population led by cultured mandarins. They lived in harmony with heaven and earth, with beliefs in spirits and guided by principled philosophy and wisdom. As they did not possess powerful modern weapons, South Vietnam, or Cochinchina, was easily conquered by the French and became their colony. The North, or Tonkin, and the Centre, or Annam, had the status of French protectorates. French Indochina was constituted by Vietnam, Cambodia, and Laos, and this beautiful peninsula was lusciously green, and rich in mining resources.

South Vietnam was a fertile and happy land. The fields yielded good crops. The population had a better and more relaxed life than in the North.

1

It shaped their characteristics. They were easygoing, less austere and rigid than the northerners, generous, and joyful. Their lifestyle was influenced by French culture, and they took the best from the French and made it Vietnamese. Over the past centuries, there were Chinese, Cambodian, and Indian immigrants who coexisted well and survived with small trade. The unique culture was also an assimilation of diverse cultures and populations our ancestors found on their way from Tibet, where they began their journey. They descended slowly along the Mekong River to the extremity of Camau, the pointed end of South Vietnam. Vietnam was characterized by two fertile rice baskets, which were the Red River delta in the North and the Mekong delta in the South.

North Vietnam was mountainous. The land was arid and the climate windy and cold. North Vietnamese had a tough life and suffered often from famine. Revolutionary ideas and resistance against the oppressors were more ebullient and violent in the North than in the South. North Vietnam bordered South China, and over the past millennia, the North Vietnamese had had to fight against Chinese invasions. China had always aimed to annex Vietnam as a Chinese province. The Chinese had been permanent enemies of the Vietnamese, and feelings of hostility between Chinese and Vietnamese never died.

I remember the beautiful postal stamps of Cochinchina from when I was a child. They showed the pictures of Emperor Bao Dai, Empress Nam Phuong, and Fr. Alexandre de Rhodes, a Portuguese-born Catholic missionary of the seventeenth century who invented the modern Vietnamese language by harmoniously combining the Latin alphabet and the six musical accents he heard from the local population. The Vietnamese talked like birds, and each word had six different accents that imparted six different meanings. Classic Vietnamese had derived from Chinese words. Scholars like our Father knew both classic and modern Vietnamese. Younger generations in general knew how to write and speak only modern Vietnamese.

The traditional Vietnamese society and family can be found in this definition written by the sociologist Phan Thi Dac: "In Vietnam, community life (large families, villages, districts) appears so conform to natural laws that the Vietnamese have a tendency to consider all those who neglect it or who detach themselves from it as ungrateful and selfish. The

Vietnamese found disrespectful the manifestations of the 'Me' too obvious from occidentals. In all walks of life, society controls the Vietnamese and do not let them forget that they are members of the group and that they owe everything to the group."

Happiness was perceived as the perfect harmony between human beings, including parental approval, the family honor (genuine or mistaken), and public opinion (justified or not). A respectable man was born among traditions and rites. As an adolescent, he learned perfection through culture. As a mature man, he aimed to attain wisdom in following the paths of spirituality. This way of life often led to tolerance and detachment.

Rural Vietnam was divided in districts and villages. Imperial authority had no precedence over village customs. The Vietnamese village was remarkably organized and constituted the religious, social, and political life of its inhabitants. The traditional village offered a peaceful landscape. Its fragile houses standing in mud, straw roofs, small vegetable plots, fruit trees' blossoms, coconut trees, bamboo groves, buffaloes, and pond with lilies and croaking frogs offered a vision of happy life. Children playing flutes and singing whirled around venerable elders; meanwhile, from beneath the shadows of the banyan trees, one could hear the monks and nuns' monotonous prayers and the sounds of the gongs.

Marriage and destiny were inseparable. Marriage was a formality with or without love. Marriage was not an institution for the happiness of the individual but an institution for the family. Its purpose was to solidify the continuity of the family and the assurance given to parents becoming ancestors that their cult would be honored and their tombstones would be well taken care of. The wife had to be submissive to her in-laws.

Confucius had declared that the greatest impiety for a woman was to be sterile and not able to give birth to children. A child was a blessing from heaven. That legitimized polygamy. The more children a man could have, the greater were his blessings. Children would guarantee his posterity, the cult of the ancestors, and the family name.

During the course of our history, Vietnamese women were famous for their participation in the wars against invaders. Before the arrival of the French, those invaders were the pirates coming from the seas, the Chinese during thousands of years, and the Mongolians in the thirteenth century. Vietnamese women were cultured. They were fine musicians and poets.

The national heroes of Vietnam had praised the virtues of their mothers, wives and daughters.

The Vietnamese after 1930 had access to French schools in Vietnam and French universities in France.

The status of women had historically always been almost equal to men. The new constitution of 1967 recognized that absolute equality between men and women in all walks of life. Continuous wars obliged women to get out from their homes. They replaced the men who had gone to battles or had died. They were often left alone to administer large estates, to enter the workforce, and to raise, alone, their children.

My Family

My brother Francois Nguyen Vo Trung, born in 1939, and I, born two years later, came into this world at the clinic of Dr. Henriette Bui Quang Chieu, the first Vietnamese female doctor of Vietnam. Her private clinic was also the first of its kind in Saigon. Dr. Henriette Bui, the first Vietnamese woman who graduated with a medical degree from the University of Paris in 1934, was a pioneer in the field of medicine. She stood up against discrimination under a French colonial regime.

I was born as a French citizen. In 1940, my father, the Doc Phu Su Nguyen Van Ba, and my mother were granted French citizenship. This was a rare privilege. Only some Vietnamese officials obtained it. My five brothers and two sisters, born before 1940, did not have French citizenship.

Father, born in 1901 in Mytho, and Mother, born as Nguyen Thi Liem in 1905 in Travinh, had celebrated their wedding in 1924. Mother was the youngest daughter of an agricultural mandarin from the province of Travinh. It was an arranged marriage, but the union was made in heaven because Father began a promising administrative career and Mother was a sweet beauty with refined features, an ivory complexion, and eyes in the form of a dove. She was young and healthy, and that was a good sign of fecundity.

Our custom taught the daughter to be submissive to the father and the wife to be submissive to the husband, and afterward, if she became a widow, to the eldest son. The family was dominated by the father, who was considered as the patriarch. The wife was a dependent and had to be submissive to her in-laws—especially to her mother-in-law. Well-behaved children had to be silent. It was impolite and inadmissible for them to talk without being asked a question, or to discuss their opinions with their parents.

Confucius had said, "How could an egg teach wisdom to a duck?" and Confucius was always right.

They were blessed with the arrival of five sons and three daughters.

My siblings were Vietnamese citizens, but they benefitted, like me, from an excellent French education at the two French lycées of Saigon. Lycée Chasseloup-Laubat was founded for boys, and Lycée Marie Curie for girls.

Rene Nguyen Vo Quan, our eldest brother, Brother Two, was followed in succession by Henri Nguyen Vo Dieu, Anna Nguyen Vo Le Khanh, Albert Nguyen Vo My, Annie Nguyen Vo Le Hanh, Maurice Nguyen Vo Duc, and Francois Nguyen Vo Trung. They were called by French names, but French names did not appear on their birth certificates.

I was the youngest and eighth child. My Vietnamese first name was Le Dung, which was pronounced "Zung" in the North or "Yung" in the South. I translated it in French as "the beauty of a tear." "*Le*" means "a drop of tear" but can also mean "beauty"—one among many forms of beauty. "*Dung*" also means "beauty."

Child One did not exist. In Vietnam, children were numbered from the eldest, who was Child Two. Following the custom, Child One was an imaginary one sacrificed to the devil so it would not harm the other children of the family.

My siblings had the name Vo added to the family name Nguyen. I did not have the name Vo because I had "Alice" on my French birth certificate, and this was considered long enough.

Our ancestors were members of the Vo family. They lost their war against the Nguyen, who took the power as the last imperial dynasty of Vietnam. The Vo had to submit to the Nguyen and take their name, but Father added the name Vo to his children's names. "*Vo*" means "warriors." In our ancestral home in Mytho, built at the end of the nineteenth century, an impressive display of weaponry in bronze from past centuries stood in front of the main altar, where Buddha and the goddess Quan Am were worshipped.

Father had studied at the French lycée Chasseloup-Laubat of Saigon. He was chosen later for highest studies alongside 249 young men from the best families of Vietnam. Some came from modest families but were selected because they were exceptional students. They were trained at the National Superior School of Administration and Law of Hanoi. This school had been founded by the French government to achieve only one purpose, which was to have those young men marry eligible girls of the society after graduation and found the Two Hundred Fifty Great Families of Vietnam. Thus the class of the Doc Phu Su, well versed in French language, laws, and customs, was created at the beginning of the twentieth century to administer and govern Vietnam alongside the French or on behalf of the French.

From 1924 to 1936, Father was an administrator in the provinces of Baria and Bentre. From 1936 to 1945, he worked in Saigon. In 1944, he was promoted to the rank of Doc Phu Su of exceptional class, the highest rank of the Doc Phu Su.

My Family and World War II

During World War II, Father was among some Doc Phu Su with French citizenship who had been integrated into the inner circle of the French governor general of Indochina for consultation and advice. We enjoyed the same status and privileges as other French citizens.

Our family split for security reasons so we would not die all together in the same spot during the war.

Mother, with me in her arms, along with my sister Anna; my brothers Maurice and Francois, two years older than me; and three cousins, daughters of Aunt Five, mother's half-sister; fled to the southwestern provinces, with some male servants for protection. We headed to the Red Coconut—Mother's former home before her wedding.

Mother's group paddled along the arroyos in small barges and stopped to cook rice and pick up water spinach. They made their way through water lilies and lotus flowers. Sometimes a corpse would float by and a hand would be put over my eyes to prevent me from seeing it. Our group tried to avoid the bombing planes, the Japanese troops, and the Vietminh, which was the abbreviated name for the Vietnam League for the Independence of Vietnam, led by Ho Chi Minh. The Japanese and the Vietminh fought against each other and were both feared for their cruelty.

Father, with Annie and Albert, returned to Mytho; this was a wise move for Father's career, as Mytho was closer to Saigon.

In 1943, my maternal grandfather, Ong Phu Nguyen Trung Tri, born in 1876, died. He was the chief of the Binh Phu district and a rich landowner. The French had divided South Vietnam into hundreds of districts, and usually the chief of a district was also its most important and most cultured man. Grandfather's passing left our maternal grandmother without financial means. The peasants had occupied their land, taking advantage of the

Communist revolution, which was as violent and bloody as in China. Many landowners were killed and their land distributed to the peasants.

My maternal grandmother, born in 1883 as Le Thi Lanh, was the second wife, and Mother was her only daughter. Mother had three elder half-brothers and a half-sister, Aunt Five. One of the brothers was assassinated by the Vietminh, and another one survived by living humbly as a peasant.

Aunt Five became a widow, left with five children, and had a hard life. Aunt Five was a tall and strong woman with a tan complexion. She lived in a big house in Travinh, but she had to gather wood and fruit in the countryside in order to sell them at the market to get some money. She risked her life every day with those trips, as it was not safe with the war going on and the Vietminh killing former landowners.

Mother was lucky, being well married to a high-ranking mandarin. She was delicate, with ivory skin and refined features. I remember her walking gracefully in her silky embroidered tunics. I still remember her velvet-black eyes, and a thin red line on her lips stood out from her beautiful white powdered face. A French fragrance followed in her footsteps. Women had different styles when they tied up their hair depending, on their region of origin. Mother was a typical southern lady, which was made obvious by the way she rolled her long black hair into a bun above her neck. A large silk scarf around her shoulders was her inseparable accessory.

Travinh was Mother's province. It was beautiful, with an abundance of green rice paddies, fruit orchards, coconut trees, and bamboo groves. It was the prettiest city of the Mekong delta, with large avenues lined with venerable leafy trees. The food was similar to Cambodian food, as Travinh was near the Cambodian border.

Fermented and pickled fish and shrimp were salty and spicy, and these were eaten with unripe bananas, sour star fruit, and aromatic herbs, such as mint, basil, coriander, lemongrass, ginger and so on. The market was crowded with Cambodians, who were easily recognizable by their typical large checked scarves tied around their head and shoulders.

President Franklin D. Roosevelt commented about Indochina, "France has had the country for nearly one hundred years and the people are worse off than they were at the beginning. France has milked it for one hundred years. The people of Indochina are entitled to something better than that."

On March 9, 1945, Japan ended French domination in Indochina. In previous years, they had left the French Vichy administration in peace in Vietnam in exchange for free passage and food resources to feed Japanese troops. With the growing popularity of General Charles de Gaulle among the French, they did not trust the French anymore. Japanese soldiers arrested the French governor general and imprisoned French troops and civilians.

President F. D. Roosevelt proposed to General Chiang Kai Sheik that Vietnam be placed under Chinese control. Chiang Kai Sheik refused, saying, "They are not Chinese, they would not assimilate to the Chinese population." The Chinese leader knew very well the history of Vietnam and its two thousand years of resistance against Chinese invasions.

In August 1945, the Japanese troops capitulated. On September 2, 1945, Japan signed its surrender aboard the USS *Missouri*, which was anchored in Tokyo Bay.

Ho Chi Minh then proclaimed the independence of Vietnam with words inspired by the American Declaration of Independence: "We hold truths that all men are created equals, that they are endowed by their creator with certain unalienable rights, among these are life, liberty and the pursuit of happiness."

The Vietminh emerged during the Second World War as the only Vietnamese organized force fighting French colonialism and Japanese domination. They helped the American pilots shot down by the Japanese, with expectations that the Americans would support them later in their struggle for independence.

British General Douglas D. Gracey was in charge of Vietnam after the Japanese capitulation. He disobeyed the orders of Lord Louis Mountbatten to remain neutral between the different factions in Vietnam and to not interfere. Having experienced a British colonial past, he sided with the French and rearmed them, with the help of Japanese soldiers. He ignored the Vietminh delegates.

US General Douglas MacArthur, from Tokyo, commented with disgust, "If there is anything which made my blood boil, it is to see our allies in Indochina deploying Japanese troops to reconquer the people we have promised to liberate …It is the most ignoble form of betrayal."

General Charles de Gaulle, the leader of France, wanted to restore his nation's former colonial power in Vietnam. Indochina was the most beautiful and the richest colony of France, and they would not let it go.

My Family and the Indochina War (1946–1954)

Ho Chi Minh went to France to negotiate the independence of Vietnam, but the negotiations failed. He returned to Vietnam on an ocean liner so he had time to meditate and decide on the next move. He declared war on France. The French returned to Vietnam with tanks and troops commanded by General Jacques Phillippe Leclerc. The Indochina War began on December 19, 1946, with atrocious massacres from both sides.

Our family reunited in Saigon in 1946, and we took residence at number 172, Chasseloup-Laubat Street.

The Indochina War began as a colonial war.

Ho Chi Minh predicted that "it would be a war between an elephant and a tiger. If the tiger ever stands still, the elephant will crush him with his mighty tusks. But the tiger will not stand still…He will leap upon the back of the elephant, tearing huge chunks from his side, and then he will leap back into the dark jungle. And slowly the elephant will bleed to death. That will be the war of Indochina."

The Vietnamese were divided between two choices: siding with the Vietminh or siding with the French. Ho Chi Minh was a Communist. The Vietnamese wanted independence, but they did not want to live under a communist regime. The tragedy of Vietnam was that Ho Chi Minh was communist and the independence of Vietnam under communism was his goal. The Vietminh assassinated rich people and landowners in the name of social justice.

The Vietnamese did not consider the French living in France as their enemies. They hated only the French colonialists coming to Indochina to exploit the resources of the country for their own greed. Along with the colonialists came also the good people, such as scientists, doctors, teachers, humanitarians, and missionaries.

As a privileged child, I grew up in the French culture. My teachers were French, and I looked up to them as my educators and role models. Every year, the French doctor and his team came to the French schools and performed routine medical checkups on the children. We were given injections and vaccinations against major tropical diseases.

I saw in the streets the coolies, the cyclos, the "pousse-pousses" (pedicabs) pushed by meagre and sick men sweating under the scorching sun of the tropics, beggars and lepers in the streets, children walking without shoes, and prisoners chained to one another, probably about to be shipped off to the Island of Poulo Condor to languish there, or to be tortured or executed. Any time we walked under the walls of the Chi Hoa jail, I heard that it was a terrible prison and that political prisoners were tortured there.

Studying at the French lycée Marie Curie, I returned home to the smell of delicious food, played with my brothers Maurice and Francois, and read with them the series of Spirou and Tintin books. My favorite books were Becassine, the tales of the Countess of Segur, and the tales of Charles Perrault.

From 1946 to 1948, we lived near the Saigon Zoo and Botanical Gardens, and my early childhood after school was spent in those public gardens with my brothers, sisters, and cousins. We fed small monkeys peanuts, and we were familiar with the jungle animals—for instance, the gorillas, elephants, tigers, the birds of paradise, parrots, and giant butterflies. The Saigon Zoo and Botanical Gardens were internationally famous for their orchids and their museum of ancient Asian cultures.

In 1948, we moved to another house inside a courtyard. I had been told not to play with the children of the neighborhood. We had to keep our distance from others, and we were not to trust people, not knowing where the enemy was hidden. Social class also played a role.

I kept myself busy catching butterflies and dragonflies in a corner full of tall grass. Maurice and Francois rode their bikes. I had no bicycle small enough for my size. As the baby of the family, I had no one of my age to play or exchange ideas with, so I became a loner.

No one in Saigon knew what would happen at the end of World War

II. Father was a French citizen and was French educated and trained in French law and public administration, so naturally he chose to side with the French. He was a Doc Phu Su and the Doc Phu Su were the highest-ranking administrative mandarins and loyal supporters of Emperor Bao Dai. Ho Chi Minh, unfortunately, was a Communist leader, and the Vietminh were known for being cruel toward landlords and governmental officials.

The Doc Phu Su Nguyen Van Hai was Father's best friend at the Superior School of Public Administration and Law of Hanoi and was born in Ban Me Thuot. The two had opposite characteristics. Nguyen Van Hai was handsome and tall, with a strong personality. He was a born leader. He rose from the ranks because of his outstanding intellectual and leadership qualities. Father was timid and vulnerable. Nguyen Van Hai acted like an elder brother to him and protected him. After graduation, Father invited his friend to his family home in Mytho, and Nguyen Van Hai married Father's sister, Aunt Three.

The Doc Phu Su Nguyen Van Hai became Uncle Three to us. He was appointed chief of the provinces of Baria, Ha Tien, and Chau Doc, which were dangerous provinces far from the central government of Saigon. He came once a month to Saigon to present his report to the government. He traveled back and forth with a convoy of French soldiers to protect him and other travelers. As the Vietminh ambushed and attacked travelers, they needed armed protection.

As he resided in a very dangerous faraway province, Aunt Three was forbidden by her family to join him and live with him. She stayed in the Mytho house to keep Grandmother company. It was a normal duty for a daughter, even a married one, to stay with her parents to look after them. The blood that united family members was much more important than alliances and marriage ties. Members of a family composed of parents and children, brothers and sisters, were a tight-knit entity because they had the same blood.

Nguyen Van Vinh, Uncle Ten, was Father's youngest brother. At eighteen years old, after sailing aboard a French ocean liner to discover the world, he chose to follow the Vietminh, and one night in 1946, he fled the Mytho ancestral house to join Ho Chi Minh in the North. Our family never spoke with him or about him anymore. He ceased to exist.

His war name in the Vietminh army was Vo The Phong. He fought with Ho Chi Minh's troops against the French, and afterward against the Americans, always believing that he was defending his country against foreign aggression and imperialism.

In 1947, Ong Phu Nguyen Van Tai, our paternal grandfather, born in 1874, passed away. I remember once seeing him. He was sitting on a carved black armchair, in his traditional Vietnamese tunic and turban, with a meagre beard, smoking a French cigarette.

I was fascinated by Grandfather's long, curved, spiraling fingernails, which indicated his status as a mandarin who did not do any manual work with his hands and fingers. On the day of his funeral, the House of the Ancestors became silent and the elders who came to present their respects whispered when they talked.

It was typical for men to smoke cigarettes and drink beer, due to the influence of French colonization. South Vietnam was a big producer of rice, tobacco, rubber, tea, and coffee. Beer, introduced by the French, became a renowned Vietnamese national product. French companies prospered, and Saigon glittered with huge signs reading, for instance, "Brasseries de l'Indochine," "Distilleries de l'Indochine," "Cigarettes Marlboro," "Cigarettes Gauloises," and "Pneus Michelin."

Inside a Vietnamese home, a warm teapot stood in permanence on a tray with teacups, and a servant came at regular intervals to replenish it with boiling water. We could drink tea anytime we wished.

We drank coffee in large glasses with milk—usually canned sweetened condensed milk imported from France. We did not have cattle and cows for fresh milk. Butter and cheeses were imported from France. We drank coffee and milk for breakfast before going to school. Vietnamese-made French baguettes were eaten as much as rice. That crusty bread, stuffed with cold cuts and pickled carrots, was delicious.

Mytho was Father's province and town. Seventy kilometers from Saigon, it was a busy, prosperous trading and commercial city on the border of a branch of the Mekong called the Tien Giang, or Upper River. Mytho was famous for its floating market full of sampans selling fruit, vegetables, and all kind of goods. It was also famous for its noodle soup, called "*huu tieu Mytho.*"

Every morning, for breakfast, a servant was sent to the central market near our House of the Ancestors to buy this famous soup. A weekend spent in Mytho included savoring the huu tieu Mytho during breakfast or the afternoon break. Vietnamese had an ingenious system to carry takeout food. Round containers made of steel were stacked one above another along two long rods so different food items could be stored in individual containers.

As the eldest of three sons, Father inherited from Grandfather and was also in charge of the cult of the ancestors. A portion of the inheritance, called "*huong hoa*" was put aside to cover the costs of the cult of the ancestors. Vietnamese wanted to be sure that after their death, they would be well buried and well honored with altars, food offerings, and Buddhist prayers. If they were neglected, they would become lost wandering souls. Children were expected to look after their elders when they were alive and to honor them with a cult after their deaths. It was considered a blessing to have several children.

Father inherited immense rice fields, orchards, and the Mytho house, but that house was not our primary or permanent residence. We resided in Saigon. Grandmother lived in the Mytho house, and Father made it mandatory for us as our pious duty to visit her during weekends. The address of our ancestral house was 36 Do Huu Vi Avenue. It was named after a Vietnamese pilot who died for France during World War I. Along our avenue were also lined-up properties that belonged to our family. Grandfather divided his estate into properties and gave them to Uncle Five, Aunt Six and Aunt Nine. Great Aunt also had her house and garden next to our other cousins. Relatives having the same bloodline lived next to each other along this large avenue leading to the central market and the grand theater.

Outside the house's gate, we could sit on a marble bench and watch passing people and the activities along our avenue. An iron gate, enlaced by the branches of an old bougainvillea tree, gave access to the house. The purple flowers were alive but looked dry like silk paper. I never saw this tree being watered, except by rains.

When we entered the front yard, the first thing we saw was an aquarium with a huge fish. It could not move, and it looked very old. It was obviously alive, because its mouth had bubbles going in and out. It could live beyond one hundred years and symbolized longevity. Planters held miniature orange trees, and the fragrance of the tiny white blossoms perfumed the air. We sat on pink marble benches, enjoying the fresh breeze.

The busy and large kitchen was linked to the main dining room, where elderly women, grandmother's friends, sat on low divans in wood and socialized. We, visitors from Saigon, ate at a round dining table. Four generations gathered to spend the weekends together.

In the front of the house was located the principal reception room, where we honored Buddha, the goddess Quan Am, and our ancestors up to the seventh generation. This huge room scared me with its pictures of the ancestors, the dim lights, the scented smoke of the incense sticks, the cold drafts, the mice, the sleeping bats hanging from the wood beams, and the tortoise shells displayed on the walls. We bowed and prayed in front of the altars. When I was alone in that room, I was filled with fear of the supernatural.

Our paternal grandmother, born in 1879 as Le Thi Dau, lived in that house. She had a long life of over one hundred years. After grandfather's passing, she had a daughter, our Aunt Three, living with her. Grandmother was also well looked after by servants.

This house was considered as a temple to honor Buddha and the ancestors. The servants prepared the daily meals to be offered to them. Every day, some elderly ladies visited Grandmother and spent the day with her. They chewed betel rolls and spit the red liquid in small individual brass containers, ate, and played cards. They gossiped. Grandmother was reserved and distant. She listened but rarely talked.

Weekends in Mytho were often crowded with visiting family members. We lived inside a large extended family or inside a community. Those of us who preferred solitude or individualism were classified as oddities. We had to share space with parents or siblings or cousins. That did not disturb me. I was scared of ghosts, and I would never want to sleep alone in a dark room in the Mytho house!

During nighttime, I trembled with terror because the toilets were outdoors and I was scared to go out to pee, as I thought the ghosts might pull out my entrails.

Great Aunt lived across the avenue, and she was Grandfather's elder sister. She was tiny, and blind, looking like a wrinkled apple. She could recognize voices and footsteps and she would called out our names. "Is it you?" Every morning, Grandmother crossed the avenue and visited Great Aunt. She had to pay her respect because Great Aunt was older. That was the custom. Great Aunt lived beyond one hundred years.

A curtain made with beads and pearls formed a screen at the entrance of Great Aunt's house. As a child, I was tempted to pick up some beads and pearls. Hearing the noise, she would yell, "Who is the little devil who is stealing my beads?" In her bedroom was displayed a cute coffin, custom made with the finest and most expensive wood, and lined with silky satin. She was very proud to show off her coffin because it gave her the assurance that she would be well buried.

Nguyen Van The, Father's younger brother, whom we called Uncle Five, enjoyed going to the Mytho Market in his youth to drink beer with his friends and smoke cigarettes. This market near our house also had a grand theatre to entertain the public with popular Chinese opera singers and dancers. Uncle Five was not as well educated as Father. Maybe he was not intellectually gifted, or maybe our grandparents chose to invest more resources in Father's education because Father was the eldest son and the heir. Uncle Five mingled with lower-class people and was clearly at ease with them. One day, he fell in love with a local singer and abandoned the wealthy and aristocratic bride chosen to marry him.

Grandfather was very angry. He never forgave Uncle Five for this disobedience to his authority and disinherited him. Uncle Five, his wife (the singer), and their ten children then lived in poverty, but theirs was a united and happy family. When the children grew up, they worked, helped each other, and weathered the storms of their life well. We visited them anytime we visited Grandmother and Great Aunt.

Uncle Three and Father reached the top of the hierarchy of the Doc Phu Su. The men who married Father's other three sisters (numbers two, six, and nine) were mandarins of a lower rank.

In September of 1947, Henri Nguyen Vo Dieu, our Brother Three, was sent to France for university studies. Henri had been a revolutionary youth—an ardent patriot rioting against French colonialism. The French advised Father to send him to study in France. We went to the Saigon Harbor to say goodbye to Henri.

There were hundreds of Vietnamese youths, boys and girls, mostly from the elite, being sent to France for studies. They crowded the deck of the huge French ocean liner and waved white handkerchiefs to their families. Henri's years of study and career in France from 1947 to 1955 were happy ones, as he had the company of Vietnamese friends of his generation studying with him and belonging to the best families of Vietnam. This group nurtured a strong bond of friendship and solidarity between them that lasted all their life.

Henri attended the University of Bordeaux and continued his law studies at the University of Montpellier.

Independence of Vietnam:
the State of Vietnam (1949-1950)

The French were unable to defeat the Vietminh and realized that the Indochina War, which had begun as a colonial war, was lost.

On March 8, 1949, Emperor Bao Dai signed the Élysée Accords with the president of the French Republic. France recognized Vietnam's independence within the French Union. France retained special privileges for its citizens and armed forces in Vietnam. It retained control over the economy and finances.

On December 15, 1949, the second phase of the Indochina War began, and it would be the war against Ho Chi Minh and communism.

Emperor Bao Dai became head of the State of Vietnam, and on February 7, 1950, the State of Vietnam was recognized officially by the United States and more than fifty other countries of the world.

In 1950, Father continued his career as a Doc Phu Su of exceptional class with the State of Vietnam. As a French citizen, he had higher privileges than a Vietnamese Doc Phu Su with Vietnamese citizenship. He served as director general of the Economic Affairs of Vietnam from 1950 to 1954. His office was on the first floor of a building that housed *Le Journal de L'Extreme-Orient*. When I visited Father, I poked my head inside the main room of the newspaper in the hope to see my classmate, Jacqueline Porcher, whose father was a French journalist and whose mother was Vietnamese. I liked her. She was a beautiful Eurasian.

Father went to work driven by a chauffeur in a black official car with license plate GVN (which stood for "Government of Vietnam"), returned home for lunch, and went back to work in the afternoon. He never talked about politics or war at home. He was cautious.

We were glad that he was not at home most of the day. We breathed better without his presence. Mother was happy in Saigon and in Travinh. In Mytho, the House of the Ancestors belonged to Father, but Mother and us children were not at ease at the Mytho house. We were introverted and incapable of affectionate demonstrations with our paternal grandmother. Mother was a daughter-in-law and a sister-in-law, and usually hers was not a comfortable position. Thanks to Father's high level as a public servant and Uncle Three's protection, no one was mean to her.

In Saigon, Mother, head of the household staff, was busy with responsibilities and the daily food preparation. With the help of servants, and with her daughters Anna and Annie and our cousins Nguyet and Ngoc Lan living with us, she cooked and baked excellent Vietnamese dishes and sweet goodies.

Mother had also assimilated the rites she had to perform with Father all year round to honor Buddha and the ancestors. I accompanied my parents when they went to their favorite pagodas to pray, burn incense sticks, and deliver their offerings. The smoke of the incense sticks enveloped us as a sign of our union with the deceased and with a divine world. Outside the pagodas, there were old banyan trees, and it was believed that they sheltered the souls of the monks who had passed away. I felt no love, connection, or attraction toward the massive golden statues of Buddha looking down on me, an insignificant creature. There was no love lost between those statues and me.

Uncle and Aunt Three had four sons. Aunt Three did not live with her husband in Saigon, because she had to care for Grandmother in Mytho. Three of their four sons had settled with us in our home of Saigon because they studied at the University of Saigon. My parents cherished them. Nguyen Quoc Hung became a judge; Nguyen Minh Chau, a doctor, specialized in obstetrics; and Nguyen Xuan Hue became a public servant.

Uncle Six, the Doc Phu Su Tran Van Ninh, was appointed chief of the province of Travinh and, afterward, of the province of Bien Hoa.

Uncle and Aunt Six had five children. Their third son, Tran Van Au, lived with us because he studied medicine in Saigon. The youngest and fifth son, Lac, stayed a short time with us and was sent to study in Paris, France.

Uncle and Aunt Six invited us to spend our summer vacations at their gorgeous residence in Travinh. The residence of the chief of the province of Travinh, beautiful and romantic, looked like a château surrounded by iron fences. It had a tennis court, lawns, flowers, and tall leafy trees full of storks' and herons' nests. There were hundreds of white storks and herons flying every day to the swamps and rice fields of Travinh, looking for fish; they would return in the evening with fish to feed their little ones. The ground under those trees, of course, was littered with rotten fish.

The usual architectural plan for the residence of a chief of a province included a gate, and when one entered the compound, there were buildings. One housed the treasury and administration, and the other house was the jail. Prisoners in black shirts and pants, with conical straw hats, could be seen working on the grounds and planting flowers, under the supervision of armed guards.

Meals were delicious. One day, we had a roasted rabbit. In the middle of the dining table, the rabbit's head was displayed to confirm that we were eating a rabbit and not a cat. Another day, we had a soup of storks.

We played tennis. Mother was often absent because she preferred to sneak outside the compound and visit her relatives. Travinh was her province and her town, and she had many cousins to visit. Aunt Six was not happy with Mother's escapades because they were dangerous. We had security and bodyguards all around the place, but Mother left carelessly, and it was not safe.

Uncle Six started his days by touring the countryside with his bodyguards and his soldiers, and he pinned medals on the uniforms of courageous soldiers from our side who had victoriously resisted enemy attacks. He returned in the late afternoon.

Going from Saigon to Travinh could mean a long day of traveling, because we had to cross the Mekong River on a ferryboat. Depending on the traffic, sometimes the wait time was quick. Sometimes we had to wait long hours before boarding the ferryboat. This location was very crowded and busy. Local people sold Vietnamese sandwiches, roasted quail, and freshly cut pineapple to feed people while they waited.

When Uncle Six was posted later as chief of the province of Bien Hoa, north of Saigon, the ride by car was much shorter. We had to drive along a steel bridge guarded by Senegalese troops leading to the gates of Bien Hoa. It was forbidden to throw anything from the windows of cars. The Vietminh aimed to blow up bridges that were vital for travel, communication, and trade. The Senegalese soldiers made an unforgettable impression on me because they were black and very tall with shining white teeth.

The residence of Bien Hoa, a modern villa, held nothing exciting. Bien Hoa was renowned for its grapefruit and pomelos. Later, in the 1960s, the Americans built the Bien Hoa Highway to connect Bien Hoa, a strategic military location, to the North (the direction of North Vietnam) and to the South (Saigon).

Uncle Nine, the Doc Phu Su Le Minh Tung, served as mayor of the first district of Saigon from 1950 to 1968. The family lived in the heart of Saigon, above the police headquarters and across from the National Assembly Building, formerly the Grand Opera House.

Le Minh Tung was a handsome young man with a white complexion and curly hair, and Aunt Nine, born as Nguyen Thi Ngoc "Pearl", was celebrated as Miss Beauty of Mytho. She was extraordinarily talented in music, poetry, and arts (silk painting). She was romantic and chose to marry for love. Her husband was not as wealthy as her other suitors, but he was the best-looking young man. They had three sons and one daughter, all of whom studied abroad after graduating from the French Lycées of Saigon.

In 1950, Rene Nguyen Vo Quan, our Brother Two, was sent to France to study textile engineering at the University of Lyon. After graduation from Lyon, Rene worked at the Petroleum Institute of Paris as an engineer.

In 1950, the new National Army of Vietnam was created. Fifty young officers were sent to France to be trained as the future leaders of our national army.

General Nguyen Van Hinh, son of the Doc Phu Su Nguyen Van Tam, president of the Council of Vietnam, already trained in the French Air Force, was appointed commander-in-chief of the new National Army of Vietnam. Duong Van Minh was among the senior officers.

General Duong Van Minh was born in 1916 in Mytho. Father had become like a substitute father to young Duong Van Minh after his father died. The two men met in Baria in the 1930s as colleagues and friends. The general's father was a wealthy landowner, and worked in the finance ministry of the French colonial administration. After his death, Father helped his friend's family, and I remember as a child seeing Duong Van

Minh, his wife, his mother, and his sister frequently visiting us. He was older than our brother Rene, so he was considered our elder brother, and we called him Brother Big Minh. He was tall and big with rough brown skin, and he had some replacement teeth covered in gold and a gap between his teeth. When he was a young soldier in *le corps indigene*, part of the French colonial army, he was captured and tortured by the Japanese military police. They knocked out his teeth. Later on, he was captured and tortured by the Vietminh.

Father asked Minh what career he wanted to choose, and Minh, without hesitation, answered, "I want to be a soldier." Father helped him to go to France in 1952 and be further trained at the École Militaire de Paris. He was the first Vietnamese officer to be honored to attend this prestigious establishment. After his return to Vietnam, he was commander of the Saigon-Cholon Garrison in 1954.

In 1950, after Vietnam gained independence, the French troops remained in Vietnam to help the new State of Vietnam in the new war against communism.

In 1950, General Jean De Lattre de Tassigny was appointed commander-in-chief of the French expeditionary forces in Indochina and high commissioner of France (a replacement name for governor general of Indochina). Charismatic and respected, he could have saved a desperate situation for France, but he died from cancer in Paris in 1952. He was promoted to marshal at his deathbed. His only son, Bernard, had been killed the year before during the Battle of Vinh Yen.

Vinh Yen was a fortified city in North Vietnam, not far from Hanoi. In January of 1951, General Giap attacked it. The French responded, fighting back with a detachment of the Muong (hill tribes) soldiers and a detachment of Moroccan soldiers. General De Lattre ordered that all available resources be thrown into the battle. The Vietminh retreated. The French won that battle, but General De Lattre lost his only son, Bernard, who was killed on top of a hill.

His famous speech in Saigon at the French lycée for boys, where my brothers Albert, Maurice, and Francois studied, was very emotional. He proclaimed in front of those young faces of Vietnam, who were hesitant about what side to choose in that war, "Behave like men. If you are Communists, go and join the Vietminh. There are people there who fight well for a bad cause but if you are patriots, fight for your country because this war is your war. And France will fight for you only if you fight with France."

During the following days, inspired by his appeal, a large number of young men joined the new national army. Emperor Bao Dai signed an emergency decree proclaiming officially that the country was at war.

General Henri Navarre replaced General Jean de Lattre de Tassigny and arrived in Saigon in May of 1953. He would be the last French general in Vietnam.

The Battle of Dien Bien Phu; the Defeat of France; The Geneva Agreement (1954); Two Vietnams: The Democratic Republic of Vietnam (North) and the Republic of Vietnam (South)

General Henri Navarre decided to engage in battles with General Vo Nguyen Giap deep in the mountains of North Vietnam. He chose to build a fortress in the valley of Dien Bien Phu as his base of operations, and this was a fatal strategic mistake.

Colonel Christian de Castries was in charge of the Battle of Dien Bien Phu, which would be decisive for France's military prestige in Vietnam. General Giap built a formidable force in the mountains surrounding and looking upon Dien Bien Phu. The French could not move out from this valley and were entrapped.

General Vo Nguyen Giap, the Vietminh commander-in-chief, broadcast his final message to his troops on March 11, 1954: "Remember this historic battle. Determined to destroy the adversary, keep in mind the motto. 'Always attack, always advance'. You must master fear and pain, overcome obstacles, unite your efforts, fight to the very end, annihilate the enemy at Dien Bien Phu and win a great victory!"

At home, we followed the events happening at Dien Bien Phu in French newspapers, and we listened to the news broadcast through the radio. We did not have TV.

On May 6, 1954, Col. Christian de Castries radioed for the last time with Gen. Rene Cogny, and within minutes, Colonel de Castries and his men were submerged by waves and waves of Vietminh soldiers and were taken prisoners. They had to walk in long columns to prison camps. France was humiliated.

A French pilot who flew over Dien Bien Phu reported, "It was complete silence. Only the smell of death rose from the valley."

In 1954, when France lost the Battle of Dien Bien Phu, Vietnamese people were extremely proud to have defeated a former colonial power. Psychologically, it was the victory of the colonized yellow people against the white colonialists. It was a great feeling of empowerment and victory for them.

The defeat of the French army at Dien Bien Phu signaled the beginning of French troubles in other parts of its colonial empire. One example was Algeria. Algerian soldiers returned home and, stimulated by what they saw in Indochina, fought for the independence of Algeria. The Algerian War was atrocious too because the French did not want to lose their colony, but Algeria won its independence in 1962. Moroccan soldiers were not harmed by the Vietminh when they were captured. They married Vietnamese women and were politically brainwashed before they returned to Morocco with wives and children. Senegal became independent in 1961. So Indochina led the way for other French colonies to fight for independence. Ho Chi Minh also became a legendary figure for socialism in South America and Cuba. Fidel Castro was a fierce follower of the Marxist-Leninist doctrine of Ho Chi Minh and his military strategy regarding how to win a guerrilla and subversive war.

On July 20, 1954, the French signed the Geneva Agreement with Ho Chi Minh's delegation. This agreement separated Vietnam at the seventeenth parallel.

The United States, South Vietnam, and Cambodia refused to sign this agreement so they would not be tied up by it in the future. Colonel Christian de Castries and his military men, captured at Dien Bien Phu and taken as prisoners of war, were liberated.

After the partition, the Democratic Republic of Vietnam (North Vietnam) was led by President Ho Chi Minh, and the Republic of Vietnam (South Vietnam) was led by President Ngo Dinh Diem.

Ngo Dinh Diem, a Catholic nationalist who wished to become a monk, was appointed prime minister by Emperor Bao Dai, pressured by the United States. Ngo Dinh Diem had spent years abroad and had a reputation of nationalism.

Our Residence; Family Life; Celebrations

In the spring of 1950, Father was offered one of the sixteen governmental villas, each of which had half an acre of lawn.

This elegant, beautiful green governmental neighborhood was full of history. Those villas faced the private French Saint Paul Clinic across Legrand de la Liraye Avenue (later renamed Phan Thanh Gian). The second row of those villas, behind the first row, faced Ba Huyen Thanh Quan Street. Those villas, similar in architecture—French colonial style—formed a large official compound and had been built during the colonial past for French top officials. They had been taken over by the new Vietnamese government and were very sought after as official residences for high-ranking public servants.

Aunt Five, Mother's half-sister, a widow, had her two eldest daughters join the Vietminh in 1946. They had fled home, seduced by the Vietminh propaganda and later had married their Vietminh comrades. In order to shield her other three children from the Vietminh, and so as not to lose them in the same way, Aunt Five sent her two younger daughters, Nguyet and Ngoc Lan, to live with us in Saigon, and she sacrificed every penny to send her only son, Bernard Ngoc Hue, to study abroad. Sending sons to France was a way to protect them from being drafted into military service and being sent to war. University studies in France were a privilege afforded by the wealthy class. Aunt Five was poor, but she saved every penny for her son's departure. Mother helped her too. The two sisters were always very generous with each other. Ngoc Hue studied at the Academy of Fine Art of Rome. He won the first prize for sculpture at the Academy and later married a French girl and settled as an artist in Normandy, France.

Aunt Five visited us and her two daughters from time to time in Saigon, bringing us fresh fruit, live ducks, and hens as gifts.

In the early 1950s, our neighbor was the Doc Phu Su Thai Lap Thanh, governor of South Vietnam. He died by assassination at Tay Ninh along with the French General Chanson. His two daughters Alice and Jacqueline were friends with our sister Annie, and the friendship lasted all their lives.

In 1954, we had for neighbors the vice president Tran Van Huong and another respected cabinet minister, Vu Van Mau. Both of them lasted very long on the political scene until April 30, 1975. Tran Van Huong was a quiet, moderate, and conciliatory public servant. He did not make enemies. Vu Van Mau was a renowned pious Buddhist. In 1955, he was secretary of state for foreign affairs.

We had lived in this governmental residence for seven years across from the large, storied, and sprawling St. Paul Clinic. Across the street on our right side stood the National College Gia Long, a college for Vietnamese girls. Dressed in Vietnamese long white tunics and pants, most of them rode to the College on bicycles, their heads sheltered from the tropical sun by conical hats. Our sister Annie took a position of French teacher there.

Our residence was built in the middle of a half-acre lot. Mother planted roses and peonies on the front lawn, which had already a huge cactus, a jasmine tree, and palm trees. There was a fountain where a servant washed the laundry by hand. Mother raised chickens and ducklings. They ran everywhere. When they became big and fat, they ended up on the dining table. The hens cackled in pain all day long while laying fresh eggs inside a large poultry shed. I played with tiny turtles.

No one in the neighborhood ever complained about the farm noises coming from our property—especially the endless clucking, the cackling of the hens, and the crowing of the roosters at sunrise. Mother could not be happy without farm activities. She was profoundly nostalgic about her childhood in a rural environment. She was a flower of the Mekong River transplanted into the city, and the Red Coconut of her childhood never left her heart.

Our family was always outdoors, joyful, and full of activity. The other residences were quiet, silent, and without much light or life. None of them were seen outdoors. Some had soldiers guarding the property for fear of Vietminh assassination.

On the right side of the house, Mother planted culinary herbs, fruit trees, vegetables, and banana trees. Those trees provided us with bananas, and we chopped up the tender flowers and shoots for salad and soups. We wrapped food inside banana leaves. We picked papayas, guavas, and plums. Vietnamese people liked to eat sour fruit with salt instead of sugar. We stuffed zucchini flowers, fried them, or boiled them in soups. Sometimes we had a live goose or a live turkey offered by Aunt Five.

We did not then have freezers, fridges, or electric ovens. Food was cooked and preserved inside banana leaves and other edible leaves. There was a pantry called in French the *garde-manger*, where perishable food was kept. Food was cooked with lemongrass, garlic, ginger, and peppercorns, and it could therefore be kept longer than usual. Every morning, the cook walked to the market to buy meat and fish to be used for that day. Live hens were killed in the backyard. For freshness, Mother did not buy already killed and processed chicken or duck at the market.

I had witnessed how our cook, as was the practice of other cooks in China and Vietnam, killed a live hen, duck, or goose while sitting on a stool in the backyard. She slowly slit the throat of the bird and collected the dripping blood in a large bowl. This blood later congealed into a dark red block which would be boiled, cut into square pieces, and mixed in a stew or soup with the bird's giblets, heart, and liver. Afterward the bird would be dropped in a huge caldron of boiling water so the feathers could be removed easily from the skin. In China and Vietnam, nothing was wasted. Everything from the bird was cooked in a delicious way, from its entire head to its feet, including the skin and neck. Of course, all was very well cleaned. This kind of killing appeared barbaric, but it was the way they did it in order to drain the blood from the bird.

The cooking was done above ovens made of earthenware (terra cotta), and we used charcoal and wood.

Mother collected the cooking oil herself from bacon, pork fat, and duck fat. She cut the fat into small cubes and fried it, collecting the grease she saved in huge jars. She made caramel sauce and poured it into big jars too. This was used to cook caramelized pork or fish. She also made fried pickled vegetables with curry paste. Curried food came from the culinary influence of India. She pickled bean sprouts. Most of the vegetables and aromatic herbs came from our garden. Our banana trees in the backyard were very useful. We ate the bananas, and we chopped the banana blossoms for salads. When I was sick with a white-coated tongue, Mother scraped the white fungus from my tongue with banana sap. For vitamins, we had to swallow cod oil. We used penicillin as an antibiotic in the form of a pill or liquid, and it cured all kind of diseases.

President Ngo Dinh Diem was a nationalist. The first thing he did was change French colonialist names to Vietnamese names—mostly names of our national heroes. The names of streets, places, and institutions with French names were speedily changed to Vietnamese names.

The French had to rename Lycée Chasseloup-Laubat (the name of a colonialist admiral) to Lycée Jean Jacques Rousseau. Petit Lycée became Petit Lycée St-Exupery. Lycée Marie Curie, the Pasteur Institute, and Pasteur Street remained untouched. Marie Curie and Pasteur were respected scientists.

Legrand de la Liraye Avenue became Phan Thanh Gian Avenue. Legrand de La Liraye was a colonialist officer. Phan Thanh Gian was a mandarin who came to France at the beginning of the century to negotiate the independence of Vietnam. When he failed, he committed suicide and recommended to his sons, "Never trust the French." Chasseloup-Laubat Street became Hong Thap Tu Street (Red Cross Street). Charles de Gaulle Avenue became Tu Do Avenue (Independence Avenue). The palace of the former French governor general became the Independence Palace or Presidential Palace.

Do Huu Vi Avenue in Mytho changed to Nguyen Hue Avenue. Nguyen Hue was one of our greatest emperors.

In 1955, the French government awarded Father with the Medal of the Legion of Honor. It was its ultimate farewell gift to Father, renowned for his loyalty and integrity as a public servant.

We did not celebrate the New Year on January 1. We celebrated the Lunar New Year, called Tet (an abbreviation for Tet Nguyen Dan), which started with the new moon on the first day of the New Year and ended on the full moon fifteen days later.

Several months before the arrival of a new lunar year, the Saigon Market and the adjacent commercial streets were decorated with strings of bright lights and sophisticated artistic arrangements of fruit, such as apples, grapes, and pears. They were expensive, imported from France and Japan. Vietnamese fruit and gorgeous boxes of candied fruit and vegetables were also displayed. At the flower markets, it was the custom to buy spring branches of peach, cherry trees and other trees with white, yellow, pink, or red blossoms.

The Tet celebrations lasted for seven days, and no physical or domestic work was allowed during that time. Nobody was to clean or cook. Offices and stores were closed. Special food packed inside bananas leaves and other edible leaves, such as betel leaves, were prepared in advance and stored to be savored during Tet. For several weeks before the arrival of Tet, the kitchen was busy, with Mother, my sisters, my cousins, and the cook preparing the caramelized pork, sticky rice, candied fruit, and pickled vegetables. Favorite Tet fruits were watermelons, tangerines, dragon fruit, pomegranates, lychees, and pomelos. The favorite flowers were chrysanthemums, marigolds, flowering branches of the peach tree, and cherry blossoms.

Servants returned to their villages to visit their families. We spent time visiting relatives, eating, and snacking on roasted watermelon seeds, candied plums, fruit, ginger, lotus seeds, and dried tomatoes. We played cards and table tennis (which we called ping-pong.) People visited family tombstones, dusted them, deposited fresh flowers, and prayed. The smoke from burned incense sticks rose in the air.

On the eve of the New Lunar Year, we said goodbye to the gods of the kitchen and sent them off to heaven, where they would present their annual report regarding our family's behavior during the past year. We bribed them with good offerings so their reports would be excellent about us. When midnight came, deafening firecrackers exploded in the yards, welcoming the New Year. Under President Ngo Dinh Diem, firecrackers were forbidden because they sounded like real gunfire, and in wartime, it would be difficult to discern the difference.

People put on new clothing, such as bright dresses, and women showed off their gold or jade necklaces, bracelets, rings, and so on. Gold and jade are said to fight off evil spirits. The red color represented happiness and prosperity. Money given as a gift was put inside a red envelope. Yellow was the color of the emperors and symbolized power. Mourners were dressed in black and white. People made sure they did not do any physical work. They were not to swear, fight, or show a bad temper. Whatever they did during the New Year would be the reflection of what they would be doing during the coming year. Children bowed in front of the elders, wishing them happiness, prosperity, and longevity, and they received in exchange small envelopes of money wrapped in red silk paper.

On the first day of the Lunar Year, Father showed up in his ceremonial tunic, wrapped his turban around his head, and disappeared from home until late afternoon. He had been solicited to visit people. Requests for his visit had been planned in advance. Following our custom, the first person who entered our home on the first day of the New Year, or Tet, had to be a person who symbolized good luck, happiness, honor, and prosperity.

Our parents celebrated Buddhist festivals and anniversaries, and they performed the associated rites. They went to the pagodas, knelt, prayed, and made money offerings.

Vietnamese also venerated the national heroes who had saved the country in times of war. Magnificent temples were built for them. I remember the temple of Marshal Le Van Duyet, who was buried there with his wife. He had been Emperor Gia Long's companion during his battles and had helped him reunify the country. I remember also the temple of General Tran Hung Dao, who, in the thirteenth century, vanquished an army sent by the Mongol emperor Kublai Khan.

Vacations; Cap Saint-Jacques; Dalat

Studying at French lycées meant that we had two weeks of vacation during Christmas holidays and three months of vacations during the summer. As Buddhists, we did not celebrate Christmas.

For the summer vacations, Father sent Mother and us, the children, to Cap Saint-Jacques, where he had the use of a governmental vacation house overlooking Front Beach and the ocean. We could see the passing ships far away. We bought fish from the fishermen. I remember the coconut trees on the beach and the giant almond trees on the sidewalk. Father remained in Saigon for his work. Aunt Three was invited so Mother had company. Mother and Aunt bathed in the sea fully clothed and with conical hats on their heads. Annie, always modern and fashionable, put on a bikini.

We picnicked at Back Beach. We could go around in a carriage pulled by a donkey. Cap Saint-Jacques was a well-known vacation resort created by the French. Later the name was changed to Vung Tau.

Anna's youth had been wasted by tuberculosis and the war. She had endured unhappy circumstances and had not attended university. She resided in Dalat to enjoy fresh and pure air, which was beneficial for her lungs.

Dalat was another French-built vacation resort on a hill at an altitude of 1,500 meters, and it enjoyed a temperate climate like that in France. I remember the posh Dalat Palace Hotel, the romantic pine trees, the Lake of Sighs and the Lake of Spring Perfume. Strawberries, avocados, asparagus, and an abundance of beautiful flowers, such as roses, gladioli, and lilies bloomed in an explosion of colors. There were no vineyards, because grapes did not grow well. Vietnam was not a wine producer. We imported wines from France. The population drank beer. Vietnamese beers were excellent and renowned.

Emperor Bao Dai chose his summer palace in Dalat as his favorite residence; it was far from the political stress he endured in Saigon. He liked to hunt deer, boars, and tigers in the surrounding forests. Empress Nam Phuong owned a villa inherited from her grandfather.

The Congregation of Our Lady had a convent, Convent des Oiseaux, in Dalat. The convent had boarding rooms for girl students, and the fees were expensive. Dalat was also known for Petit Lycée Alexandre Yersin. Yersin was a Swiss-born French doctor who, along with Paul Doumer, a former governor general, promoted Dalat as an ideal location to treat respiratory and lung health problems. They had built a sanatorium there. After 1954, the Dalat National Military Academy became the best military academy of South Vietnam. During the Ngo Dinh Diem regime, tourism was developed, and I remember our picnics on new beaches near Cap Saint-Jacques and the waterfalls near Dalat. The most notorious were the Datalan falls.

The Bamboo Curtain and Passage to Freedom (1954-1955)

In 1954, the Geneva Agreement on Vietnam stipulated that the population had three hundred days to choose where they wanted to live. Almost a million people, mostly Catholic people from the Red Delta, Phat Diem, and Bui Chu villages, fled to South Vietnam. Their exodus was called "Passage to Freedom" or "The Blessed Virgin goes to the South."

Refugees from the North Vietnam exodus were everywhere. They were known to be hardworking people. American aid poured in, and people sold in the streets big containers of margarine, cooking oils not yet known in Vietnam, flour, powdered milk, underwear, nylon petticoats, radios, and all kinds of equipment. The American Women Club distributed bras to the highland women who walked bare-breasted. They did not succeed in changing the customs of our ethnic tribes.

President Ngo Dinh Diem resettled the refugees in newly created villages and economic zones. He relied on the Catholic refugees from the North as his best anti-Communist supporters.

Dr. Tom Dooley was a young doctor from St. Louis and was stationed in Japan with the USS *Montague*, part of the US Seventh Fleet, when they received the order in 1954 to sail to Vietnam and pick up the North Vietnamese refugees at sea. During his first day on board, rescuing a huge number of very sick refugees, he suddenly found the purpose of his life.

He wrote in his book *Deliver Us from Evil* that while standing on his ship during his first night, he was struck by the white light of revelation and God's calling. He then chose the vocation of missionary doctor, dedicating his life to help the poorest of the poor. He founded MEDICO, which sent teams of US doctors to help poor people in remote and perilous areas. He spent two years in Vietnam and three years in Laos before dying from cancer at age thirty-four in New York. He was known for his American patriotism and his Catholic faith. He became a legend.

He wrote, "It is impossible not to respect their driving compulsion for freedom, impossible not to admire the story of such a valiant people. The difference between them and us is that we have our freedom and our hearts command us to keep it. The Vietnamese does not possess it and his heart's command is to struggle against all odds to achieve it."

President Ngo Dinh Diem awarded him the Medal of Merit of Vietnam with those words "Dr. Dooley, you are one of the rarest Americans I and my people like."

The United States and the Republic of Vietnam

The support for the Republic of Vietnam started with President Dwight Eisenhower under the domino theory. If South Vietnam fell into Communist hands, the theory stated, communism would spread to other neighboring countries. Therefore, communism had to be stopped in Vietnam.

The United States viewed Vietnam as a faraway exotic little country and they faced no difficulties whatsoever in dealing with its problems. The US generals reasoned the same way they had during World War II: "Bomb them and they will be destroyed!" They could not foresee that the Vietnam War was a totally different war: a war in the jungles, a psychological war, and a war to win the hearts and minds of people, even with using terror. They came to Vietnam without a thorough knowledge of its past history and the complexity of its populations and cultures. They were unprepared.

In 1955, with the US commitment to help South Vietnam against the Communist aggression coming from North Vietnam, Saigon breathed with relief and the population celebrated with enthusiasm and exhilaration. With military and financial help from the United States, we had hope for our future. We believed that nothing could go wrong and that we had been rescued from communism.

In Saigon, the construction of American buildings surged, built for American military, economic, and aid organizations. American help in the forms of food items and medicinal drugs poured in to be distributed to refugees from the North and to the poor. American agencies and families needed staff; this benefitted many Vietnamese, who were able to secure jobs with the Americans and were well paid.

There was a large cultural gap between the Americans and Vietnamese.

The Americans offended their hosts by boiling water to purify it or by being reluctant to sample Vietnamese food. They also offended people by patting old people on the head, as the head was considered sacred. If they touched a woman, that was a sexual gesture. The differences between cultures and behaviors were huge. The Vietnamese consulted fortune-tellers and refused to cooperate in developing parcels of land or villages, build houses, or dig wells if the sites were not judged well suited for a given project, based on superstitions.

That explains how things were already difficult at the start of the alliance between two countries so different from each other.

Ngo Dinh Diem appointed by Bao Dai

Ngo Dinh Diem, the new prime minister, had graduated from the School of Public Administration and Law at Hanoi, which was the same school attended by Father and Uncle Three. He was known to be nationalist and anti-Communist. In 1950, he visited Europe and the United States, where he lectured at universities explaining the political situation in Vietnam and made friends with important personalities. The Americans had pressured Emperor Bao Dai to offer the premiership to Ngo Dinh Diem. The Americans saw him as the best choice they had at that time.

Ngo Dinh Diem entered the political scene and encountered fierce obstacles. The French, emperor Bao Dai and supporters, the feudal sects that fought with the French against the Vietminh, disliked him. He then relied mainly on the Americans and the Catholic refugees who had fled North Vietnam for support.

On April 28, 1955, we suddenly heard gunshots and troops running along our avenue. Street battles in Saigon and Cholon had broken out between the Binh Xuyen and the governmental troops. General Duong Van Minh, leading the Ngo Dinh Diem troops, overran the Binh Xuyen positions and chased them to the Rung Sat swamps. Bay Vien, the Binh Xuyen leader, escaped to France. General Duong Van Minh relentlessly pursued the Cao Dai and the Hoa Hoa troops. The Cao Dai pope fled to Cambodia. Ba Cut, the leader of the Hoa Hoa, was captured, sentenced by a tribunal, and beheaded. Those sects, powerful during the past French era, were decimated.

General Duong Van Minh had saved the regime of Ngo Dinh Diem. He became a national hero in the South and was immensely popular for having exterminated the dissident and feared sects. However, Ngo Dinh Diem and his brother Ngo Dinh Nhu did not like to see General Minh becoming too popular. They considered him a threat to them and sent him away from Saigon, first for further military training in the United States and afterward to become first commander of field operations in the war against Vietcong guerrillas. Ngo Dinh Diem, always paranoid, began to distrust General Minh.

The flag of Vietnam was chosen as a yellow flag with three red stripes symbolizing the three united regions of Vietnam. Yellow was the color of the emperor but also the color of the earth. That flag, the symbol of Vietnam, had never changed from 1950 to 1975.

On my way from our residence to Lycée Marie Curie, I walked in front of the residence of the Doc Phu Su Nguyen Van Tam, president of the council. In 1955, his son General Nguyen Van Hinh, who had been trained by the French Air Force and was married to a French woman, was appointed as the first commander-in-chief of the new National Army of Vietnam. However, Ngo Dinh Diem accused him of plotting against him. Hinh fled to France. Mr. Nguyen Van Tam also preferred to immigrate to France.

The Referendum of 1955; Abolition of the Monarchy and the Class of the Doc Phu Su; President Ngo Dinh Diem and the Republic of Vietnam

President Ngo Dinh Diem launched the referendum for people to choose between him and Emperor Bao Dai. He crafted a new constitution. It was said that the elections were rigged in his favor. He proceeded to get rid of Emperor Bao Dai, who was exiled to France with the imperial family. Bao Dai's possessions were confiscated.

Empress Nam Phuong was respected, so she was allowed to keep properties she had inherited from her grandfather, Ong Huyen Si, the richest man of Indochina. In the first half of the twentieth century, he founded some Catholic churches in South Vietnam. His son Nguyen Huu Hao had two daughters who had been sent for studies in France. One had married Baron Didelot; and the other, Marie Therese Nguyen Huu Thi Lan, had married Bao Dai and had become empress of Vietnam.

Emperor Bao Dai, born as Nguyen Phuc Vinh Thuy, was the thirteenth Nguyen Emperor and had ascended to the throne at age thirteen. The Nguyen Dynasty was founded by Emperor Gia Long in 1802.

As a student in Paris, Bao Dai fell in love with Marie Therese Nguyen Huu Thi Lan. He married her on March 24, 1934.

Empress Nam Phuong (who was known as the Perfume of the South or the Empress of the South) was beautiful, with refined features, ivory skin, and eyes shaped like a gazelle's. She was born to a wealthy Catholic family from the South and was well educated at the Convent des Oiseaux of Paris. Her family agreed to the wedding on the condition that the emperor elevate his wife to the same title and give her the same rights as himself. No emperors' wives before had acceded to this equality of rights. Empress Nam Phuong was conferred the same status as Emperor Bao Dai. The second condition was that she remain Catholic and all their future children be baptized according to the Catholic faith. Bao Dai accepted their conditions, but for himself, he would remain Buddhist, following the religion of his ancestors and of most of the Vietnamese population.

Tu Cung, Bao Dai's mother, and the ladies of the Imperial Court of Hue, had their favorite young girls to introduce to him for marriage, but he ignored them. He even blackmailed his mother by telling her that if he was not allowed to wed the young girl he had himself chosen, he would never marry and she would be left without grandsons and with no heir to the throne.

The young emperor Bao Dai had lived with French families carefully chosen by the French government and was educated in France. He was like a prisoner in a golden cage. Politically he was crushed in his nationalist aspirations by the French, who kept him busy and corrupted him with women, casinos, nightclubs, and hunting expeditions.

In 1945, Bao Dai abdicated in favor of the Vietnamese revolution led by Ho Chi Minh, who proclaimed the independence of Vietnam at the end of World War II and chose to live as an ordinary citizen. However, the French returned to Vietnam to reconquer their former colony. There was no other prince to replace Bao Dai and they kept Bao Dai as emperor. Ho Chi Minh and the Vietminh were pushed back to the jungle and they waged war relentlessly against the French. The French finally realized that the colonial war was lost and at the end of 1949, signed the Treaty of Independence of Vietnam with the representative of Bao Dai. Bao Dai was nominated as the head of the new State of Vietnam.

In 1955, exiled in France by Ngo Dinh Diem, Emperor Bao Dai and Empress Nam Phuong went their separate ways. The tensions created by the political turmoil in Vietnam, as well as the passion of Bao Dai for hunting wild animals in French forests and womanizing, destroyed their life as a couple. Empress Nam Phuong was profoundly Catholic and virtuous, and she chose a reclusive life of prayer and devotion.

Bao Dai wrote in his autobiography, "As for us, during twenty years' reign, we have known much bitterness."

In 1955, President Ngo Dinh Diem proclaimed the First Republic of Vietnam.

Our brother Albert Nguyen Vo My was sent to France to study at the National Institute of Agronomy of Toulouse. Albert's big dream was all about helping the country, developing forestry and agriculture, and raising cattle.

Our brother Henri Nguyen Vo Dieu returned from France. Always a patriot, he had refused to return to Vietnam as long as the French troops were still stationed there, even if they were now our allies. Under the regime of Ngo Dinh Diem, a massive number of Vietnamese returned enthusiastically to Vietnam from abroad to serve their country.

Henri had graduated in law from the University of Montpellier, and he had worked at the Bank of Indochina and Suez in Paris. In Saigon, thanks to his expertise, he was rapidly promoted and became executive director of the Commercial Credit of Vietnam from 1965 to 1971. He bought for the bank as an investment a merchant ship christened *Vietnam Thuong Tin*. He was also appointed as chairman of COGIDO, the National Manufacturing Paper Company of Vietnam.

Henri was very well liked. As a banker, he lent money to people without discrimination. He lent money to refugees from the North and to former Chinese immigrants to develop their businesses. As an employer, he had a keen eye for choosing people who could be efficient, and he promoted them. He built cafeterias and vacation houses for staff and their families. He was generous and innovative.

In 1956, behind our residence was built the most modern and most politically active Buddhist pagoda of Saigon, the Xa Loi Pagoda on Ba Huyen Thanh Quan Street.

Cousin Juliette Mi returned from France in the arms of her new husband, Mr. Giang. In her youth, she had followed a French officer to France, and they had a daughter, Rita. After their divorce, she met Mr. Giang, a millionaire businessman who had made his money in real estate in France. He was a good man, and all the women involved with him and the children they had from him were very well provided for.

In Vietnam, among Mr. Giang's business acquisitions, he bought a plantation in the highlands near Blao, a big cinema, and a merchant ship. I remember being invited with my family to their plantation. Life on the plantation was simply marvelous. I liked the wilderness, the jungle, tiger hunting's stories, the deer, the squirrels, and the good life there. It was, for me, a paradise on earth. During the colonial era, the French plantation owners lived like kings as Indochina was very rich in resources. They had to leave after 1954 and the Vietnamese took over. Under the First Republic of Ngo Dinh Diem, emphasis was put on forestry, land development and creating new economic zones.

The workers on the plantations were mostly tribal people. They worked hard for little money. The highland tribes were different from the Vietnamese in physical aspects, cultural customs, and beliefs. Those tribes lived in remote areas—hills and mountains far from the cities—and suffered greatly from the wars raging in Vietnam. As minorities, they suffered at the hands of the Communists. They showed loyalty to the French and to the Americans, helping them but as the French and the Americans were defeated, the tribes were left on their own. Hundreds of thousands of tribal people died in Vietnam and Cambodia because they had sided with the French and the Americans.

The French troops left Vietnam in 1956. During the Indochina War, the French military forces in Vietnam consisted of the French expeditionary forces recruited in France on a volunteer basis and the troops sent by its former and current colonies, called the French Union troops.

One distinct military group would be the men of the French Foreign Legion. They had a distinctive uniform—a white kepi with flaps on the ears, crimson epaulets, and a distinctive scarf. They were handsome and physically fit, and they fought very well. When they applied to join the French Foreign Legion, they were not asked about their country of origin or their past. It was an ideal destination for European men who had been through the Second World War and who wanted to live a future with adventures and military action without having to disclose their past. German and Eastern European languages were the most often spoken languages among them. They were led by French officers. At the Battle of Dien Bien Phu, they were decimated, and afterward, the French Foreign Legion never regained its past glory.

On January 19, 1956, President Ngo Dinh Diem ordered the French troops to get out of Vietnam. He said, "The presence of foreign troops, no matter how friendly, was incompatible with Vietnam's concept of full independence." In April, the last troops of the French Expeditionary Corps bade adieu to Vietnam. Eurasian children and orphans fathered by French men were taken to France. France was opened generously to Vietnamese who had sided with them for the past century of French presence in Vietnam.

Lycée Marie Curie (1946-1958)

We must believe that we are gifted for something, and
that this thing, at whatever cost, must be attained.
—Marie Curie

From 1950 to 1954, we students were often gathered on the sidewalks anytime we were informed that an official motorcade carrying Emperor Bao Dai, the high commissioner of France, or a French general or top-ranking officer would be riding along our avenue, from the airport to the palace of the high commissioner. We waved tiny flags of France and Vietnam at their passage. I saw history in front of me. I saw French generals in charge of the French expeditionary forces in Indochina, one after another, over the years. They were Generals Raoul Salan, Jean de Lattre de Tassigny, Rene Cogny, and Henri Navarre. At the end of the school year, they distributed to us a package of French books tied up with a beautiful ribbon.

At school, the teacher made me sit next to a French boy or girl because I was to speak French and not Vietnamese. I had also a special status because I was a French citizen. On July 14, French National Day, there was always an impressive parade of French military forces. Lycée Marie Curie participated in the celebrations, with its students performing gymnastics and ballets. I walked in the military parade in white shorts and blouse, along with the soldiers of the French Union, because I had French citizenship. I remember once marching with the Moroccan Division. I never asked questions. We were children and did what we had been told to do by our French teachers. I grew up, never knowing that I was a French citizen and my Vietnamese school friends were Vietnamese citizens.

My sister Annie and I graduated from Lycée Marie Curie. My final year there was 1958. Annie was enrolled in the Pharmacy Studies Department of the University of Saigon, but she dropped out. She preferred to work as a French teacher at the Gia Long National College for Girls.

Our Family Life and Events (1957-1960)

My parents and I became Vietnamese citizens in 1957.

President Ngo Dinh Diem advised Father to renounce his French citizenship and embrace Vietnamese citizenship. Father did not want to live in France. He could not leave behind Grandmother and his ancestors' tombstones. He hated Western civilization, which he judged as evil, corrupt, and immoral. Therefore he had no other choice than to renounce his French citizenship, and he did so also on behalf of Mother and me. I was not yet eighteen years old, so I had no say in the matter. On my birth certificate, he explained that he made this decision under pressure from moral and professional obligations.

In May 1957, Ngo Dinh Diem visited Washington and was greeted by President Dwight Eisenhower with great honors. Eisenhower said, "President Diem, you have exemplified in your part of the world, patriotism of the greatest order." Diem thanked the United States for "the faith in [his] country that accomplished the miracle of Vietnam."

In 1957, a Catholic University was founded in Dalat by Archbishop Ngo Dinh Thuc.

In 1957, Uncle Three died suddenly from an embolism in his villa in Saigon. Aunt Three, still tied up by her filial piety toward her mother, resided in Mytho but came occasionally to Saigon to visit her husband. He held the position of director general of finances at the time of his death. That day, he had lunch with my parents, went into his room for a nap, and never woke up.

For the wake and funeral visits before the burial, his closed casket was shown in a room at his son's house. Dr. Nguyen Minh Chau was an eminent obstetrician of Saigon. My family and I were there, as we had to greet the visitors and bow back to them any time they bowed in front of

47

the coffin. I did not see Uncle Three's body; I saw only his coffin. We were there as his relatives, taking turns bowing in front of the visitors to thank them for their visits. It was the custom.

In the late hours of the night, I saw Aunt Three embracing her husband's coffin and sobbing. She thought that she was alone, so she let out her despair. It was the first time that I saw Aunt Three so genuinely distressed and sobbing like an endless stream. She had been always reserved, distant, and cold. I believe that she was thinking about her life, loving this man, and being separated from him for decades.

Uncle Three's funeral was grandiose in Saigon, as it was the burial of one of the last remaining Doc Phu Su. This class has been abolished by President Ngo Dinh Diem. After the long procession along the streets of Saigon, the hearse was driven to the Gate of Mytho, eighty kilometers from Saigon, and he was buried in his wife's family cemetery. My parents were devastated. They had lost their best friend. Uncle Three had always been there to advise and protect my parents like a big brother. Mother deposited inside his coffin her gift for his travel to the other world. It was a bracelet with a river of diamonds on it. Uncle Three had always protected both Father and Mother—who was sweet and vulnerable; she adored him.

After Uncle Three's death, Father became more and more depressed. He had resigned from a brilliant career. He had lost his former colleagues and friends, the Doc Phu Su, who were either imprisoned, mostly on charges of corruption, or had chosen to live in France. Being a traditionalist, he feared revolutionary times.

Our sister Annie, Sister Six, was well born, beautiful, talented, educated, and healthy. She had graduated from Lycée Marie Curie, where she was renowned for her elegance and beauty. Annie was multitalented. She was excellent in cooking French gourmet cuisine. She baked delicious cakes, and she designed herself her own outfits. Her hands were magical. She was stylish, innovative, and modern.

Her friends had married doctors, lawyers, and wealthy businessmen. Annie had been a maid of honor at their weddings. Many men proposed marriage to her. Father always found them unworthy to marry his daughter Annie. He always found negative factors to deride them and turned them away. Her destiny could be to have become a wife, a mother and a brilliant socialite. She remained unmarried. That was Father's doing. Her future as a happy normal woman had been deviated from its normal course.

Our sister Anna asked Father for some money to set up a business to occupy herself. He yelled, "What would people say? That we are poor and my daughters have to go out to earn money?" Anna wept. She felt powerless and she was very unhappy.

In 1957, President Ngo Dinh Diem initiated a series of rural reforms, and there was a law that would reimburse the landlords for parts of their land that had been occupied by the peasants since the Communist uprising in 1945 and beyond. The former landlords would receive an indemnity for their lost land, and at the same time, the peasants would become the legitimate owners of the land. The former landlords were ecstatic to receive money for the land they thought they had lost forever. Mother fell into that category and had to return to her former property to sign the appropriate papers.

Mother had the opportunity to pay a visit to the Red Coconut, her childhood property, and she took me with her for the trip. I remember how friendly and deferential the peasants were with us. They called her "Mistress Six." Although poor, they killed and roasted a pig, cooked a duck with rice soup, and served boiled giant snails picked up in the rice fields. Everything was delicious, with garlic, ginger, and lemongrass added in the sauces. I shared the same passions as my mother. I loved the land, life in the countryside, and simple fresh food. We ended the afternoon at Mother's family cemetery, among rusted tombstones in ruins. For decades, no one went there to look after them. The trees were dead, and some black crows sat on top of them.

In 1957, President Ngo Dinh Diem offered to Father the position of representative of the government in the South, which was equivalent to the former position of governor of the South. Father declined and tendered his resignation. He bowed in front of the president and respectfully explained that he had become old and needed to look after his aging mother. The truth was that Father could not adjust to a new and modern republican era.

Father was awarded the Medal of Merit of Vietnam by President Ngo Dinh Diem in 1957. This medal was the highest medal awarded to public servants.

Retired from public service, Father became increasingly worried about the future. He was paranoid, pessimistic, and negative. He told us that the Communists very soon would take over the country and that we should learn how to survive under communism. The first fundamental rule was to learn to live as humble people. He disapproved of Annie's luxury tastes. He begged her to change her lifestyle. I personally did not like the prospect of living under a communist regime.

After moving out from our official residence on Phan Thanh Gian Avenue, we lived now in a rented villa in Saigon. My parents did not buy a house in Saigon. Father had planned to retire later in the Mytho house. After receiving money for her land, Mother invested in building houses for rental income in Travinh, and this was a bad idea. Travinh was four hundred kilometers far away from Saigon, and she did not get much money from this project.

Father had lost the privileges of his former career. Now we had no official residence, no car, and no driver, and we had to pay the wages of servants ourselves. We downsized to keep only one servant. The driver had been with Father during his whole career, and his wife and children had lived with us, camping inside the garage. It was very emotional for them to leave us.

Father had spent money for the university studies of three sons in France and for his mother, who lived in the Mytho house. Our parents had welcomed several nephews and nieces to live with us in Saigon for their studies and for security reasons. They were generous with the food they provided to a large number of people, including the servants. Mother would not buy anything that was not of the best quality or freshness. My parents had to live up to a high standard of hospitality and generosity.

Father had renovated the Mytho house with additional space to accommodate relatives coming to visit and with modern washrooms so Grandmother would not stumble into the big hole that served as the toilet before 1950. When I was a child, the toilet location consisted of a big room with no roof, for natural ventilation, and a huge hole in the middle. I sat on some stone and bricks above the hole, watching with horror as hundreds of maggots crawled up and down the hole. I was scared that they would reach my sandals and feet. Going to the toilet was a nightmare. Once a week, an old Chinese man or woman would walk along the streets with two containers along a pole over their shoulders and take the human waste to fertilize their vegetable fields. After his or her passage, a strong horrible smell persisted for a long time in the streets.

Modern toilets were built. The dark, rotten walls of the old house were replaced with new wood. Dozens of big jars were displayed along the outside walls of the house to catch water from the rains. Father upgraded the house with electricity and running water. He paid for the maintenance of the Mytho house and for the food offered every day to a large group of Grandmother's friends, relatives, and servants.

The abolition of the class of the Doc Phu Su by President Ngo Dinh Diem meant that we no longer saw those Doc Phu Su and their families, because the majority of them had moved to France. France was very generous with Vietnamese who worked with them, and they got excellent pensions and benefits in France. In Saigon, my parents became lonely without their Doc Phu Su friends.

When Father had his career as a Doc Phu Su, Mother's social life in Saigon revolved mostly around other Doc Phu Su's wives. They were her dearest friends, and those ladies got together, had tea, and played cards. It was a harmless activity. However, they had immigrated to France. Mother felt lonely and lost. She became depressed—especially with Father always breathing down her neck and complaining about everything.

The return of Henri from Paris saved our family from financial difficulties. Henri helped our parents by buying a house in Saigon for them. He restored our former prestige. He helped all his brothers and sisters to the best of his abilities. Henri emerged quickly as an important player in the world of business. He became a big banker and was part of the elite of Saigon.

Father was a victim of his own traditional Vietnamese education. He had never evolved with the times. He was submissive to the traditions and to the elders. He was obsessed with being a role model as a good mandarin, a good Buddhist, and a good son. He lived with this obsession. "What would people say?" Public opinion was paramount for him.

Other people would focus on marriage for their daughters and sons. Strangely, my parents never envisaged that eventuality and never groomed their daughters to marry nice and rich men.

Father did everything for the careers of his sons. However, he did not envisage them getting married. He also did not care about his daughters getting married. We were praised as good and pious girls when we worshipped Buddha and the ancestors and were obedient. My parents lived day after day as if life would always remain the same and as if, as a united close family, we would live together forever under the same roof.

Our brothers, Rene and Albert, got the best of university education that money and prestige could afford. They were sent to France and graduated. But they were not brought up to look after themselves. Before going to France, they had mother, sisters, and servants to look after their needs and pamper them. They were not taught about practical life, realities, or relationships with girls. Should our parents have had introduced nice girls to Rene and Albert, maybe this could have changed their destiny for a better one.

Rene, a handsome and sweet young man, was lonely in France and married a totally wrong Vietnamese woman for him. He endured a long, miserable life with her. They had careers and money, but the home was not a happy home.

Albert—handsome, idealistic, and altruistic—was never interested with his personal life and never had a romance or a romantic feeling for a girl or a thought about marriage. He was totally obsessed with serving his country and being a good son and a good brother. He believed that his country, his parents, and his sisters needed him. "Country and family" was the purpose of his life.

Francois, an introvert, was not sociable. He stayed in his room for hours and was not talkative. No one worried about his moods—a sign of mental illness. He could have been treated at the onset of his illness with communication, affection, and empathy.

Francois and I did not get any significant attention in a family whose members were rather cold, reserved, and introverted. Francois and I grew up in our own solitude. I worked out my own plans to leave home because I was imaginative and daring. Francois did not look for an escape. He locked himself in his room.

Our parents never knew what really happened in the minds and lives of their three daughters. They never understood our dreams and aspirations. Anna was like a sacrificed lamb. She had no personal happiness, no health, no beauty, no university studies, no money and no independence. During the last decades of her life, she found solace in becoming a Buddhist nun in Paris. The Vietnamese Buddhist Institute of Paris became her home and the other religious men and women became her spiritual family. On the surface, she looked happy and in peace as if she had found her vocation. Annie soothed her frustrations and solitude by indulging her passion for luxury, elegant dresses and jewelry, and I, Alice, was obsessed with leaving home and I was dreaming of the green valleys beyond the frontiers of my natal country.

When I was a child and an adolescent, Father humiliated me by slapping me violently in front of the servants and family members, and he annihilated my self-confidence and self-esteem. For him, punishing me was a matter of strict discipline. For me, it was public humiliation. His great mistake was to have humiliated me in public with physical violence. I was a Scorpio in the Western horoscope and a Serpent in the Asian zodiac. These two signs were deep and strong signs. Therefore, I did not accept the humiliations inflicted upon me.

When I was a child, a French teacher said that I was cute. I was very proud to be found cute. When Father heard me telling this to Ngoc Lan, a cousin who lived with us, he screamed at me. "You are ugly. You should never praise yourself. You should learn the virtue of humility." That destroyed my self-confidence. All my life, I had an inferiority complex, and there was no reason behind it.

Looking back at my childhood and adolescence, I see that I was driven toward the wrong direction, with terribly old-fashioned education, and was headed for disaster. The Western standards for education and success were the opposite of Father's education of me.

Parents should never humiliate their children and should never hit or spank them. In order to build my self-confidence, Father should have praised me, motivated me, and never stated that I must be humble and that I was not beautiful and intelligent because the virtue of humility forbade me to be satisfied with myself. That was a recipe to create an adult who thought she was inferior to others, and this lack of self-confidence later led to mental issues. I was distressed, frustrated, and left feeling powerless. I had the ability to retreat inside myself as a refuge to nurture wild imagination and lonesomeness. I lived in my own world of fantasies. Fortunately I found people in later years in the outside world who loved me. Father had destroyed my self-worth, but I found my mental salvation with strangers.

I could have written a novel titled *The Three Daughters of the Doc Phu Su Nguyen Van Ba.* I could never forget that our lives—Anna's, Annie's, and my own—had been very unusual. Our lives could have been totally different had we had another father. That was my personal opinion, which was probably not shared by any of my siblings. They were bound by filial piety and respect. They did not psychoanalyze their life story.

My friends at Lycée Marie Curie had young and modern parents who educated their daughters for success, and the results were brilliant. My bad luck was to have parents too old for me. They were in their forties when they conceived me. My friends were eighteen years old with parents no older than forty. What a dramatic difference this made!

Rene, Henri, and Albert studied and lived in France, and they did not witness the changes at home. Anna and Annie, although unhappy, were good daughters. They talked with each other about their frustrations but were not rebellious. Maurice and Francois were of a silent type, shy and introverted. They were not rebellious either.

I had another mindset. I was not submissive. I hated my life in that house, in that family, and in that country. I wanted to get out of my home and be independent. I looked up to Annie as a role model. I dreamed to one day be like Annie, to have money to buy whatever I wished to have, and to be beautiful with powder and red lipstick on my face. I had been deprived of so many things—for instance, pretty dresses, elegant shoes, dolls to play with, and fashionable haircuts. Father said that toys were a waste of money. We were not to play with toys but were instead to worship Buddha and the ancestors.

Father did not encourage any attempt by my sisters to play musical instruments or to sing. For him, playing music was futile and a waste of time. We were to focus on religion. Mother was not a role model, because I never heard Mother singing or playing music. Mother was not a singer, musician, poet, or intellectual. She had been raised in a rural area, whereas Father's sisters had been raised in a city. My aunts were sophisticated, artistic, and cultured.

In the spring of 1958, an itinerant Buddhist nun entered our new rented villa in Saigon. It was a custom in Vietnam to have itinerant monks and nuns—with shaved heads, wrapped in brown or yellow robes, sporting bare feet—walking along the streets with a bowl in their hands. They would eat whatever people poured inside their bowl. Our largely Buddhist population respected them.

Mother and I were alone at home. The elderly nun looked at me and said, "Child, the noble contour of your face and the depth in your eyes indicate an extraordinary destiny. You will leave the land of your ancestors, cross the four seas, and study the sciences of the occident. You will reach fame and wealth. You will marry, far away, and will have four children. This is written in the celestial book thanks to the one thousand virtues of your ancestors."

Her prediction empowered me. I shall have a magical destiny. That prediction sheltered me from fear and uncertainty. I knew then that I would cross the four seas.

During the academic year of 1958-1959, I began my first year at the University of Saigon, and I hated it. I did not speak Vietnamese well, having been educated mostly in French. Almost all of my classmates had gone to study abroad, mostly with university scholarships offered generously by some countries of the Free World. The exams to win those scholarships were easy, and almost no one failed. They tested your English or French language knowledge, and you needed to have obtained your high school diploma. It was certain that students graduating from French lycées could not fail. I did not apply to go, because I assumed that Father would not let me go overseas.

I attended my first ball at the Faculty of Law. The students were very enthusiastic. They prepared themselves for a great party. They were young, in their twenties, and they flirted. One young man came and invited me to dance. I found him repulsive, short, and ugly—absolutely not my type. However, I was forced to dance like everybody else and could not say no. When he squeezed me hard against his body, I had nausea. I broke free and went to sit on the steps of the back porch of the house.

I hated that evening, the University of Saigon, and those young men. I had no attraction toward them. I found them ugly. I would not say the same for Vietnamese girls. They were smart, smooth-talking, clever, and pretty. In Vietnam, a good marriage would be the combination of a man

55

who was rich and professionally successful and a wife who was a beauty and had musical talent.

I would not say that all young Vietnamese men were not my type. In Europe, I had seen handsome young Vietnamese and Chinese at university in Europe. They were aristocratic with delicate ivory skin. They were thin and tall with refined facial features, and they were educated and pleasant. I could have married one of them. But life was strange. In the Western world, most of the Vietnamese girls married male Westerners and most of the Vietnamese young men liked to marry Western girls. It was an attraction of opposite physical features, but mentality and traditions had also their say. Young and modern Vietnamese people studying in the West were westernized, and found it painful to return to the old Vietnamese mentality.

During that dancing evening, I cried, sitting on the steps of the back porch of that house, and some girls asked me, "What happened to you?"

I said, "I want to go home. I am sick."

I did not belong in that environment. I felt like an alien at the University of Saigon. I missed my former Marie Curie classmates who studied in France, the United States, Canada, Australia, and New Zealand. I envied them. I envied them even more when they married foreigners from the west side of the globe. It was my dream. The ideal man for me was a man as handsome as Gregory Peck and the white missionaries and doctors I saw in movies adapted from Pearl Buck's novels, such as *The Keys of the Kingdom* and *The Inn of the Sixth Happiness.* My other favorite books were Emily Brontë's *Wuthering Heights*, Charlotte Brontë's *Jane Eyre*, Han Suyin's *A Many-Splendored Thing*, and Daphne du Maurier's *My cousin Rachel* and *Rebecca*.

In 1959, two years after her husband's passing, Aunt Three died in a car accident on the road between Saigon and Mytho. The car was being driven by her eldest son. My father was also a passenger, and he was not physically hurt; however, he had severe mental trauma from holding his beloved sister in his arms as she bled, dying from her injuries.

Aunt's body was transported back to Mytho from Vinh Long Hospital. Grandmother grieved in silence the death of her daughter, who had also been her companion. She never uttered a word. Aunt was buried in our family cemetery next to her husband.

I do not remember going to Mytho and attending Aunt Three's funeral. I was scared of dead people and stories of ghosts. The House of the Ancestors was, for me, a sinister place full of dark rooms and corners, cold drafts, oil lamps, and the altars honoring the dead ancestors.

After her death, the relatives sleeping in this house where Aunt Three had spent most of her life before her sudden demise said that they saw her in the middle of the night, dressed in white cloth, weeping, and whispering to them, "I don't want to go. This is my home." People were very superstitious, and this was a period of mourning when her sons and relatives were still traumatized by her sudden death. They saw what they wished to see. Her ghost appeared in their imaginations during their fresh grief. There was also a belief that ghosts returned to the location where they had died in a gruesome manner because they could not find peace to move on. The only way to help them was to erect an altar for them, pray for their souls, and burn incense sticks for them. It was normal that Aunt Three's ghost would come back to haunt the house where she had spent almost all her life.

I had not gone to her funeral. I stayed in Saigon. I did not see her dead body, and I did not see her casket. I stayed away from funerals because I was so scared of dead people and had nightmares. I should have been educated with the notion of death going hand in hand with life. No one really explained any of this to me. All I heard in my childhood were stories about ghosts.

Aunt Three's passing was another huge blow to Father. She was his favorite sister and his moral support. Father had always been weak and vulnerable. He needed Uncle and Aunt Three and became lost without them.

I was at war with Father. He was an old man of his times and was even worse than his contemporaries. I had been educated with French individualism and the quest for personal freedom. I was fed up with Father's obsession with Buddha, Confucius, and the dead ancestors

Father saw sins everywhere. My indifference to Buddha and the cult of the ancestors sparked his rage. His face became sanguine like a red tomato, and he used all the force of his hands to slap me. I never forgave him for these big shows in public. He wanted the servants to see that he, a great mandarin, did not hesitate to punish his own daughter, with violence, should she be disrespectful towards anybody from the ancestors to the servants. He once threw my French books in the garbage bin, yelling that it had been a mistake to send me to French school. My bad manners and my insolence came from the French culture. Mother witnessed that incident from the beginning to the end. She had warned me in advance, "Obey, my child. He is very angry." The more he disciplined me, the more I nurtured my rebellion and my desire to leave home.

This was not the father I wanted to have. I was determined to get out of this house and find the father I dreamed of having, even if I had to walk on a long journey to the other end of the world. I overheard one day that when I was born, a wealthy Vietnamese couple who were friends with my parents begged Mother to give me to them. They had no children and wanted to adopt me. They later lived in France, and I resented my parents for not having given me to them. That explained my attitude toward adoption. Adoption was a godsend—a blessing for the child. It was not a bad thing.

I disliked Father, but I loved Mother. She was beautiful and kind. On Sundays, I liked to go to Saigon Central Market with her. I would ask her to buy me a pair of shoes or a piece of material. I liked to accompany her when she visited her lady friends. I was proud of her. Even in her older years, she was still an elegant lady, well dressed in silk and brocade, her face well powdered; and she smelled good. She always had a French perfume on her dresser. She never raised her voice to me or hit me. When she visited her friends, I would sit in their kitchen. When I got bored, I would sprinkle salt around in their kitchen. Superstition told me that would help to end the visit.

I did not have a normal life like my schoolmates. They competed for success at school. They flirted with their male French teachers or with the boys from Lycée Jean Jacques Rousseau, our male counterparts. Their parents focused on their education, social success, careers, and marriages.

I also knew girls who lived with only their mothers. Those single or divorced or widowed mothers were ambitious and clever concerning the futures of their daughters. They paid for the daughters' music, ballet lessons, and elegant dresses. They were largely rewarded. One girl from Lycée Marie Curie went to Paris, won the first prize for music at the conservatory, and married a young and handsome French count. As mothers and daughters in Vietnam were inseparable, they would continue to live under the same roof. In this case, a young, modest Vietnamese widow went to live in a French château after her daughter's wedding.

Annie and I had everything in our favor to marry among the best men of Vietnam and France. We were well born, we had family prestige and honor, and we were pretty and healthy. However, because of Father's lack of social ambition for us and his maniac religious obsessions, we ended up with a worse fate than that of ordinary girls. They would rise up to become ladies, thanks to clever mothers. We were on top of the social ladder and had our wings cut off. I was always bitter about this.

Father had only one obsession; his duty toward his mother was his priority. He was happy to keep the daughters at home. Other parents would be happy to forge an alliance with other great families through their children's marriages. Not our father. After all, daughters could become companions and supporters to elderly parents. His other obsession was sex. He could not imagine that any man having sex with a daughter of his. I found this a very bigoted and hypocritical viewpoint from those men who conceived an average of ten or eight children and afterward declared that sex was a sin and was dirty.

Father did not allow me to attend parties given by some of my classmates. Among them were invitations from Nancy Shen, the daughter of the consul of China, and Jacqueline Diep, whose father was ambassador to Japan. Father said that dancing with boys was scandalous. For him, boys were to stay with boys and girls were to stay with girls. It was indecent for a girl to talk with a young man, and it was scandalous to dance because of the physical contact. Sex was a sin.

Decency ordered me to have friends only among girls. I never had a boyfriend. I spent my time with some of my Lycée Marie Curie girlfriends. We walked along the large avenues of Saigon holding hands, because that was what friendship meant in Vietnam. We were not lesbians—just friends. Looking back at those times, I found it pretty ridiculous for girls to walk in public holding hands with girls or with their arms encircling each other's waists. All physical affectionate gestures were natural friendship demonstrations.

The American Cultural Center, Saigon (1959-1960)

In 1959, I decided to take evening English courses at the American Cultural Center on Mac Dinh Chi Avenue, which was not far away from our new residence in Saigon. My goal was to make things to happen in my life and to be able to go to America.

I left home after dinner and returned at ten o'clock. Father, of course, was furious to see me going out in the evening, but it was for English classes and he could not forbid me to advance my education.

On November 3, 1959, I was eighteen years old.

I was the last student at the American Cultural Center to remain inside my English classroom, and my eyes met with the eyes of my professor, a handsome, young US Army officer. I was young and cute. We smiled to each other. He came to me and asked, "May I walk you home?" We strolled along the large, quiet avenue leading from the American Cultural Center to my home under the leafy branches of old flame and magnolia trees shining under the moonlight.

I told him, "Today is my birthday. I am eighteen."

He stopped, circled my waist, and kissed me on the cheek, saying, "In Texas, where I was born, we always kiss a girl on her birthday."

Arriving at home, I left him with a goodbye.

That night, for the first time in my life, I felt like I had a miraculous opportunity. A door had opened. I was enchanted to have met such a handsome, young, and wonderful American. I was Alice in Wonderland, and I had broken the glass ceiling!

The next Sunday, I was washing my hair when I heard the doorbell ringing. Our maid, Chi Sau, opened the door, and there were two

Americans asking for me. Chi Sau was very excited and she ran to me, announcing. "Miss, you have two American visitors."

"Tell them that I am not home," I told her. It was catastrophic for me, because I had my hair all wet and no makeup on my face. Father was going to kill me if he saw two US military men visiting me. In Vietnam, people like Father were prejudiced. Only bad girls went out with the French and US military men. I did not think I would even be allowed to date a Vietnamese military man. For Confucius, a soldier ranked much lower than an intellectual. When a Vietnamese family had three sons, they wanted them to become a doctor, a pharmacist, and a lawyer. Those careers were associated with wealth and prestige.

Our maid did not speak English, so she gestured to them with large movements of her arms and a huge smile to make them understand that I was not home. They hesitated for a while and decided to leave. I watched them from a window. Unfortunately, my professor turned around to look again at the house and saw me! He looked puzzled and deceived. I felt bad. I would have loved to be with him, but I could not because of prejudice.

During the next English lesson at the American Center, my professor acted as if he did not know me. He ignored me.

In December 1959, at the American Cultural Center, I signed up to be invited by an American family for Christmas 1959 to experience how Americans celebrated Christmas in America.

The family who invited me consisted of a burly US officer; his wife, who was a small brunette; and two young daughters. I spent Christmas Day with them. It was the first time that I saw an ornate American Christmas tree, and I was invited for an American Christmas turkey meal. The family took me to an American baseball game, where I had my first Coca-Cola can; and in the evening, we ended up at the US officers' club.

The year 1960 changed my life. An Australian professor, Kenneth, met at the American Cultural Center, invited me to go with him to his Australian friends' home for the New Year 1960. I would get an Australian experience of celebrating the New Year.

At home, Mother had already stored special food for our Vietnamese New Year, which would take place later in January. I reversed the invitation situation. I said to the Australians that I would take Vietnamese specialties and introduce them to our delicious delicacies. Mother did not mind my pillaging her food provisions. Vietnamese people were hospitable and generous.

Instead of me experiencing Australian New Year food, it was the Australians who sampled Vietnamese food. They loved it and found it terrific. The husband was an engineer, and he was very tall and skinny with a mustache and red hair, and he wore a khaki colonial outfit. He looked as if he were going on a safari trip and hunting a tiger. His wife was young and beautiful, with blond hair and blue eyes. The twins were adorable; they had blond hair and blue eyes like their mother.

At the end of the dinner, the hostess announced, "I want to show Alice how an Australian housewife does the dishwashing." So both of us disappeared into the kitchen and soon had our arms immersed in hot water with lots of bubbling soap. At home, our cook did the dishwashing with cold water from the tap and a piece of hard soap. Hot water that poured from the tap did not yet exist for us. To bathe, we took showers with cold water. The weather was always very warm, as we lived in a tropical climate.

The Purpose of My Life (1960)

In the spring of 1960, I read a long article in *Paris Match* that detailed the life and achievements of Fr. Dominique Pire, a Belgian Dominican monk who had been awarded the 1958 Nobel Peace Prize. Father Pire asked the readers, should they wish to be Good Samaritans, to send letters and gifts to the children living in his SOS villages in Europe.

I responded to Father Pire, offering to do so. His request was easy for me to respond to, as I loved to write and loved to offer presents.

To my great surprise, Father Pire answered with a long letter. His trademark was to write with what looked like minuscule flea strokes steeped in violet ink. He invited me to come to Belgium to help him with other international young people to build the University of Peace, his dream and vision. I possessed the ideal criteria he wanted in his young followers. I was born into high society, I was educated, I was fluent in Vietnamese and French, I came from a country at war, and I wanted to save the world. He had a dream, and he wanted to train his young followers as the future builders of peace around the world.

In reading Father Pire's letter, my life, so bleak so far, was suddenly lit up like a lamp switched on and shining in the present darkness. I found the purpose of my life. I would go to Belgium. The gods had spoken and shown me where I must go. It was easier to dream than to get it achieved. How could I go to Belgium? With a father like mine, nothing was possible. I knew what he would say: "I have no more money to send a child to study abroad. You are a girl, and you stay home with your parents. Good girls don't wander alone overseas. They would become lost girls."

Our next-door neighbor, Chi Ba Tu, taught at the kindergarten of the convent Regina Mundi of Saigon. I told Chi Ba Tu that I was very unhappy at home. She suggested to me to go and see the French mothers of the convent. She was convinced that I would connect well with the French nuns and find there people who understood the complications of my soul. I went to the convent and was enchanted by my visit.

The Congregation of Our Lady from France had already sent twelve French nuns who left Marseille for the shores of Vietnam in 1935. They had built a convent, Our Lady of Langbian, in Dalat (1936) and one in Hanoi, Our Lady of the Rosary (1937). The convent Regina Mundi of Saigon, more recent, was founded in 1950. The Canonesses of St. Augustine were in charge of the education of the girls of the high society. It was private education, and the fees were very high, but to study there was prestigious. The mothers there had been born as aristocrats. When they were being ordained and took their vows, they donated what they owned to their congregation.

Reverend Mother Superior Marie Zoila became my favorite among them. She was elderly, tall, thin, pale, and majestic in her immaculate long white religious habit. She welcomed me into her office any time I came, and I told her my stories and my dreams.

One day we looked through her open windows and saw Mrs. Ngo Dinh Nhu with her children arriving inside the courtyard of the convent. Her children studied at the convent. Mrs. Nhu was President Ngo Dinh Diem's sister-in-law and called herself the first lady of Vietnam.

Mother Marie Zoila confided to me, "In 1935, I was the one who accompanied the young Empress Nam Phuong of Vietnam on her return from France to Vietnam. We traveled by sea on a French ocean liner. I was her teacher, her companion, and her confidante. She sailed toward her destiny as the empress of Vietnam. She gave me the mandate to educate the girls of high society."

I said to Mother Marie Zoila, "If I go to Europe, I shall contact Empress Nam Phuong and shall ask her to be my godmother in the Catholic Church. For me, she is the first lady of Vietnam, and my godmother would be the first lady of Vietnam."

Mother Marie Zoila noticed that I was staring at a tiny statue of the Virgin Mary on her desk. She said with a soft, tender voice, "She is our Mother. Pray to her, and she will help you. Only our Mother has the power to help you."

In the fall of 1960, for the first time in my life, I entered the Notre

Dame Cathedral of Saigon. It was built between 1863 and 1880 using Norman architecture, with two bell towers; the materials used in its construction came from France. The bricks, red and pink in color, were shipped from Marseilles. In 1962, Pope John XXIII elevated its status to that of a basilica. It became Basilica of Our Lady of the Immaculate Conception.

I, raised as a Buddhist, prayed for the first time in my life to the Virgin Mary: "Please, Saint Mary, please help me; please let me go to Belgium. I promise you that I shall convert to the Roman Catholic Church." The Virgin Mary was my ultimate refuge and my last hope. The Virgin Mary heard my prayer!

Father said, as a strong and valid argument, that he had no money to send me abroad for university studies. My brother Henri suddenly proclaimed that he would pay for my travel ticket and for my university studies in Europe for as many years as it would take. He sided with me, understood my feelings, and thought that I had no future in Vietnam. Life in Europe would be his gift to me. "Father paid for my university studies in France. Now I shall pay for your studies. Go to Europe and live your dreams as you wish. Live your life in Europe. You are still very young, and if I can help you, I will do it."

I applied for my passport and supplied two mandatory documents, one confirming that I was enrolled at the Catholic University of Louvain in political and social sciences, and two certificates confirming my housing in Brussels and Louvain.

Michel de Grave was my Belgian pen pal through the program of international correspondence between schoolchildren. I got names and addresses through Lycée Marie Curie. He entered his first year in economics at the Catholic University of Louvain. His parents provided me with a certificate confirming that I had accommodation with them in Brussels. The chaplain of the Vietnamese students in Louvain, Fr. Andre Bourguignon, registered me at the Sedes Sapientiae, a boarding center for girl students in Louvain.

The passport office was located inside the Presidential Palace. President Ngo Dinh Diem liked to control everything whenever possible. He had just signed a decree forbidding people to leave Vietnam because we had become engaged in a big war, and no one could exit the country except some students and some emergency cases. Out of curiosity, he read the applications for passports and stumbled upon mine. I was the daughter of a man he respected and liked, and I was going to study at the Catholic University of Louvain, his favorite university. He had been there and had wished to become a monk. I chose to study political and social sciences, which belonged to the category of approved studies abroad because the University of Saigon did not offer them yet in their program. President Ngo Dinh Diem approved my application to go to Belgium. I got my passport! Do you believe in miracles?

On November 3, 1960, I was nineteen years old. While I was packing, Father turned around and around me. He spoke to me: "After graduation, you must return to Vietnam to serve your country. Don't marry a foreigner; you will bring shame to the family if you marry a foreigner. You must not convert to the Catholic religion. Priests and nuns are very smart to convert such a naive girl like you."

I answered. "Yes, Father. Yes, Father." I zipped up my luggage as fast as possible, delirious with joy to leave home. I had dreamed of that moment for many long years.

I visited the convent for the last time to say goodbye to Reverend Mother Marie Zoila. I was thrilled. I had succeeded in going to Belgium! Mother Marie Zoila was less enthusiastic than I would have imagined. In fact, she had never wished me to be able to go. She had never believed that I could accomplish what I set out to accomplish. She mumbled to another nun, "Oh, those priests, inviting such a young girl to go to Europe. They are irresponsible." I promised to Mother Marie Zoila that I would write to her from Belgium.

A young and pretty French nun looked at me and said, "My child, are you going to save the world?" I was furious.

My Departure to Europe
(December 1, 1960)

Two roads diverged in a wood, and I, I took the one less traveled by, and that has made all the difference.
—Robert Frost

On December 1, 1960, my parents, brothers, sisters, cousin Therese, and Uncle and Aunt Nine came to Tan Son Nhut Airport to say good bye. Another Vietnamese family was there, sending off their son to study in France. Our two families did not know each other but bowed to each other and made us promise, as we would be the only two young Vietnamese on the plane, to look after each other in the plane and in Europe.

I walked quickly to the Air France Caravelle, which was scheduled for its last trip from Saigon to Paris. The plane was very old. I was afraid that at the last minute I might be stopped and my great dream of freedom would be shattered. I could hear my family shouting behind my back, "Goodbye, Alice, Goodbye!"

When the plane took off and climbed up to the skies, I looked down and saw for the last time the rice fields and the sinuous rivers of my ancestral land. The plane was crowded with American and French people. The young Vietnamese student and I were the only Vietnamese passengers. We appeared like two privileged youth because we had been able to get out of Vietnam during wartime.

I sat between a French publisher from Hachette Editions and an American journalist named Richard who was writing for the *Christian Science Monitor*; he became my first friend during my journey. I was pampered by the young Air France steward. He told me that he had served Mrs. Ngo Dinh Nhu, who was President Ngo Dinh Diem's sister-in-law and the most powerful woman in Vietnam. She had showed him her impressive jewelry. Passengers in my vicinity gave me their names and addresses in France and America. They said, "Write to us if you need something." My fellow Vietnamese student looked pale and greenish with travel sickness. He slept the entire time.

I was triumphant. I talked with Richard, telling him about my idealism, my love for President John Kennedy, Dr. Thomas Dooley, and Fr. Dominique Pire. Richard seemed to listen attentively, and I was pretty sure that I amused him with my naivety.

The old Air France Caravelle had technical problems over Pakistan, so it landed there for repairs for three days. The passengers had two nights in the most expensive hotel and restaurant of Karachi, all paid by Air France. I stuck like a piece of gum to my American journalist, who looked after me like a big American brother watching over a Vietnamese little sister. I had a waiter in the dining room dressed in a gold-and-red uniform with a sword at his side.

A hotel maid greeted me in my hotel room and with a sweet smile, asked me if I knew how to prepare my bath. I kept silent, not knowing what to say. We had bathtubs in Saigon, but I always took a shower. She proceeded to open the faucets of the bathtub and prepared my hot bath with lots of pink bubble soap and fresh flower petals in the warm water. A naive little girl from Vietnam started her journey. I was in Pakistan!

I had an old man with a long white beard guarding the door of my hotel room. He slept across my door, forbidding me to go out. I wanted to give to Richard, my American journalist, some delicious *nem* (Vietnamese sausages) Mother had prepared for my journey. I believe that he forbade Richard to sneak inside my room, because Richard looked at me with a strange expression the next morning, as if I were an oddity because I had my room guarded and secured. Who had instructed the hotel? Surely it was Father and Henri from Saigon. I assumed they were panicked at the news that the plane did not reach Paris and that I was stranded in Karachi.

Arrival in Paris; Brussels; Louvain

After Karachi, we were again in the plane, off to Europe. My brother Albert picked me up at the gates of Orly. I said farewell to Richard, such a handsome young American, and watched him disappear in the crowd in his beige overcoat. I wished that I could disappear with him.

Albert had graduated and had an excellent career in Paris. I resented him because, from Paris, he had opposed my departure for Europe. Henri had let me go to Europe. There had been a clash between my two brothers. Albert said that I should have stayed in Vietnam, gotten married, and had children. Why study in Europe? According to Albert, it would be a lonely student life and a waste of the best years of my life.

We walked along the Champs Élysées boutiques, and he offered me a black velvet coat with a mink collar. I said proudly to the saleswoman, "This is my brother!"

She commented, "I have never seen a brother offering to a sister such an expensive present."

Albert asked his landlady, "Could my sister stay in my room?" The landlady knew him as a very decent young man and acquiesced. She showed up out of curiosity to have a furtive look at the so-called sister.

Albert took me out for meals. I had been told not to eat much because Western meals would make me fat. I was very dainty and ate little. Albert picked up a chicken leg from my plate and ate it. He always had an ironic smile on his face, and he truly got on my nerves. I guessed what he was thinking: "Why did the family send her here?" He surely scratched his head about this nonsense.

Albert tried to persuade me to stay in Paris and abandon the project to study at Louvain. He said, "Paris is the cultural and artistic center of Europe. Have fun in Paris and enjoy your youth here. Louvain is a monastery. Why do you want to bury yourself in Louvain?"

Exasperated, I answered, "You don't understand. Please leave me alone."

On December 15, 1960, Albert and I arrived in Brussels by train on the wedding day of King Beaudouin I of Belgium and Dona Fabiola di Moro y Aragon at the Cathedral of St. Michael and St. Gudula. The streets were empty. People stayed home, watching the wedding on their TV screens.

I was welcomed at the Brussels home of Michel de Grave like the sixth child of the family. Maurice and Marie Louise de Grave treated me as if I were their own child, and their children (Michel, Andre, Jacqueline, Jean Pierre, and Bernadette) were sweet and friendly. It was a very loving family. Maurice was an engineer who built homes and garages and also rented space for cars in his garages. They belonged to the middle class, had money, and were generous. Meals were abundant and excellent.

In December 1960, I arrived in the middle of a general strike that paralyzed Brussels and Belgium. Another big problem was that the Belgian Congo had been granted independence in the summer. Most of the Belgians who lived in the former colony returned to Belgium. They had to adjust to a new life, and most were not happy to have lost their former colony. There was also a permanent linguistic problem between the Walloons and the Flemish. The country was linguistically deeply divided, and that problem had never ceased to exist.

Albert returned to Paris in the evening and left me in the care of Maurice and Marie Louise de Grave.

I arrived on December 20, 1960, in Louvain (Leuven in Flemish) to begin my studies at the School of Political and Social Studies. The courses had already begun in September, so I was late. The university had two separate sections—the French one (Walloons) and the Flemish one. I studied, of course, in the French section.

I had a room at the Sedes Sapientiae, the largest student boarding center for girls—especially for foreign girls. The Sedes and its extension, Les Renards, were managed by three women. Huguette was the eldest and the leader. Sabine was her sister, and Anna, from Spain, was another member of this lay religious congregation. They had civilian clothes. During my first lunch at the Sedes cafeteria, I chose a dish called American steak tartare. It was raw ground beef mixed with mustard and other condiments, and decorated with a raw egg yolk. This remained my favorite dish. I wondered why they called it American, because beef tartare was a popular dish in Belgium, France, Switzerland, and Germany.

I found two Vietnamese girls at the Sedes. Tuyet was leaving for Paris, as she had finished her studies in medicine, and Kim Dung had finished her studies in sociology. The Sedes administrators told me that they had beautiful and talented Vietnamese student girls as my predecessors and that Vietnamese were very well liked there. I asked Tuyet if she would like to have a walk with me. In Saigon, I had taken walks with my girlfriends along the spacious avenues of Saigon. Tuyet laughed and said, "I am too busy. No time." She then advised me, "Don't ask other girls to go for a walk with you. They prefer to look for a husband." Kim Dung had a Belgian boyfriend, Jacques, and she found herself in a dilemma. She had to choose between Jacques or Vietnam. After many months of soul-searching, she opted to return to her family and Vietnam.

The de Grave parents invited me to spend Christmas 1960 and the New Year 1961 holidays with them in Brussels. I had a permanent guest room at their house, and my affection for them extended well beyond the Louvain years. I returned many times to visit them during the following decades.

The Catholic University of Louvain;
the Great Friendships (1961-1964)

Claire de Bethune was my first friend at the Sedes and in Louvain. By coincidence, Claire arrived at the Sedes at the same time as me. I was standing outside the building, looking at the public park in front of me, when a Belgian girl, driving her car, stopped and asked me with a shy and friendly smile, "Do you know if I can park in that spot?"

I responded, "Sorry, I have no idea." That was my first encounter with Claire de Bethune, one year younger than me, the daughter of Baron Jean Baptiste de Bethune, who resided at the Chateau de Marke near Courtrai (Kortrijk in Flemish). It was also her first day at the university, where she was studying archeology and art history at the Flemish faculty of the university. She spoke French and Flemish. She was tall, thin, beautiful, refined and elegant.

We became great friends. Claire was receptive to foreigners, and she liked Asian populations and cultures. Physically we were the opposite of each other. Claire was very tall and very thin. I was very small. We walked on the irregular cobblestones of Louvain, Claire curving her back and wearing flat shoes so she would not appear too tall, and me walking in high-heeled shoes. Terrible sufferings for my feet! Claire and I became lifelong friends.

The Catholic University of Louvain (Leuven) was established in Leuven on December 9, 1425, by a papal bull issued by Pope Martin V. It had been part of the Duchy of Burgundy.

I studied at the School of Political and Social Sciences, which later upgraded to institute and faculty. My favorite professor was Pierre de Bie, professor of sociology. He was very handsome, and people told me that female students fell in love with him when he was a professor at the

University of Lovanium in the former Belgian Congo. I was also friends with his eldest daughter, Myriam, who was a boarding student with me at the Sedes, so I was frequently invited over by Pierre de Bie and his family. Myriam left soon after for England.

The rector of the university, Msgr. Van Weyenberg, and the vice-rector, Msgr. De Vroede, were elderly, and we loved them as if they were our grandfathers. They were approachable and friendly. We could often see Msgr. Van Weyenberg touring Louvain, his university city, driven in a big limousine, wrapped in all the splendor of his bishop's dress, distributing large smiles and blessings. He often visited us at our Vietnamese student foyer, sharing the joys of our festivities.

I once stopped by the office of Msgr. De Vroede and offered him red roses, to the great amusement of his secretary, to thank him for waiving my tuition fees. I had arrived in Louvain with family funds to pay for my studies. The Vietnamese government restricted the monthly transfer of money to students to five hundred dollars, converted to Belgian francs. I had extra money thanks to my brother Albert, who worked in Paris. Most of the male Vietnamese students in Louvain had scholarships from the university and no tuition fees. They advised me to ask for my tuition fees to be waived, and my request was successful.

The university was very generous with the Hungarian students, refugees from the Revolution of 1956, an uprising against the Soviet Union, and with the Vietnamese students, refugees from 1954, which saw the exodus of one million Vietnamese from North Vietnam to South Vietnam, fleeing communism.

In January 1961, the world was tuned to hear the inauguration speech of President John F. Kennedy, my hero. I loved it. "If the path ahead was long and difficult, if it would demand the utmost of strength and sacrifice, then this was the price the nation would have to pay. I do not shrink from the responsibility, I welcome it…We would pay any price, bear any burden, meet any hardship, support any friend, oppose any foe, to assure the survival and the success of liberty."

In the context of the Vietnam War, the Vietnamese could interpret his speech as a speech intended for the Vietnam War. That was not the intention of the president. He addressed a host of problems, internal and external, pertaining to the United States, but as a Vietnamese person, I was ecstatic. With the help of the United States, which was a superpower, we would be safe and protected, and we would never have to live under a communist regime.

President Kennedy also created the Peace Corps for American youth to enroll in and serve the world.

In Brussels, I was soon connected with Monique Godenne and her family. In January of 1961, Father wrote to his friend the Doc Phu Su Nguyen Huu Hau, who was living in the sixteenth district of Paris, announcing to him my arrival in Belgium and asking him to look after me. This was typical Vietnamese behavior. They always asked relatives and friends to look after their children. I knew this family well. I knew Mr. Nguyen Huu Hau as Father's colleague and friend. Mrs. Hau worked at Lycée Marie Curie in the administration department. Their daughter was my sewing class teacher. Father and the Doc Phu Su Nguyen Huu Hau were close friends, and they both had French citizenship, which formed a bond of solidarity between them.

The Nguyen Huu Hau family introduced me to Monique Godenne, the daughter of a man who had been a senior French officer during the Indochina War. Monique had studied medicine in Paris with their son. She married a Belgian doctor, Jacques Godenne, and they lived in Uccles, a posh district of Brussels. They had two adorable children: Isabelle and Olivier. Monique often invited me to her home in the suburb of Uccles.

Monique introduced me to Andre Molitor and his family. She was a cousin of Andre Molitor's spouse, Edith, and she told them about this Vietnamese girl, the daughter of an eminent mandarin, who studied in Louvain. Monique thought that as Andre Molitor was a professor at Louvain and his children Michel and Anne were students at Louvain, they could be an excellent connection for me.

Andre Molitor, born in 1911 in Kermanshah, Persia, from Belgian parents, was a professor at Louvain in the constitution and administration of Belgium. In 1961, he was appointed principal private secretary (*chef de cabinet*) to King Baudouin I of Belgium. Andre and Edith Molitor had five children. Michel, the eldest, my age, studied political and social sciences with me. Anne studied psychology. Luc, Pascal, and Marc were still at school.

Andre Molitor, a man of duty, believed that it was his moral duty to look after this Vietnamese girl because she studied at a Belgian university and because she was member of a prominent family. Therefore, I became a frequent guest at his Brussels home.

The Virgin Mary had again blessed me with those two encounters. I was now invited into the most distinguished and safe homes of Belgium. I became a member of the de Bethune and Molitor families, although those families did not socialize with each other. The barons de Bethune belonged to the old aristocracy of Belgium.

The Royal Belgian family after World War II became deeply unpopular in Belgium. During the war, King Leopold III had spent his time as a prisoner of the Germans, and the royal family had lived in exile in Switzerland. He had married Lilian Baels, a commoner and the governess of his children, to whom he had bestowed the title of Princess de Rethy. Leopold III abdicated, and young Baudouin then became king in 1950 at age twenty.

Andre Molitor was appointed as his principal secretary and advisor (*chef de cabinet du Roi*) on June 1, 1961. Andre Molitor was a disciple of Emmanuel Mounier, and after the war, he had founded *La Revue Nouvelle*, a Catholic review that grouped French-speaking intellectuals in search of progress and change.

His role with King Baudouin was that of a moderator, a guide, and the conscience of the king. He wrote an academic book titled *The Royal Function in Belgium*, which taught how exactly he viewed the monarchy, using such statements as *"the king reigns and does not govern."* The king saw his political power diminished, but his moral power grew bigger.

King Baudouin, Queen Fabiola, and Andre Molitor reformed the monarchy and its constitution. The three of them were completely devoted to the well-being of the Belgian population.

Nothing was a coincidence. In 1961, Claire de Bethune and Andre Molitor crossed my path by divine providence.

Fr. Dominique Pire; Huy (1961-1962)

The future belongs to those who believe in the beauty of their dreams.
—Eleanor Roosevelt

In 1961, I visited Fr. Dominique Pire, the 1958 Nobel Peace Prize winner, during weekends in Huy. He had arranged for me to have transportation back and forth with Jacqueline de Terw, a student in medicine in Louvain. I shared a room with Jacqueline and three other girls in a house they rented on Marie Therese Avenue, close to the station. Jacqueline was a nurse who had been forty years old when she decided to study medicine. She was determined to become a missionary doctor in Africa. She also learned how to pilot a bush plane. Father Pire, a parish priest, had known her family for a long time. They lived in a château on the outskirts of Huy along the Meuse River, on the road to Liege.

During my first visit, Father Pire asked me to talk about Vietnam at his Mahatma Gandhi Centre. I put on a beautiful Vietnamese outfit and talked passionately about my country, and I ended with quotations from President John F. Kennedy, who promised to us "a new frontier" and aid in the fight against communism.

Back in his office, Father Pire cupped my tiny face in his large hands and said, "I am very proud of you, Alice. You will become a great lady." At that moment, I would have killed myself for him if asked to do so. Those few words had metamorphosed a tiny ordinary child into a brilliant and pretty young girl. I became a beautiful butterfly. That was the power of praise and appreciation.

I stayed in one of his three guest rooms that were located inside a huge building, 35 rue du Marche, which he used for his offices and his warehouses. He had dozens of staff. As a Nobel Peace Prize winner, and because he was undertaking international humanitarian projects, he had the authorization from his church hierarchy to work outside the convent and to circulate and travel as he wished.

I had a privileged status. I was his cherished follower and child. I could walk everywhere in his building. He showed me his office with a huge map of the world covering one wall. Colored pins marked the locations of his projects in Europe. During the Second World War, he was active in the Belgian resistance against the Nazis. After the war, he helped "the displaced elderly people"—a term for the elderly refugees, mostly from Russia and Eastern Europe. He founded the SOS Children's Villages.

His executive assistant, Andree, or his junior secretary, Monique, would sleep overnight in the bedroom adjacent to mine so I would not be left alone in the building during the night. Father Pire had to return every evening to his Dominican Convent de la Sartre. I also had the exclusive authorization to climb to the rooftop where he had his private garden. He cultivated roses, tulips, and prayed and meditated while looking over to the Meuse River. He was a priest, and I was twenty years old. People said that I was cute. I was possessive, and he was my whole universe. That was the reason for our separation at the end of 1961. Father Pire decided that we should not see each other for some time because I was too emotional and too possessive. I needed maturity. He was a priest, and he was afraid. He said to me, "Stop being a little girl who plays with dolls in a world on fire!" I was very upset. My journey had taken an unexpected turn. I traveled to Belgium in 1960 with the purpose of being a follower of Father Pire, building the University of Peace with him, and being one of his young builders of peace in the world. Now my purpose was changed, not by my own will but by the Providence of God, again in mysterious ways.

That day, I returned to Louvain with Jacqueline, a down-to-earth, practical, and sarcastic woman. She looked at me like a salivating cat with bright eyes looking at a mouse, with her perpetual ironic smile, and she commented, "What did I tell you? You are in love with him. You see a halo on his head because he has the Nobel Peace Prize. For me he is only an ordinary parish priest."

I told her. "Please, leave me alone. Shut up."

My lease in the same student house with Jacqueline de T. and others had expired. Things worked out well. I had resided there only to get a ride with Jacqueline to travel to Huy. She acted like an elder sister to me, but I did not like it. I was a dreamer and a fantasist. I was sentimental. She was practical and tough. We clashed because we were so different from each other. Each morning, when I was slow to tidy up my bed, she would say ironically, "Are North Vietnam and South Vietnam still fighting on your bed?" She controlled my mail and what I read. One day, there was a leaflet concerning a bad comment about the church, and she jumped on me, screaming that I read evil literature. One day I complained about a stomachache, and she called her professor at the hospital to prepare a bed and operate on me immediately, because she believed that I had appendicitis. I had to beg them to back off. I stopped complaining about any illnesses I had.

I remember going back once to Huy with Jacqueline in the summer of 1962 and staying at her château for the weekend. Jacqueline thought I wanted to spend the weekend there, just for a vacation. I did not tell her that it was the inauguration day of the University of Peace and I was determined to go and see it. In the afternoon, I said to Jacqueline, "I am going for a walk." I walked on the road to Liege, taking shortcuts through the fields, and I did not know really the directions. Suddenly I saw the University of Peace in front of me in the middle of the fields. It was Inauguration Day. The university was ultramodern with large glass windows. I could see lots of people, professors, and students. They had drinks in their hands, and they talked. Father Pire dominated the crowd with his tall stature and his white Dominican monk's robe. I stood outside the university in the middle of a field like a little ghost. Suddenly Father Pire saw me. He became pale, was shaken, and vanished.

In June of 1961, on the Feast of the Pentecost, Father Pire and I took a long walk there, and he explained to me the meaning of Pentecost. It is the Church's commemoration of the descent of the Holy Spirit upon the apostles, fulfilling what Our Lord promised before ascending to heaven. Father Pire and I stood on this bare land, and he said, "It is here that we will build the University of Peace." We were at the peak of our tender affection for each other. He was my divine light, and I was the apostle. The Holy Spirit descended on us. It was what we thought. Everything then looked so blessed and wonderful.

I walked back to Jacqueline's home. Jacqueline scrutinized me with her piercing eyes and said, "Where have we been? Oh my God, did you walk up there to see him? I understand now why you wanted to go to Huy with me. You wanted to see him. I told you to forget him. Turn the page. It is not good for you to be friends with him."

Father Pire and Huy had been my whole universe. My heart was broken in thousands of pieces. Back in Louvain, I had no choice other than to immerse myself entirely into my student life. I had to replace Huy by Louvain. Soon after, the man dearest to my heart would be Andre Molitor. I was searching for the perfect father I could have on Earth, and God gave me Andre Molitor.

In one of his letters, after our separation, Father Pire wrote to me, "You don't know yourself well. You must look into yourself and know yourself. In the Antiquity, that was the advice of the Greek philosophers. When you know yourself well, this would the first step on the road to perfection." He added, "You turned your back to me and Andree because we told you the truth about yourself. You needed to grow up. You reacted like a spoiled child. We told you the truth because we loved you."

I told Father Pire that I had the intention to convert myself to the Roman Catholic faith and that I chose him to be the priest to baptize me. I found this as a way to go back to him and see him again. His reaction was vehemently negative. He said, "When I called you from Vietnam, I had no intention to convert you. You must respect the religion of your country and your parents."

I pointed out, "You don't understand. My decision was already taken before I met you. I made a promise to the Virgin Mary before I left Saigon. My conversion was for our Mother Mary, not for you."

His sermon about my desire for baptism upset me. I later chose Canon Jean Giblet, eminent professor of theology at the University of Louvain, to be the priest who would baptize me. Andre Molitor had introduced Father Giblet to me for my theology lessons.

My Student Life in Louvain; Aucam; Ad Lucem

*Over every mountain, there is a path, although
it may not be seen from the valley.*
—Theodore Roethke

The Providence of God had other plans for me. The Huy chapter was closed. The Louvain chapter opened. I found my next accommodation at the AUCAM House for girls. AUCAM stood for Catholic University Association for Aid to the Missions. We were about ten girl students there. The foreigners were welcomed to make it an international group. The foreign girls were Olga, a Russian from the United States; Kiwako, a Japanese; Marie-Jeanne Kao, a Chinese from the United States; Marie-Josee, a Congolese; and me, Alice.

My best friends there were Marie-Jeanne Kao and Francine Pauly, daughter of a Belgian judge. His position in French was *Procureur du Roi*. Marie Jeanne and I were like sisters because we cooked and ate Chinese and Vietnamese food, went shopping together, and went to Mass together. I was an ocean of fantasies; meanwhile, Marie-Jeanne was a serene lake. Kiwako took up a room in the attic. She cooked her Japanese meals in our kitchen but never joined me and Marie Jeanne for cooking or for eating. She was always by herself.

Francine invited me during weekends to her home in Brussels, and I was lovingly welcomed by her parents. We also visited her uncle, whose hobby as an elderly retired man was cultivating flowers and creating new species of roses, tulips, and dahlias.

At our student house, the salary of the cleaning lady and coffee expenses were subsidized. We were allowed to invite male friends for coffee in the living room. We were located at number 12 Place de l'Universite. Sitting at the edge of my upstairs window, I looked at the student crowd crisscrossing the Place de l'Universite below.

The Walloon and the Flemish students had different caps and scarves. Sometimes they had fights because they did not like each other. That was a political linguistic problem in Louvain that later would seal the fate of the university.

Nearby stood the AUCAM building, which housed the administrative offices and the male students. There they had their rooms, a big kitchen, and a large dining table. The AUCAM boys and girls saw each other often, and marriages often happened between them. A boy and a girl also teamed up every day to do grocery shopping, cooking, and dishwashing. We shared the cost of the meals, which were frugal, such as spaghetti, meatballs, and a salad. This was appropriate for a student budget and for a missionary vocation.

Fr. Jean Giblet, chaplain of Ad Lucem, Louvain, introduced me to Ad Lucem, an international association. I joined Ad Lucem. This association was founded in Paris by a French doctor, Dr. Robert Aujoulat. Members were mostly French and Belgian professionals and students who wished to serve the Catholic Church as missionaries, especially in Africa. The members were handsome young men and sweet girls. I was the only Vietnamese and the only non-Belgian member of our Louvain group.

We had a weekly Mass in our chapel at a building on Marie Therese Street. Fr. Charles Lambin, an elderly retired Jesuit, lived there alone, dusting donated books, repairing them, and sending them off to the missions in Africa. He rented the upstairs rooms to students who were Ad Lucem members. Another renter was Ignace, a Congolese studying medicine who was married to a Congolese named Elizabeth; he was not an Ad Lucem.

Any time I felt lonely, I walked to Father Lambin's building. It was a long walk from my AUCAM girl house, but the streets of Louvain were safe, even at nighttime. On my way, I stopped to buy some popular Belgian street food: french fries, pickled mussels, and a sausage called *cervelas*. In the middle ages, this province belonged to the Duchy of Burgundy. The economic life of Louvain revolved around its population of students, academics, and religious congregations. The Catholic elite of Belgium studied at the Catholic University of Louvain.

Fr. Charles Lambin was like a grandfather for me, and he loved me as a granddaughter. As hobbies, he raised tiny little birds and guinea pigs in his backyard. He fed them withered lettuce discarded by grocery stores nearby. They were his children, and instead of talking to himself, he talked to them. He lived there alone and independent; I heard that he did not get along with his Jesuit congregation. He wore the long black cassock of priests with a black sash around the waist.

I liked to spend the day there and cook for me and for Father Lambin. We were not alone, because the handsome young men upstairs—namely Jacques, Eric, and Walter—joined us and cooked for themselves, and we were a joyful family. Father Lambin would have liked me to marry a nice Belgian, but I was too immature. I did not even think of them as young men; they were my brothers in Ad Lucem.

I walked with the Ad Lucem students in pilgrimages to Notre Dame de Lourdes and Notre Dame de Chartres. We also had spiritual retreats in almost all the famous monasteries and convents of Belgium. I got a ride in Fr. Jean Giblet's car. Father Giblet was our spiritual leader. During the summer, the Ad Lucem groups from France, Belgium, and England converged at the Ad Lucem summer camp in the Beaujolais region of France. The missionary doctors, engineers, and economists coached younger people with advice about the future and helped them to land professional positions. Ad Lucem was funded and subsidized privately by its own professional members.

I enjoyed the Ad Lucem summer camps. We started the day with a Mass. Afterward, we had breakfast with bread, butter, jam, and large glasses of milk and coffee. During the day, we split into discussion groups according to our interests. Some shared kitchen tasks, such as peeling potatoes and cooking for our lunches and suppers. Some men cut the wood for our evening outdoor bonfires. For my part, I enjoyed walking and exploring the countryside. We drank the Beaujolais wine like water. I met new Ad Lucem friends from France there. They invited me to Lilles, Toulouse, and the Basque country, beyond the Pyrenees.

My Baptism in the Roman Catholic Faith (December 8, 1962); Empress Nam Phuong of Vietnam; Claire de Bethune; Andre Molitor

I had maintained a correspondence with Reverend Mother Marie Zoila from Saigon. I had promised to write to her about my life in Europe. I remember also that I wanted Empress Nam Phuong to be my godmother in the Catholic Church.

In the spring of 1962, I wrote to Empress Nam Phuong and introduced myself as the daughter of the Doc Phu Su Nguyen Van Ba and a friend of Mother Marie Zoila. The Doc Phu Su had been the administrative and loyal pillars of the imperial regime up to 1955, when this special class of high ranking mandarins was abolished by President Ngo Dinh Diem. Father was also born in Mytho—the same province where the family of our empress came from. Mother Marie Zoila was the empress's teacher at the convent des Oiseaux of Paris, her confidante and companion during her return from Paris to Vietnam on a French ocean liner as Empress Nam Phuong of Vietnam.

I could not have had a better introduction to win the empress's heart and trust. She agreed with affection to be my godmother. I chose the baptism day to be the Feast of the Immaculate Conception on December 8, 1962, in honor of the Virgin Mary, for whom I held a special gratitude and love. My godfather would be Andre Molitor, senior private secretary to King Beaudouin I. In French, this position was called *chef de cabinet du roi*. The location for the baptism would be a big church in Louvain or Brussels.

At the beginning of December 1961, I had asked Andre Molitor to be my godfather. He told me that he would give me his answer at Christmas

1961, when I would come to spend Christmas at his home. He needed some time to reflect about it. During Christmas 1961, he bowed courteously in front of me as the perfect gentleman he was and said, "I would be honored to be your godfather."

I wrote to the empress my daily life stories in Belgium. She read that my best friend was Claire de Bethune, the daughter of a Belgian baron. Originally, the empress asked me to choose Claire to represent her by procuration in case she could not travel to Belgium. But one month before the baptism, she wrote to me and said that after having deep thoughts on the subject and after praying to God to guide her, she had arrived at the conclusion that my godmother must be Claire de Bethune.

She explained that she was no more a sovereign, only a former empress in exile. She wrote, "Under the tragic circumstances of our country, I shall be a liability for your future, not an asset. Claire de Bethune would be the ideal godmother for you." She continued, "My dear child, you are too young to understand my decision. I chose to live in self-reclusion away from the world. If one day, God would allow me to return to Vietnam as a sovereign, I shall call you to be at my side. To be your godmother means that I have responsibilities to be there for you, to be your spiritual mother and I find it impossible to fulfill that role. Please understand that I love you and pray for you on the day of your baptism and always,"

Claire said that the empress was wise in her decision because of the political circumstances of Vietnam. It was how Claire de Bethune, instead of being a procuration on behalf of Empress Nam Phuong, became my real godmother in the Catholic Church.

The man who would take an important place in my heart and destiny was Andre Molitor. He knew his responsibility as godfather and the challenges that came with it. He accepted me into his family and into his life with affection and pride.

I loved the Virgin Mary, but that was all I knew. I did not care more or less about anything else concerning religious matters. My attendance at Father Giblet's theology courses was mandatory, but it did not mean that I listened or understood anything. I would be there, but my mind was absent, thousands of miles away.

Andre Molitor agreed to be my godfather because he was convinced that it was God's will. I needed help, and God put him in my journey to help me. It did not matter what my problem was. God gave me to him as his spiritual daughter, and he accepted God's gift.

During one weekend spent at his home on Pere Eudore Devroyes Street in Brussels, he gave a reception for friends. My room was in the attic. Anne was sent to invite me to attend the reception, but I was not willing to go downstairs and see the guests. I was shy. My godfather then climbed up the stairs and said, "You are my spiritual daughter and Anne is my biological daughter. You are a member of my family. Come down and be hostess to the guests with Edith and Anne."

At the beginning of my flow of letters addressed to him, like a wild stream, he tried to direct me to exchange correspondence with his wife, Edith. He thought that what I needed was a woman friend and I shall confide myself to Edith as a woman to a woman. He was wrong. It did not work out. I had no inspiration and no desire to write to Edith, and the feelings were mutual. There was no chemistry between us. Our letters to each other were very short, flat, and boring, I returned to my passion to write to my godfather, and he answered. He understood that it was only him I wanted as my confident, not his wife. He enjoyed my letters as he was a reader and a writer. He was amused with my letters full of fantasy, and he believed that it was his duty to be my spiritual mentor and guide.

He encouraged me to write, especially about my childhood and my current daily life, so he could know me better and be informed. He also said, "Maybe I shall publish one day a book, *Letters from my Goddaughter.*" He seemed serious about this project, but I do not know when exactly he abandoned it. He was swarmed by my numerous long letters and had no time to sort them out. One day he told me that getting published would not be easy, stating the example of his father. "My father wrote a very interesting book but was not published. It is not easy to get published."

Twenty years down the road, when I confided in him that I had converted only to have him, Andre Molitor, be my beloved godfather, he answered, "I always was aware of it. On the day of your baptism, you had not encountered Jesus Christ. But I also knew that one day, you would meet Jesus Christ and that you would receive him in your life."

I was baptized in the Roman Catholic faith on December 8, 1962, at the Abbey of Rhodes St. Genesis near Brussels. I had promised to the Virgin Mary in the Cathedral (now Basilica) of Saigon in the fall of 1960 that I would convert to the Roman Catholic Church should I be able to go to Belgium.

It was not by chance or by coincidence that Claire de Bethune and Andre Molitor, perfect strangers, had crossed my path. Providence had put them in my life to become my godfather and godmother. I now had the perfect spiritual family I had always dreamed of.

Claire de Bethune belonged to the Belgian aristocracy and had five brothers: Jean Louis, a priest; Emmanuel, a politician; Guy, a doctor; and Jacques and Francois, both Benedictine monks, Jacques in the Abbey of Maredsous and Francois in Clerlande. The Chateau de Marke stood proudly through more than two hundred years of history, and inside they had a library that contained rare precious archives, unique in Belgium. A priest came on Sunday to celebrate Mass in their private chapel and have lunch with the family.

This family gave three sons consecrated to the service of God. It was the family that Our Lady of the Immaculate Conception gave to me in Belgium.

I had planned my baptism as a magnificent ceremony. I went to a salon of haute couture in Louvain and ordered a custom-made long dress with precious white lace matched with a long purple velvet cape. It was the most beautiful day of my life, and I was willing to spend a lot of money for my baptism. It was a gorgeous wedding dress. I invited the boutique lady who made the dress for me, and she came with her daughter. Before the ceremony began, she adjusted my dress and pinned a fresh orchid on it as her gift.

The Ad Lucem students organized the ceremony. The Vietnamese students took the pictures. The nuns of the Abbey served lunch. The nuns, in their long black habits and veils, stood on the back benches of the chapel, stretching out their necks to look at the ceremony.

I was flooded with gifts such as crucifixes, crosses, statues of the Virgin Mary, books, and flowers. Father Giblet gave me a collection of books written by Paul Claudel. My godfather gave me a Bible and other religious books. Claire de Bethune gave me a long white candle and a silver crucifix.

During the months preceding my baptism, I had chosen as my favorite authors Thomas Merton, a Trappist monk, and Edith Stein, a Carmelite nun. *The Seven Storey Mountain*, written by Thomas Merton in 1949, which became a classic, became my bible. That book never left me. Thomas Merton and Edith Stein were in my life and in my heart, my inseparable and invisible companions.

I liked Raissa Maritain's book *The Great Friendships*, in which she described the special relationship between her and her godfather, Leon Bloy. I could relate to her and to her godfather because I also wanted to write *The Great Friendships* and describe my special relationship with my godfather, Andre Molitor.

Edith Stein would be beatified by Pope John Paul II in Cologne, Germany, on May 1, 1987, and later canonized as a saint. She became Saint Theresa Benedict of the Blessed Cross. When I read her book and gave her my love in 1962 and beyond, she was only a Carmelite nun who had converted to Christianity from the Jewish faith and died in a gas chamber at Auschwitz. I believed deep down in my soul that she had protected me since my baptism day. Without knowing it, I had loved a saint, and even if I had not prayed for her intercession, she surely had blessed me.

I had a childish crush on Jacques Deplan, a young doctor, who had rented a room upstairs at Father Lambin's big house. It did not work out. He devoted his medical career to the service of handicapped people, and I did not like crippled people. Jacques married his nurse, a young Belgian woman who shared his missionary ideals. She was pretty and sweet. I was very mad at him and jealous of her. They knew it, and they came to my baptism, kneeling in the church, praying and offering me an olive branch.

Fr. Charles Lambin was disappointed that I did not succeed in hooking Jacques, such a kind, young and handsome doctor. I cried on his shoulders, and he said, "My dear child, the world is full of nice and promising young men. It will work with the next one. Just say to yourself, 'This one does not deserve me. I will find a better one.'"

In Saigon, in 1962, our brother Henri married Julie Nori Huynh Hoa No. He had met her through her uncle, who was his client at the bank and a friend. Julie had graduated from Cambridge University in England, and her Vietnamese parents lived in Phnom-Penh, Cambodia. Henri went to Phnom-Penh several times to visit Julie and her family, fell in love with her, and proposed.

Henri had found his soulmate. Julie came from an excellent family, but she was not richer than him, and she was not assertive, as were the wealthy girls Henri had known before. Julie was sweet and diplomatic. Henri was a very proud young man and would never marry a girl for her money. In past times, Miss Ngoc Dung loved him and wished to marry him. He refused to propose to her because she was a pharmacist and came from a very wealthy family. She had to marry another friend, a senator.

With Julie, Henri felt comfortable. Julie knew how to please him and not to hurt his pride. Henri did not accept any negative comments about his parents, sisters, and brothers. Julie knew what happened to a former girlfriend, Margaret, when she commented to Henri, "Why do your parents keep your sisters like anchovies in a jar?" Henri was furious and broke off the engagement. Margaret apologized and begged him to reconsider his decision, but he remained inflexible. He did not tolerate any criticism of his family. Julie learned to keep her mouth shut and integrated well in our family. It was a happy marriage, and they had four children.

Our parents were scandalized by Henri and Julie's modern ways and for their kissing like Westerners did. Mother said to Julie, "My beloved daughter-in-law, can't you kiss discreetly in a corner?"

My Confirmation (March 1963)

The Sacrament of Confirmation was conferred upon me on March 20, 1963, by Msgr. Albert Descamps, the bishop and new rector of the University of Louvain. It was an intimate ceremony. We were only the four of us—namely Mgrs. Albert Descamps, Andre Molitor, Claire de Bethune, and me. The event took place in the chapel of the Chateau d'Arenberg, which belonged to the university. After the ceremony, the four of us had lunch at a new modern student center, privately owned by Mr. and Mrs. Morin.in the middle of the woods.

Overseas Student Catholic Organization (Osco)

Francis Bacon wrote that "travel in the young was education and in the old was experience."

During my years in Louvain, I had the opportunity to travel a lot, discovering Belgium, Nederland, France, Switzerland, Italy and Austria. Travels had been a profound formative experience for me. Living in a community inspired me to live like other students. It meant going to the Catholic Mass, searching for spirituality, opening up to the vast world, and nurturing a missionary spirit.

In addition to Ad Lucem, I also joined OSCO (Overseas Student Catholic Organization). One of the Vietnamese students in Louvain, a PhD graduate, Nguyen Duc Thang, was its secretary general, and that is how I became an executive member of OSCO. I was part of the committee, which included Ronald Da Costa (from South Africa), Kiwako (Japanese), and Eddy (a Burmese medical student in Padua, Italy), and our chaplain was a young student priest from India.

OSCO gathered a large number of overseas (mostly Asians and Africans) Catholic students in Europe. We were linked by solidarity because we were Catholic and in my case, born in developing countries or third-world countries. We were perceived as the elite of our countries. OSCO was subsidized by the Vatican and by Catholic organizations. We had our OSCO conventions in Louvain, Padua (Italy), and Nimegen (Holland), and we traveled together by chartered bus or by train.

While in Nimegen, hosted by the students of the university, we had the opportunity to visit Rotterdam and Amsterdam. In the bus to Rotterdam, the student guide kept telling us that the Netherlands was destroyed in the Second World War but the Dutch had rebuilt their country from its ashes. Amsterdam was a charming town with its waterway. We had a cruise along the canal. In the evening, while going to a restaurant for dinner, our male friends tricked us into venturing into the red-light district, and they laughed, looking at our horrified and scandalized faces. We were mad at them.

We organized vacations for our members in searching for host families in Austria and the Netherlands. I stayed in the Netherlands for two weeks of vacation as guest in a family. An Indonesian woman married to a Dutch man invited me for an Indonesian lunch. One of her friends was a fortune teller, and I asked him to predict my future. He carefully examined the palms of my hands. He exchanged agitated words in Indonesian with the hostess, and none of them would tell me what he saw in my hands. By the gloomy looks on their faces, I guessed that it was not good news, but they refused to tell me what it was.

Nguyen Duc Thang had married a Vietnamese girl, and I was godmother to Lan, their daughter. "Lan" means "lily." After Thang had obtained his PhD from Louvain, his mother came from Vietnam, bringing with her a Vietnamese girl to marry Thang. Her name was Ngoc. I liked her. She was pretty and a honey-sweet talker. She was rich, and Thang had a PhD as a prelude to an excellent career. It was an arranged marriage between money and education. They settled in Brussels, got jobs, and opened a Vietnamese restaurant.

The Vietnamese students in Louvain formed a joyful and united group. The baptism of Thang's baby was a church event for the Vietnamese association. The godfather was a Vietnamese student married to a Belgian girl. Most of our young Vietnamese men in Louvain married Belgian girls they met at university. They were lonely, and there were not many Vietnamese girls around. I liked their Belgian girlfriends and wives. They were quiet, sweet, and they were good wives and mothers.

We Vietnamese students attended another church event—the ordination of our dear friend, a young Dutch Salesian priest, Fr. Jean Donders. Vietnamese students loved him. He was joyful and always smiling, radiating fervor for his vocation of missionary priesthood, and he chose Vietnam to be his mission country. After his ordination into priesthood, Father Donders flew to Saigon, where he would dedicate his life as a St. John Bosco's priest to the orphans of Saigon. He picked up the orphans from the streets of Saigon, sheltered them, and taught them some skills so they would be able to earn a living.

In the spring of 1963, in Paris, our brother Rene married Jacqueline Trinh Dinh Thao. He worked as an engineer at the Petroleum Institute of Paris, and she was a dentist. They had known each other since childhood. She was the eldest daughter of lawyer Trinh Dinh Thao, who in 1968 chose to side with the Vietcong (South Vietnamese Communists).

South Vietnam Was on Fire

Riots against the Ngo Dinh Diem regime erupted violently in Vietnam. The regime became increasingly unpopular in South Vietnam. The president was a victim of circumstances. He lived in an ivory tower, and he was unaware of the realities of Vietnam. The real power was in the hands of his brother, Ngo Dinh Nhu, and wife, Mrs. Nhu. The other brothers included Ngo Dinh Can, hated in Central Vietnam for his corruption and cruelty; Ngo Dinh Thuc, the ambitious archbishop; and Ngo Dinh Luyen, ambassador to England. Mrs. Nhu's father was appointed ambassador to Washington, but he and his spouse chose to distance themselves from their own daughter, disapproving of her politics and attitude. He resigned from his ambassadorship.

President Diem believed that God had chosen him to lead Vietnam and presented himself as a Catholic crusader for God. The Ngo Family clashed with the Buddhist monks everywhere in Vietnam, from the Buddhist University in Hue to the pagodas in Saigon. The Ngo family underestimated the power of the Buddhist religion, which was strongly seeded in the hearts and minds of the South Vietnamese population. They persecuted the monks and nuns and showed lots of contempt for the Buddhist religion. Army trucks arrested the screaming monks and nuns, dragging them out of the pagodas and imprisoning them

In June of 1963, demonstrations against the government began. Some monks and nuns immolated themselves by fire in public places and made sure that pictures were taken by foreign journalists. They succeeded in igniting the fury of the Buddhist population against the Ngo. The Xa Loi Pagoda, behind our former residence in Saigon in the 1950s, was the headquarters of the Buddhist insurrections. It sheltered the heart of the venerable monk Thich Quang Duc, who died by self-immolation by fire on June 11, 1963; his heart did not burn even after a second cremation of his remains.

The Vietnamese living overseas reacted at the same time as the Vietnamese at home. The Vietnamese students in Louvain were linked with the Vietnamese students from Paris. Those students from Paris were political activists. They often came to Louvain to socialize with us. One day, Nghia, our young leader in Louvain, told us that our group had joined in with all other Vietnamese student associations in Europe to protest against the Ngo Dinh Diem regime. It was an act of solidarity, and our group, although mostly Catholic and cherished by President Diem, could not stray from other student groups.

When Mrs. Ngo Dinh Nhu and her daughter Ngo Dinh Le Thuy visited Paris as part of their official trips in Europe and the United States to win support for the Ngo Dinh Diem regime, the Vietnamese in France organized a huge demonstration against Mrs. Nhu.

In 1955, Albert was an ardent supporter of the agricultural reforms and the development of the highlands promoted by President Diem. In 1963, he had turned against the Ngo regime because of its Buddhist persecutions. Albert was one of the leaders of the huge Paris demonstrations, where participants shouted anti-Ngo Dinh Nhu slogans and threw tomatoes and eggs at Mrs. Nhu and her entourage. As such, with some others, he was arrested by the French police. The crowd yelled, "French police with us!" and the policemen, smiling, responded, "You should have thought about it long ago." They alluded to the fact that the Vietnamese had replaced the French with the Americans. The French seemed contented that the Americans were now stuck in a quagmire in Vietnam, as they had been before. There had not been a happy ending in this long war.

Albert spent one night in jail and was released the next day after the departure of Mrs. Nhu from Paris. She was in Paris as an official guest, so she had to be protected by the French government. Public sympathy went to the rioters more than to the Iron Lady, or Tiger Lady, who called the monks "barbecued monks." Her attitude had contributed in great part to her downfall. Should she have been present in Vietnam, she would have been killed alongside her husband. They were hated by the population.

The US ambassador Henry Cabot Lodge had been contacted by some generals who wanted to make certain that the United States would approve or at least remain quiet and neutral should they try to overthrow the regime of President Ngo Dinh Diem. Henry Cabot Lodge tried to persuade President Diem to dismiss his brother Ngo Dinh Nhu from power because Nhu was the main individual people hated the most, but President Diem refused. Diem refused any other compromise and said stubbornly, "I am doing my duty." The US ambassador then urged him to get out of the country with US help. President Diem refused.

The Generals' Coup; Assassination of President Ngo Dinh Diem (November 1, 1963)

The president and his brother Ngo Dinh Nhu fled the presidential palace through an underground secret tunnel that led them into a Chinese church in Cholon. From there, they called the generals and surrendered. They were assassinated inside a military truck sent to pick them up. Their bodies were thrown into the French St. Paul clinic's morgue and were left to rot for two weeks, as no one dared to come and claim them. Finally the generals called one of their relatives to take their corpses away. The generals decided to spare the lives of the Nhus' three children and sent them off to their mother, Mrs. Ngo Dinh Nhu, who was in the United States and not allowed to return to Vietnam.

General Duong Van Minh, the leader of the coup, assumed power as the new president of the Republic of Vietnam.

On November 3, 1963, I was twenty-two years old. That day, I visited Venice with Kiwako and Eddy. We had our OSCO congress in Padua organized by Eddy, who had graduated from medical studies in Padua.

I was sad at the death of President Ngo Dinh Diem and at the same time, I rejoiced that the new president was our big brother Minh. Minh was like a godson to Father, and he was like an eldest brother to me and my siblings.

President John Kennedy's response to the news of the assassination of President Diem was emotional. He had expected President Diem to be removed from office but not to be killed. He exclaimed, "O my God, they had killed him! After all, he was our allied for the past nine years. He was a great nationalist. He did not deserve to die like this."

Lyndon B. Johnson wrote later in his memoirs that "President Diem is the Churchill of the decade…in the vanguard of those leaders who stand for freedom."

Ho Chi Minh was in a meeting when one of his companions came with a piece of paper on which he had scrawled that President Ngo Dinh Diem had been killed. Later on, this man revealed that Ho Chi Minh answered, "Diem was my fierce enemy. Now our victory is certain. We will take over South Vietnam."

After the fall of the Ngo Dinh Diem regime, November 1 was chosen as the National Day of the Republic of Vietnam.

On November 22, 1963, President John F. Kennedy was assassinated in Dallas, Texas. A bitter Mrs. Ngo Dinh Nhu, who always had blamed the US government "for stabbing her family in the back" was quick to say that it was the judgment of God to avenge the death of President Diem and her husband, Ngo Dinh Nhu.

I was in Louvain. I remember that the radio suddenly fell silent for a while and afterward played only classical music, mourning President Kennedy's death. Students entered churches in Louvain to pray. It was a day of prayer and grief all around the world.

The violent deaths of both presidents changed the course of the Vietnam War. The two presidents died suddenly, assassinated in the same month and in the same year. What would have been the course of the Vietnam War if they had not died?

Death of Empress Nam Phuong

On September 15, 1963, Empress Nam Phuong died in her sleep from heart failure at the age of forty-nine at her domain of Chabrignac, Correzes, France. She had moved to Chabrignac five years prior, choosing a reclusive life. Her heart gave in after so much suffering as the last empress of Vietnam in a tragic country troubled by continuous wars. She suffered also as the wife of Bao Dai, who was known to have a number of women in his life. Some of the women had children with him.

I sent a letter of condolences to former emperor Bao Dai, and he answered with his own handwriting. He said that my letter was the most moving letter among all letters received from his Vietnamese fellows. I asked Bao Dai how I could send flowers to be deposited on the tombstone of Empress Nam Phuong, and he gave me the name of the manager of her property at Chabrignac. In the village of Chabrignac there also lived an elderly Vietnamese imperial princess, older than empress Nam Phuong. The two of them never spoke with each other. They did not like each other.

December 8, 1963, was the first anniversary of my baptism. I asked Fr. Jean Giblet to drive me to the Abbey of Rhode-Saint Genesius as a pilgrimage. The road was so beautiful with its Christmas trees covered with frost and snow. The abbey was silent and empty. Both of us sat next to each other on the bench and prayed.

During the summer of 1964, with Paulette Daems, a friend I had met at the theology courses taught by Canon Jean Giblet, we went to Correzes to visit the tombstone of Empress Nam Phuong in the cemetery of the village of Chabrignac. We arrived at Chabrignac, and I had a look at the Domaine de la Perche, where the empress had resided before her passing. The gate was locked, so we just had a quick glimpse at the silent and empty château. I remember seeing two huge planters of pink earthenware at the entrance of the door that gave a touch of oriental art to the landscape.

In the cemetery, we found Empress Nam Phuong's brand-new black marble monument erected on still fresh and bare ground. There were no flowers or flowering plants. I sent Paulette away because I wanted to be alone with the empress. Paulette was surprised by my request but obliged. She disappeared. I stood in front of the resting place of my empress, the revered lady who could have been my godmother. We were reunited at last in that moment. In this remote village cemetery, there were no people, no trees, no vegetation, and no flowers, and it was cold. It was a very quiet, isolated, and sad landscape. I bowed in front of her monument.

My Last Year in Louvain (1964)

In the spring of 1964, Paulette and I decided to spend two months of vacation together touring France and Switzerland. Paulette drove a small Citroën, a popular car for students in Belgium. Paulette's program was to visit the *chateaux de la Loire*. Her passion was history and art; therefore, we visited most of the renowned châteaux along the Loire and Garonne Rivers.

We visited the cemetery of the village of Chabrignac in Correzes, France, where Empress Nam Phuong was buried.

After Chabrignac, I asked Paulette to drive to Northern France to the village of Mouilleron-en-Pareds in Vendee, where Marshal Jean de Lattre de Tassigny and his son Bernard were buried. We found their two tombstones aligned next to each other, immaculately white, with the French and Vietnamese national flags painted on their crosses.

I had seen General Jean de Lattre de Tassigny in Saigon in 1951, and I had liked him. I had received a hug from him at Lycée Marie Curie. As a French citizen, I was chosen as the flower girl alongside my French classmate Danielle Bardouillet. Both of us presented flowers to personalities. Danielle was blond with blue eyes, a sweetheart, and we were friends. I was invited to her home for birthday parties. Her father was director general of Les Distilleries de l'Indochine.

General Jean de Lattre was a symbol of nobility and sacrifice for the glory of France. He did not hesitate to sacrifice his young and only son to the altar of honor and patriotism. When he arrived in Vietnam, he made it clear that he would not keep Bernard safe behind a desk. He said, "If I were to send other people's sons to war, my own son would go with them." Bernard died at the Battle of Vinh Yen. With him died the legendary name of de Lattre de Tassigny. The general and his wife accepted Bernard's death as their ultimate sacrifice to France, but it was a terrible blow and loss to them. They never recovered from it.

He was promoted posthumously to marshal at his deathbed. At his state funeral in Paris, it was heartbreaking to look at the elderly, thin, and frail Mrs. de Lattre de Tassigny, dressed in black, walking alone behind his coffin. She had lost her son and her husband. They had died for France and for Vietnam.

At the law faculty of Louvain, I discovered that the Academy of International Law of the Hague offered grants to graduate students to attend its summer sessions. A letter of support from a law professor was required. I asked my professor, Paul de Visscher, for such a letter, and I applied to the academy for a grant. I obtained it.

I boarded a train from Louvain to the Hague and spent one month of the summer of 1964 there. The room rented for me by the academy had been rented by Edward Kennedy several years before. Edward was older than me. The elderly Dutch landlady told me that I was her last tenant. She showed me the retirement home for seniors where she would move in soon. She was happy, healthy, and wealthy. Dutch seniors had good lives.

Later I took the train for Fribourg, Switzerland, to spend two weeks of vacation at the Catholic University of Fribourg. I was invited by a young Chinese couple, Bernard and Marie, whom I had met at the Chinese House of Louvain.

In Louvain, the Vietnamese Foyer was only a house rented by some Vietnamese male students. The Chinese House of Louvain was well established in an old large building and housed several Chinese priests and students upstairs. Downstairs they had a living room, dining room, kitchen, and conference rooms. Belgian missionaries had ventured into China for centuries, and the Christian links between Belgium and China were deeply rooted. I liked the Chinese I knew in Louvain, as they were very friendly, and I liked to go to the Chinese House. I read books written by Chinese priests who had been persecuted and tortured for their faith. I persuaded Marie Jeanne Kao to go with me, but she was reticent because as a Chinese, she did not like to connect with her male Chinese fellows. They might think that she was there to look for a husband.

At the Catholic University of Fribourg, Switzerland, the Chinese and Vietnamese students looked after me well. The young Vietnamese men were quiet and nice, and they studied there in order to become priests. They took me out for picnics and walks in the woods. Most were recipients of university scholarships granted by Fr. Will Bernardin, executive director of Foyer Saint Justin, which was affiliated with the university.

Fr. Wills Bernardin, a corpulent, jovial, and smiling monk, had lunch with them at the university cafeteria and was very well liked. My new friends told me to apply for a postgraduate fellowship with Father Bernardin. "Ask and you shall receive!" I knocked on the office door of Father Bernardin, applied for a postgraduate fellowship, and immediately was granted it. I needed only to provide my address and my bank account information, and the money would be deposited directly in it for as long as I needed it to achieve my doctoral studies. No follow-up was made, and no report about the progress of my studies was asked for whatsoever. There was no supervision and no control over the use of my fellowship money. The main principle was that our university youth would be formed through our years of living abroad. Father Bernardin authorized me to study at the Graduate Institute of International Relations in Geneva.

After Fribourg, I went to the University of Neuchatel, invited to attend a seminar. A young American student told me that he was the son of Kenneth Galbraith, the US ambassador to India and a renowned economist. He told me that he was interested in international organizations and with helping developing countries.

September 19, 1964, was Claire de Bethune's wedding. She married Chevalier Dominique de Patoul. Claire's parents were not too happy about this. They wished for Claire to marry a man of a higher title. However, Claire and Dominique had fallen in love with each other, and they were determined to get married. The wedding took place at the Chateau de Marke and it was the most beautiful wedding of the year in Belgium. The Belgian aristocracy was invited. Being often invited to the château by Claire, I already knew Claire's parents well and was friends with Greta de Bethune, Claire's sister-in-law. Claire and I often visited Emmanuel and Greta de Bethune in Brussels, where they resided. I liked Jacques de Bethune, a monk at the Abbey of Maredsous in Namur. He was also Claire's favorite brother.

I once asked Jacques, "How could you become a monk? It must be terribly hard!"

He answered, "You must learn not to think about yourself."

Claire's white wedding dress was a family heirloom, a treasure of antique lace that had been her grandmother's wedding dress. Before the wedding day, it was displayed in a room of the château next to the room where the wedding gifts were exhibited. I arrived on the eve of the wedding and had a room booked at the hotel in the municipality of Marke. Some other guests stayed also there.

On the morning of the wedding, Claire, in her wedding dress, rode to the church with her father, Baron Jean Baptiste de Bethune, sitting in an antique carriage drawn by horses. The château had several antique carriages. The guests formed a cortege and walked from the château to the church. The rural population and local residents stood on the sides of the road to look at the cortege. As a sign of respect, the men took off their hats and the women curtsied as we passed.

After the church ceremony, lunch for hundreds of guests was served under tents in the gardens of the château. We had champagne, lobster, and chocolate mousse. Claire and Dominique circulated from table to table, talking with the guests. In the afternoon, the guests wandered in the gardens, admiring flowers and trees. The grounds of the château included a swimming pool, a Japanese bridge, and a vegetable garden.

The guests belonged to the flower of Belgian nobility. I and another German girl were the only foreigners. Claire was friends with a German girl she had met during her studies in some convent abroad. Convents molded aristocratic girls for entry into a world of excellence in manners, music and etiquette. Claire's parents were not happy about her invitation to her German friend, as they still resented the Germans because of bad memories from the Second World War. I saw the German girl driving her car inside the château, but she did not stay long. It was a long drive for her from Belgium back to Germany.

In the afternoon, the municipal band played in honor of Claire. At the end of the afternoon, Claire and Dominique departed for their honeymoon.

Claire's parents, Greta, and I sat on the concrete stairs leading up to the main entrance of the château. Two lions carved in stone stood guard at the bottom of the stairs. We remained silent for a while after waving good bye to the newlywed couple. Her mother then commented, "I hope that everything will go well."

Greta answered, "Why do you worry? Everything will be all right." It was the beginning of a new life for Claire. She left forever the château where she had grown up.

Baron Jean de Bethune turned to me and said, "And now, Alice, it will be your turn. We will find a nice husband for you!" He did not know that I had already made my plans to move on to Switzerland in the fall of 1964. When I left the château, it would be the last time I saw Claire's father.

Geneva, Switzerland (1964-1965)

I had spent vacations in Lausanne to visit a Vietnamese friend, Pham Van Thuan, who was an assistant professor at the University of Lausanne. Thuan was maybe the link that brought me to Switzerland. He had traveled to Belgium, had met me there at some student event, and had invited me to visit Lausanne.

After Lausanne, I visited Geneva. I went to Geneva in search of my next university move. I did not want to continue to live in Belgium. I loved Belgium and its population, but I fell in love with Switzerland and its beautiful lakes, boats, sunshine, and pretty flowers everywhere. I wanted to live in Switzerland.

In Switzerland, I felt as if I were on a perpetual vacation and as though I were living in a paradise. I wandered in Geneva in the spacious public park between Avenue de Lausanne and the shore of Lake Geneva. This was a long stretch of trees, sophisticated flower beds, and quietness—except the chirping of the birds and the song of the cicadas. I saw an exquisite landscape when I discovered the Graduate Institute of International Relations—a large, pink square house in the middle of luscious green vegetation, birds, and squirrels. The institute could be discovered from the boats that took tourists along Lake Geneva; guides told them the history of the mansions and châteaux they saw along the shoreline. One American professor crossed the lake with his canoe to teach at the institute. I decided that I would study at this institute during the year 1965.

I had asked a university professor in Geneva and his assistant, both of whom I met at the seminar at Neuchatel, to search for an accommodation for me in Geneva, and they found a room for me at Foyer John Knox.

I took up residence at Foyer John Knox. I experienced the American student lifestyle, both by studying at the Graduate Institute of International

Relations and by residing at Foyer John Knox. Both were institutions originally founded by Americans for young Americans in Geneva. The post-graduate students from this Institute were an international young elite, including a large number of Swiss and American students, who later became lawyers and diplomats.

Built and subsidized by the American churches and members of the Ecumenical Council of Geneva, Foyer John Knox was managed by two pastors, Eric Martin and Paul Frelick. The name John Knox implied that it was a Protestant center. It was a modern long bungalow in wood and glass in the middle of a spacious green lawn. The wood was painted in bright red and yellow. On the first day I moved in there, I saw young girls sunbathing in bikinis, lying in full view of the young men's windows. The student rooms were small, functional, and had windows with views. We shared a large living room, a dining room, and a kitchen with a Spanish-born woman cook who served us evening dinners. In the basement was another living room, another kitchen, and a recreational room.

Paul Frelick, our American executive director, lived with his family in a large Swiss chalet next to our student bungalow. The Swiss pastor, Eric Martin, came only occasionally. We were a group of male and female students chosen from diverse nationalities, faiths, and ideologies. There were some young married student couples. In addition there were English and German girls coming, supposedly for some studies to improve their French. They received room and board in exchange for their help in the office or in the kitchen. Rich girls from wealthy French and Dutch families stopped there too for short periods to socialize and mingle with the young men who were highly educated and at the beginning of a promising career. I remember Christine and Gerda. They were both pretty and sweet. Parents sent their daughters on world tours in selected locations so they could meet well-connected and interesting young men.

My room was at the end of a corridor. A Japanese student, Setsuko Ono, occupied the room next to me. She was the daughter of a Japanese banker and the younger sister of Yoko Ono, John Lennon's wife. Setsuko was small, thin, refined, and very smart. We became friends. At the Foyer, she was the only Japanese and I was the only Vietnamese. We were both Catholics.

Foyer John Knox was a large property buried in the middle of vegetation, meadows, and fields, built on the Grand-Saconnex Hill, along the avenue of Pregny-Chambesy. The entrance and the driveway of Foyer John Knox faced the gate of Miremont, the residence of Karim Aga Khan. Therefore, I had the frequent opportunity to see young Karim Aga Khan and his beautiful wife. They were the most elegant young couple I had ever seen. He was some years older than me and had graduated from Harvard University.

When the gate of Miremont was open, I could see the elderly gardener planting flowers here and there. One day I entered the property and introduced myself to the gardener as a student living from across the avenue. I made friends with him, and I came any time I wished. I sat on the lawn and talked with him while he was working, and I nurtured the secret hope to see Karim and his wife in the garden, but I never saw them walking around. They never appeared and never smelled the perfume of their roses. On each of my visits, the gardener gave me beautiful flowers for my student room.

My professor friend Pham Van Thuan, who resided in Lausanne, connected me with Princess Phuong Mai. She lived in his neighborhood, and he suggested to me to invite her for dinner. I answered, "Why don't you invite her yourself?"

He explained, "She looks like a nice girl, and I have nothing against her, but she is the daughter of Bao Dai, and Bao Dai is not popular. But you should contact her. She might be very happy to hear from you."

Princess Phuong Mai answered my phone call, and I introduced myself. "I am Alice Nguyen Le Dung. You don't know me, but your mother knows me."

Very sweetly, she replied immediately, "Oh yes, I know you. I know who you are. My mother told us about you and said that she would like us to meet with you and be friends."

I invited her for dinner at a restaurant that evening, and she accepted. She came to pick me up, driving a sport car. I found her extremely charming and elegant. We chose a chic restaurant at the border of Lake Leman. We talked for hours about our lives, families, and dreams about our future. I remember that I felt superior to her because I was a PhD student, and she humbly said that she had not attended university. She said, "When I was a child, we had tutors teaching us at home. As you know, our circumstances changed and I did not have the opportunity to attend university." I liked her humility and sincerity. She confided to me that she would soon return to Paris. "My father wanted me to go back to Paris to be closer to him and because I must look after my mother's estate."

She returned to Paris and took a job in a boutique on Champs-Élysées. She was invited to the Ball of the Debutantes, which was organized by Jacques Chazot every year. This ball was an ultimate posh event in Paris that was intended to introduce young princesses and aristocrats to the high society. That event allowed royals and aristocrats to get acquainted and romances to flourish.

Princess Phuong Mai married the Italian second duke of Addis Ababa and count of Sortolino. She lived in an Italian château, and they had two children: Don Pedro and Dona Manuela. After the death of her husband in the 1990s, she became the dowager duchess and her son inherited the title of third duke of Addis Ababa.

My student life in Louvain and in Geneva had offered me two opposite student experiences. Louvain was famous for its old university built in the fifteenth century, for its magnificent library, for its gothic and baroque architecture, and for its churches. Small and gorgeous old churches were crowded with religious ornaments and lit up with dim candles. Louvain was all about Catholic churches and faith.

In Louvain, during my first year at the Sedes Sapientiae, we had a curfew. We were to be back at ten o'clock, and the gates were locked with a big key. However, it was possible to get the key from the administrative manager, and a friend would open the door for you if you anticipated a late return. Rules existed but were flexible.

After the first year and during the following years, the female students rented a house and shared the expenses. The Catholic youth of Belgium studied there. There were love stories that ended with marriage and the beginning of a new life for the young couples. They generally married after graduation or during their last year in Louvain. Belgium was a Catholic monarchy with solid values, honoring traditions, religion, and family.

In Geneva, I was suddenly thrown into a completely different environment—an ultramodern American student center with American culture, American customs, and progressive and even radical ideas. The

Foyer was open to all ideologies and faiths. It promoted international dialogue and tolerance.

I was stunned on my first day at Foyer John Knox to see young men leaving bathrooms with wet hair, naked torsos, and big towels wrapped around their waists, flashing large, friendly smiles to me. They knew that I was the newcomer, and I was all confused, not knowing if I should look the other way or run away. They laughed, realizing that I was shy, naïve, and embarrassed to see them half-naked.

Breakfast was self-service with cereals, milk, and coffee. We could eat breakfast in our pyjamas or nightgowns, with no make-up and with untidy hair. Let us say that as soon as we woke up, we could go straight to the dining room, sip a cup of coffee and discussed world problems. We relaxed until noon. Lunch was not served, because we were supposed to be at the university or at the graduate institute of international relations at that time and returning to the Foyer only in the afternoon. In the evenings, we had superb dinners. Meals were subsidized by the American churches. We were pampered, as if eating at a five-star restaurant. We usually had a meat roast with all the trimmings; a mixture of salad greens, potatoes, and delicious desserts; and coffee that flowed generously like an endless river.

Most Saturday evenings were reserved for dance parties in the lower level of the bungalow. The American girls from Smith College who resided at the Hotel de Russie were invited to come and dance, but I did not see many of them. They did not come to Geneva with the goal of meeting with their fellow Americans.

Political Events in Vietnam (1963-1967)

In November of 1963, General Duong Van Minh became the new president of the Republic of Vietnam. However, he was not a good politician and administrator. He was skilled only in strategic military operations. His genius was in the battlefields. He lasted only a short time in power.

In 1964, he was sent to Thailand on a mission. When he returned, he was refused entry to Vietnam. This was how his fellow generals got rid of him. He spent the following years in exile in Thailand, cultivating orchids and reading French books. When his friends asked him when he intended to go home and fight back, he said philosophically, "Everything takes time. Look at the orchids. They take time to bloom."

On January 20, 1965, President Lyndon B. Johnson affirmed his oath as president. "We can never again stand aside, prideful in isolation." He ordered a significant military escalation in Vietnam.

On June 18, General Nguyen Cao Ky took power as the new prime minister, with General Nguyen Van Thieu as chief of state. This was the tenth South Vietnamese government in twenty months.

On December 7, Defense Secretary Robert McNamara briefed President Johnson on the situation in Vietnam and outlined that "the North Vietnamese believe that the war will be a long one and that time is their ally. They believe that their staying power is superior to ours."

On January 12, 1966, during his State of the Union address before Congress, President Lyndon B. Johnson commented that the war in Vietnam was unlike America's previous wars. "Yet, finally, war is always the same. It is young men dying in the fullness of their promise. It is trying to kill a man that you do not even know well enough to hate...therefore, to know war is to know that there is still madness in this world."

On August 30, China announced that it would provide economic and technical assistance to Hanoi. On September 1, French president Charles de Gaulle called for US withdrawal from Vietnam. On October 3, the Soviet Union announced it would provide military and economic assistance to Hanoi. In 1967, UN secretary general U Thant expressed doubts that Vietnam was essential to the security of the West.

President Johnson reaffirmed that "we [would] stand firm in Vietnam." He increased the number of US troops stationed in Vietnam to half a million.

On September 3, national elections were held in South Vietnam. General Nguyen Van Thieu was elected president, with General Nguyen Cao Ky as vice president.

During the summer of 1965, I received a letter from Mr. and Mrs. Do Van Minh, Aunt Nine's friends. Aunt Nine was the wife of Mr. Le Minh Tung, mayor of the first district of Saigon, and she was our father's youngest sister. Mr. and Mrs. Minh asked me to find accommodation for them during their vacation in Geneva and be their tour guide.

Foyer John Knox had guest rooms for a fee. I rented a room there for them. They were maybe fifteen years older than me, and Mr. Minh was a senior counsellor at the Embassy of the Republic of Vietnam in Rome. We became friends and called each other cousins.

They said, "You have already graduated from university. Why don't you come to work with us in Rome? It would be for you a stepping stone toward a diplomatic career. We don't have a Vietnamese girl at the embassy. It would be nice to have one."

Mr. Minh telephoned to Ambassador Nguyen Duong Don, and I was hired.

The fall of 1965 ended my university life in Geneva.

This important change, leaving university and starting a new chapter in my life as a working girl in the real world reminded me of something beautiful I had read: "When you leave here, don't forget why you came," Adlai Stevenson said in his speech to Princeton University graduates.

Rome, Italy—Embassy of the
Republic of Vietnam (1965-1967)

O Italy, Fatal Beauty
—Lord Byron

I informed Canon Jean Giblet that I had moved to Rome, the Eternal City. He answered, "Are you going to live in Rome, the Holy City of the Popes, or Rome, the City of All Sins?"

My godfather was ecstatic about the beginning of my professional life in Rome. He had preached to me that after graduation from university, I should return to Saigon to serve my country. He was adamant about my service to my own country of birth. Staying too long in Europe would uproot me, but I was stubborn in my resolution not to return to Vietnam. Rome was a magnificent city. Many people dreamed of being able to work or live in Rome. I was happy because I had a new purpose and a new country to discover.

Before being posted in Rome, Mr. Nguyen Duong Don was minister of national education, appointed by President Ngo Dinh Diem. He had graduated from a European university, and his German-born wife, Sophie Mohr, looked exquisite in pictures. I had not met her, but I had heard nice comments about her. After marrying Mr. Don, she went to Vietnam to live with him, and they had five sons. He started his career as a professor of math. The family lived in Hanoi, Hue, and Saigon; and as a foreigner, she adapted well to Vietnam's customs and traditions. When I was in Saigon, I had overheard my parents commenting that the German-born wife of Mr. Don was rumored to wash the feet of her mother-in-law, as dictated by tradition. Sophie died in Rome some years before I arrived in Italy.

One of the secret plans of Mr. and Mrs. Minh was to introduce

Ambassador Don, a widower, to a young Vietnamese girl from an excellent family. Vietnamese people were born spontaneous matchmakers. They thought it was a good idea to introduce me to Ambassador Don.

November 1, 1965, was my first National Day reception at the embassy. By coincidence, Dominique de Patoul was posted in Rome as an executive of the Belgian Airlines Sabena, so I again saw Claire and Dominique. They invited me to their home, and I had the opportunity to invite them for the National Day reception of Vietnam.

I had no clue about diplomatic protocol. I arrived at the reception later than Ambassador Nguyen Duong Don, and I left earlier than him. When I waved goodbye with my hands, the ambassador was stunned and looked at me with eyes as big as saucers. I learned afterward that as a staff member, I should have arrived at the reception before the ambassador and should have left after him.

When I arrived in Rome, I stayed with Mr. and Mrs. Minh in their apartment at Via Quatro Venti. I did not have to pay for my accommodation. We ate meals together at home as a family, and I lived with them as if I were their little sister. I became officially in Rome "their dear cousin." They expected me to look after their apartment during their frequent travels to Paris. Mrs. Minh preferred to live in Paris, where she had her young children left in the care of her sisters. Ambassador Don said to Mr. Minh that it was not proper for him to live alone with me, a young girl, in the absence of his wife. He ordered Mr. Minh to tell me to move out. I was not accustomed to being pushed around by people, and I believe that was the reason I felt belligerent toward Ambassador Don. I did not like his way of thinking. He protected the reputation of his friend, Mr. Minh. What about me? He should have said, "Listen, a young girl should not live with a man when his wife is away. You must not live with them. You should think about your reputation and move out." That would have better expressed his concern. Mr. Minh was a sweet man devoted to his wife, and he was an elder brother to me.

I proceeded to rent a lovely apartment in a brand-new modern building looking over the famous Via Portese Sunday flea market, the biggest flea market of Rome. Mr. and Mrs. Minh were disappointed to lose me as their houseguest, and Mr. Minh soon resigned from his position. They moved to Paris, where he died from cancer. He was already very ill when I lived with them, but they had never told me how serious it was. I thought that he was only suffering from gastric problems.

The job in Rome was my first one in the workforce, and I was not accustomed to being subservient. In Saigon, I was accustomed to seeing people bowing in front of Father with reverence and respect, and I had a sense of entitlement. I grew up with the idea that we were on top of the social hierarchy. I went to Rome without any training for an embassy job, and I considered myself as being socially on the same level as the ambassador. I did not feel inferior to him, as in Saigon, Father was friends with the highest-ranking personalities. An ambassador, to me, was not a god. I slammed the door in the face of the ambassador when we had an argument. His face became as red as a tomato, and he ran after me, screaming, "You are my employee! How could you dare to slam the door in my face?"

While having lunch with our accountant, Mr. Hop, I said to him, "Is the ambassador going to fire me?"

The accountant answered, "He did complain to me. He said, 'What am I going to do with her?' I responded, 'Nothing. Do nothing. Leave her alone. She is a nice girl. She is only too westernized. Young people in the West don't have polite manners.'" Hop assured me that my job was safe.

During lunchtime, Hop and I often ate together at restaurants, as we did not return home for lunch. Hop's wife, Maria, was Portuguese, and his having a foreign wife made him friendly with me. He spent his vacations every year in Portugal with his wife's family, and he planned to retire there in their village. They were happy with a simple life. He seemed not to have any Vietnamese family member. His wife's family was all he had.

He confided to me that Ambassador Don had found himself in hot water with our government and was going to retire. Ambassador Don's problems originated from the fact that one day, during a conversation with an American diplomat, he had praised President Charles de Gaulle's solution to resolve the war in Vietnam. President de Gaulle had preached that neutrality was the best political solution in Vietnam and that the Americans should get out of Vietnam. That political interference of the French irritated the Americans. Ambassador Don retired from this plush position he had held for nine years in Rome. After the departure of Ambassador Don in 1966, the senior political counselor, Mr. Huy, became the chargé d'affaires during the period of transition as we waited for a new ambassador to be appointed. Mr. Le Van Loi had left Rome and had been appointed ambassador and permanent representative of the Republic of Vietnam to the United Nations and its specialized agencies in Geneva. He was passionate about a multilateral diplomacy for Vietnam at the United Nations.

In 1966, Claire de Bethune de Patoul gave birth to her first son, Christophe. Claire's mother came to Rome for a visit. I lived then in the Minhs' apartment, and I cooked for them a Vietnamese soup with rice noodles, ham, and basil leaves. I did not have much money to spend, so it was all I could offer. Claire's mother was polite and said that it was good but offered no other comments. I remembered the time in 1961 when Claire's parents were so scandalized at seeing Claire eating Vietnamese food. During her vacation days spent at her château, she once concocted a bowl containing rice noodles, shredded lettuce, and some slices of meat sprinkled with fish sauce. Her parents looked at it and were horrified. Her father exclaimed, "Claire, you are going to die eating this strange food. Is it what you ate at Louvain with Alice?"

Claire laughed and said, "You should try it; it is delicious."

In 1966, my godfather and his wife visited Rome. They stayed at the residence of their friends, the Belgian ambassador to the Holy See, Baron Prosper Poswick and his spouse. They visited me, and I walked with them as their guide, proudly showing Rome to them.

Andre Molitor led an austere life. He preferred to give money to charities than to spend on faraway overseas trips for vacations. He had bought a small property in Provence, France, for vacations every year, and he shared it with his children.

At the Embassy of the Republic of Vietnam in Rome, after the retirement of Ambassador Nguyen Duong Don, I was left alone at the embassy with Mr. Huy, a political senior counsellor, and Mr. Dinh, an administrative chancellor.

One day I found at my door a young and handsome Vietnamese man. He told me that some Vietnamese students in Rome thought that I could help him. He was a pilot in the Vietnam Air Force and had defected from Vietnam, landing his military plane in Thailand. He could not stand seeing people getting killed in the war anymore. As a defector, he had made his way to Italy. From Genoa, he ended up in Rome. He contacted some Vietnamese students, and that was how they had put him in front of my apartment.

I told him that I could not give him long-term shelter or let him live with me. I had a boyfriend. It was also unthinkable as an embassy staff member that I give accommodation to somebody who had deserted. Besides, he was married with children at home.

I was ready to help, but how? He was tired of months of hopelessly being displaced from place to place, and he was homesick, missing the family he had left behind. He wanted to go home. I told him that he would be executed by firing squad should he return home. He was resigned to his fate. He did not want to continue his escape anymore. He was tired and hopeless. I was mad at the Vietnamese students who put me in that horrible situation because they thought that as a single girl occupying an apartment and having a job, I could live with him and thus resolve his problem. It was not that simple.

I called Terry Shroder, my American journalist boyfriend, and told him the story of the pilot. Terry came and asked him if he would agree to be interviewed for the *Rome Daily American*. The story would become public. He agreed.

A small article appeared on the front page of the newspaper, along with the pilot's picture. My embassy counsellors discovered that this pilot had been sheltered by me. They talked with him and negotiated his return to Vietnam. One morning as I was working at the embassy, both counsellors came to my apartment and whisked the pilot away on a commercial international airplane back to Vietnam. One counsellor went with him to Saigon.

I told Terry, "*Now* I am going to get fired!"

Terry responded, "They will not dare fire you. If they do, I shall create trouble for them in my newspaper." Ambassador Don, Mr. and Mrs. Minh, and Mr. Loi had left the embassy long ago. I had no protection left at the embassy. I was not fired, maybe thanks to my friendship with an American newsman. My enemies wrote a bad report about me, prevented any raise in my salary, and relegated me to a dark, dusty room in the back. The story of the pilot was the icing on the cake.

Fortunately, a foreign affairs director in Saigon read my file and said,

"She is the daughter of Doc Phu Su Nguyen Van Ba. I was an assistant to her father." He called Father to get confirmation that I was his daughter, and my file was happily closed.

I was treated very well by our new ambassador, Mr. Nguyen Van Hieu, the elder brother of President Nguyen Van Thieu and previously ambassador to Australia. He had graduated as a lawyer, became ambassador, and was now a widower, left with five young children. His wife had just died while giving birth to a baby. He arrived in Rome with his children, his mother, and his secretary, Miss Huong.

Ambassador Nguyen Van Hieu liked me because he saw in me a young and educated girl from an excellent family. His children were young, and he asked me to come to his house, be friends with his children, and teach French and Italian to them. He hoped that I could connect well with his children and be their friend, and ultimately, if things worked out well, he would need a new wife and a mother for his children. That plan did not work out. I was friends with the children. However, I could not be a stepmother to five children. On the other hand, I never hunted an older Vietnamese man for marriage. Mr. Hieu's mother was present at home, and I never bothered to make efforts to please the old lady. She was there like a shadow and never said anything. I was treated as a friend inside the home of the mother and the eldest brother of President Nguyen Van Thieu, and I was so young and so unaware of the great honor and opportunity I had.

The ambassador wanted me to be friends with his secretary, Miss Huong, and we did become friends. I liked her as if she were my elder sister. I was now part of a new winning team, and I worked sitting at a beautiful and sunny desk next to Miss Huong at the ambassador's office.

On December 8, 1966, on the Feast of the Immaculate Conception, Ambassador Nguyen Van Hieu sent me to represent the Republic of Vietnam at a magnificent Mass celebrated by Pope Paul VI to honor the Catholic missions in Japan, China, Korea, and Vietnam.

Ambassador Hieu and the other diplomats were Buddhist. None of them was interested in attending a Catholic ceremony and seeing the pope. Therefore, I was chosen to represent the Republic of Vietnam at this event because I was Catholic. It was exactly four years to the day, on the Feast of the Immaculate Conception, after my baptism, at age twenty-five, that I represented the Republic of Vietnam to Pope Paul VI in Rome. What an honor and privilege it was for a young Vietnamese girl to do this for the first time in history!

I did not want to go alone, so I convinced Miss Huong to accompany me. Both of us put veils on our heads, as most women did, as a sign of respect inside St. Peter's Basilica. We were the only two representatives for the Republic of Vietnam; meanwhile, the embassies of China, Japan, and Korea sent out a massive number of people—families from their embassies, including wives and children—dressed in their best costumes and showing faces full of joy and Catholic fervor. I was very impressed by the splendor and magnificence of the Mass. After the celebration, Pope Paul VI mingled with his guests and talked with us—especially with mothers and children. I had the opportunity to see him very closely. I liked him. He was elderly, and when he smiled, he exuded kindness.

During the 1965 and 1966 years of my posting in Rome, I was lucky to witness a historical event—the Second Council of the Vatican. Rome and the Vatican were buzzing with religious activities and the arrival of priests, nuns, and tourists. At our National Day reception of November 1, 1965, I saw our Vietnamese bishops, priests, and nuns coming to the Vatican to attend the Second Council of the Vatican.

In the fall of 1966, Ambassador Nguyen Van Hieu was very busy trying to settle down and reform the embassy to make it modern and efficient. He did not like our Roman villa on 58 Via Dandelo and searched for a modern building. Alternatively, he would have to build a brand-new embassy. He had been a lawyer, and although he was already in his sixties and looked like a traditionalist, he was active, progressive, and efficient.

The two Italian sisters Rita and Alda, the embassy housekeeper and the former ambassador Don's maid, respectively, and Bianca, the Argentinian-born secretary to Ambassador Don, had left. Bianca was a beautiful, tall, elegant girl, and she was the daughter of an executive of Argentine Airlines in Rome. She told me that any time she was caught speeding by a policeman while driving her car, she always got out of her car and was very polite. It worked, and she never got a fine. Our Italian driver, young Marcello, followed Mr. Loi to Geneva.

Fate wanted that when I arrived in Rome, I got acquainted with a senior counsellor posted there, Mr. Le Van Loi. He had the same title as

Mr. Do Van Minh, but they were totally different from each other. They did not like each other either.

Mr. Le Van Loi was born in North Vietnam. He had graduated from Lycée Albert Sarrault, in Hanoi; from the Sorbonne, in Paris, in political and social sciences; and from the London School of Economics. He was one of the young rising political stars of the Republic of Vietnam. He was married to a French woman, Jacqueline, whom he had met at the university in Paris.

He liked the way I looked, and he liked my European university education. He was on a search to hire his own future staff for when he became ambassador, and he wanted them to be fluent in languages and to be at ease when dealing with the international community. He judged me as an ideal recruit. He asked me, "Why are you here? If you had graduated and lived in Geneva, why come here? Do you want to return to Geneva?"

He told me that he would travel to Geneva to open the Permanent Mission of the Republic of Vietnam to the United Nations in Geneva, and he offered me the nicest diplomatic position I could dream of there. He would send me to represent Vietnam to international conferences, and he would train me to become the first Vietnamese woman ambassador to the United Nations. "Trust me," he said. He was brilliant as a diplomat, and he was friends with President Nguyen Van Thieu and with the then Minister of Foreign Affairs, Tran Van Do. He told me to wait patiently for his call.

His call to me came in the spring of 1967 when he offered me, as promised, a position at the Permanent Mission of the Republic of Vietnam to the United Nations, in Geneva, Switzerland.

At twenty-seven years old, I would be a diplomat and represent the Republic of Vietnam to the United Nations and its specialized agencies in Geneva.

However, there was an unexpected problem with this perfect plan. When I boarded the train from Rome to Geneva and headed toward my new destiny, I was expecting a baby.

The father of the baby, Jean Paul Di Leno, and I did not really talk about an eventual marriage. My position at the embassy was precarious because we were at war and my salary was very low. Jean Paul returned to Italy after years of drifting in Europe and did not have yet a job. My first encounter with Jean Paul happened at the Club St. Christopher, which was opened as a place for foreign girls to socialize. The club was not open to men, to prevent them from coming in to look for girls. Jean Paul sneaked inside, and I told him that he was not allowed to be there. That was how we got acquainted.

I fell into the arms of Jean Paul in the spirit of revenge because I had just broken up with Terry Shroder, a handsome young American journalist, after nine months of romance. He worked at the *Rome Daily American*, near our embassy. We had met in the public park near our offices. Lonely, I went into the park and read a book while sitting on a bench. Terry read a book while lying on the grass not far away. It was a chance meeting; neither of us had planned it. We went to the public park on this sunny Sunday afternoon because we were single, free, and had the idea of spending the afternoon there.

I had a book in my hands, but my mind was miles away, dreaming, imagining, and living in a surrealistic world. After some hours of reading, we smiled at each other, and Terry started the preliminaries. "Hello, what splendid sunshine, don't you think so?" I could not resist warming up to this stranger. He was young, healthy, and handsome, with blue eyes like steel, and he did not look like the young Italian men who were so annoying because they hunted girls down and followed them tirelessly with compliments and flattery. I was sure this young man was a writer or an academic in Rome. It turned out that he was an American journalist.

This was how we started a great friendship. Terry was the first boyfriend of my life. We were young and good looking; he was an American journalist, and I was a Vietnamese diplomat. He was proud of me. I was proud of him. The relationship was perfect. We were both foreigners in Rome, and maybe we were both in need of company. We became inseparable, enjoyed talking with each other, and ate at the picturesque Italian trattorias in the Trastevere.

As a reporter, he took me with his cameraman, Marco, to see the actress Ann-Margret, and another time he took me, again with Marco, to see Svetlana, Stalin's daughter, at the Rome airport when she defected from the Soviet Union, flying toward America. The crowd was huge, and people were excited by the breaking news. Marco had to knock down people with his heavy camera equipment to make a path for us. It was the biggest event of the year for journalists. Stalin's daughter had defected!

Our companionship was nice as it was, and I ruined it by talking about marriage. I was stupid. I thought that a romance should end up with a wedding. I wanted marriage, and Terry said, "I shall marry no one. Not you, not Cynthia, not any girl, Vietnamese or American. I want to be free to become a renowned writer like Ernest Hemingway or Scott Fitzgerald. I want to be free and see the world."

Cynthia was an American girl who came to visit Terry for two weeks of vacation in Rome. Terry announced it to me as if throwing a brick on my head. It was unbelievable! "I cannot see you for the next two weeks. I have a friend, Cynthia, coming to spend her vacation in Rome, and she will stay in my apartment. I am not committed to any of you. I am free to see who I want to. If they come to Rome to see me, they are my guests." I was furious.

That evening, he took me to a fantastic party given by an American lady who owned a château. I exhibited my bad mood. I was angry and broke up our relationship. That was my big mistake. I should have let Cynthia come, go, and dissipate later in thin air. Terry had known her for years, and theirs was not a love story. She was only a friend. I lived in Rome, and she was only a temporary visitor. I had an advantage over her, but I was stupid. I got on my high horse, offended that he took her into his apartment for two weeks, and I lost him.

I was very conservative and quiet, but amazingly I hung out with Day, Gisela, and the young hippies who were their artist friends. They were from an extreme leftist group and were always breaking conventional social rules. We were a joyful group. One day, Alberto, one of our Italian artists, got recognition in the United States for his talent. He succeeded in exhibiting and selling his paintings in an art gallery in New York and became famous overnight. We were very excited by the news and celebrated him as a hero. America, for us, was like a dream.

Day and Gisela remained poor because they refused to sell their art in the streets and get some money which could help them to buy food to eat. I remember eating rice with a lettuce leaf and some drops of fish sauce with them. I never understood why they did not sell their paintings and get money, and Day said, "I shall never commercialize my art." To survive, Gisela made handicrafts and sold them in the streets to tourists.

I was always embarrassed by their pranks. They were young and unconventional. They had fun to annoy people and cause public disturbances. They showed up in my apartment in the middle of the night, put on loud music, and danced, stomping on the floor. I lived in a high-rise building. I was furious with them. The next morning, I was almost thrown out of the building because of that. When we showed up at the beach and we had no space, they would shout, "Snakes!" Some people would panic and run to their cars. We got space!

I did not miss the Embassy of Vietnam, although Ambassador Nguyen Van Hieu and his secretary, Miss Huong, were absolutely wonderful with me.

When Ambassador Nguyen Van Hieu arrived in Rome to take up his post, he wanted me and Miss Huong, his devoted secretary who followed him everywhere, to share an apartment. He said that girls should not live alone, as it was not safe or respectable. I said immediately to Miss Huong, "I prefer to tell you that I want you to get your own accommodation. I don't want to share my apartment. I like my privacy." So both of us hurried to find a room or apartment for her before Ambassador Nguyen Van Hieu could force me to share my apartment with her.

In my rush, I influenced her to rent the apartment that had just been vacated by Terry. The landlord had increased his rent, and Terry had gotten into a fight with him. They were on very bad terms. Miss Huong signed the lease and occupied her new premises. The next morning, she said to me, "I looked through the window, and I think that it looks down to the morgue of the hospital. I am scared. I want to move out." I had to call Terry and explain the story to him.

Terry was mad at me. He said, "You knew why I moved out. This landlord was an asshole. Why did you get her to sign a lease there?" Terry went to the landlord, showed his fist to threaten him, and said, "Let the girl go."

Miss Huong and I again went house hunting. She found a nice room in a house owned by a German lady. The tenants could use the kitchen to cook their meals. She was very happy there.

Miss Huong was not pretty, but she had charm. She was always smiling. One of the tenants was a handsome young Norwegian, and he liked her. She was not interested in having a boyfriend. She only wanted to have a job with a salary so she could send money home to help her family. Any time I wanted to go out with her for a coffee or for a meal, she would always say, "The money I spend for a coffee could feed a family at home." She was reluctant to spend for such unnecessary frivolities. For me it was relaxing, and I tried to convince her that we needed to have some fun and not always compare life in Rome with life in Vietnam. She knew that I was looking for a boyfriend, and she introduced me to the Norwegian. He liked her but did not like me. My ego was bruised.

I was again asked to share my apartment, this time with Phuong Mai, the daughter of Ambassador Le Ngoc Chan, our ambassador to Tunisia, Algeria, Morocco, and Northern Africa. Phuong Mai studied art in Rome. Her father thought that she was safer staying with me. I could not refuse, because as an embassy staff member, I could not say no to an ambassador. Besides, Vietnamese people did not understand why a Vietnamese girl would not share her space with another Vietnamese girl. Usually Vietnamese girls loved to get together for company and friendship. The Vietnamese mentality did not fit with my desire for individualism and privacy. When I got home from work, I just wanted to be alone, cook my dinner, and watch TV. I had no desire for a girl's company and chitchat. I was introverted, was not a good listener, and just liked my solitude.

Phuong Mai was pretty, poised, cultured, and sweet. She liked me, and she defended me if she heard criticism about me. She said that I was a nice and innocent girl and that I was not sophisticated or hypocritical. Her family invited me to the International Fair of Tunis in 1966, where the Pavilion of Vietnam was judged as very beautiful. I saw President Bourguiba. He was popular and very cheerful. I did not see the king of Morocco, but he did visit our pavilion. The king admired our beautiful Vietnamese furniture, and our artists felt so honored that they donated it to the king of Morocco as a gift. That was typical Vietnamese generous behavior. Vietnamese people had a propensity to give gifts.

I was a guest at the residence of Ambassador Le Ngoc Chan. I had the greatest esteem and love for Phuong Mai and her parents. They were very nice to me. They were born in Central Vietnam. He was a member or the leader of the Dai Viet Party and was politically powerful. Their staff were very devoted to them. A servant who had been nursing Phuong Mai since her childhood traveled regularly from Tunis to Rome to check on Phuong Mai and to see if we ate well. She cooked for us and cleaned our stove.

When I left Rome, Phuong Mai took over my apartment with the agreement of my young Italian landlord, a lawyer. Phuong Mai's father had moved from Tunis to be an ambassador to London, England.

Return to Geneva, Switzerland
(April 1, 1967)

When I boarded the train from Rome to Geneva, I was already pregnant.

Half French and half Italian, slender, thin, tall, handsome, young, my age, and immature like me, Jean Paul Di Leno had been a rebellious adolescent. It was why I was attracted to him, as I understood what he went through in his youthful rebellion. I had been like him too. After years drifting in Europe, he returned to Rome to settle down with the intention to become a good young man and start a career. He reconciled with his mother and sister and promised them not to disappoint the family in the future. Jean Paul told me all that and said, "You don't know me. I did bad things as a teenager in Europe. I am not good for you."

He was still searching for the purpose of his life, and he was not yet mature. He did not yet have a career. He was anxious and unstable. My pregnancy was an accident due to a misunderstanding between us. Jean Paul thought that I was a girl with some life experience and that I had taken all steps to avoid a pregnancy. I did not even know what that meant. Terry was my first boyfriend, and I was not pregnant by Terry. I was very naïve concerning sex.

Jean Paul seemed to imply that I had made myself pregnant on purpose to force him to marry me. I was furious. He was panicked at the idea that his mother and sister would be informed of the situation. He did not care about me or the baby. He was obsessed with the fear of again having a fight with his mother and sister. I was so disappointed and furious about his attitude that I told it to Terry and Day. They decided to go and see Jean Paul at his building and ambush him to teach him a hard lesson. I said, "Leave him alone. I don't want to marry him. It is not his fault. He has no money to get married." Nonetheless, my two best friends in Rome, like two bright shining knights, wanted to fight for my honor. They went searching for Jean Paul, dragged him into an alley, and beat him black and blue. They returned with jubilant faces. Day reported to me, "He cried and asked for mercy. He was not too courageous." Terry showed off his strong muscles and seemed happy to have taken like a personal revenge on Jean Paul. I brushed him off. "It is not the time to be proud of yourself. Spare me your comments." I added, "I told you to forget about Jean Paul. I don't want anything to do with him. I don't want marriage with him."

On April 1, 1967, I left Rome to take up my new position in Geneva. At the Rome station, Terry, Gilles Trinh Dinh Day, and Gisela, came to say farewell. They were the three people who were the best friends I had in Rome. Terry gave me the address of his parents in West Virginia in the United States in case I needed help.

Day and Gisela reiterated their plan to save me from the troubles I was in. Gisela was older than me and Day, with whom she lived for several years. They could not marry because she was married to an Italian who refused to grant her a divorce. Gisela proposed to me their plan. "You marry Day. You will officially become Mrs. Day, and Day will recognize your baby. Afterward, you and Day will get a divorce, and he will be back with me. Marriage with Day would solve all problems for you."

I refused their plan.

In the train, I sobbed and sobbed. My heart remained in Rome. I had my roots there. I missed my Trastevere neighborhood, where I used to stroll with Terry, and my young artist friends who had their art studios there. I missed going to the Vatican and to St. Peter's Basilica. I missed the sunny beaches near Rome and the marvelous cities across Italy.

The train comptroller in the train from Rome to Geneva asked me why I was so distraught. I did not know what to say. The truth was so stupid. As I had a tendency to be dramatic, I said, "I am grieving a death." What I really meant was that I was mourning the end of my sojourn in Rome. The comptroller disappeared, having no intention of listening to gloomy details about death.

My New Posting in Geneva

Ambassador Le Van Loi had rented our offices in the newest luxurious modern building of Geneva, Moillebeau, in the Petit-Saconnex, not far away from the InterContinental Hotel, the United Nations, and many of its specialized agencies. Mr. Loi wanted the best diplomatic location for our mission. He was focused on our prestige on the international scene.

My ambassador presented me with a brand-new office. He surprised me one day, weeping at my desk. He asked me. "I don't understand. I gave you an ideal job. Why to be unhappy? Tell me, did I make a mistake to take you away from Rome?" I told him that I was expecting a baby. I started to sob so profusely that he handed me his handkerchief to wipe away my tears. He said. "With the American journalist?" I wished that I could say yes. That would be great but I was too honest. I did not make Terry responsible for my pregnancy because he was not.

It was a horrible start. My position at the mission was at stake. I could be fired. I also felt sorry that I had been deceptive with Mr. Loi. He had so much expectations with me, working with him as his right hand, his best colleague.

Mr. Loi offered me two weeks of vacation so I could go to a clinic and have an abortion. Geneva was the ideal city for abortion because it was legal there; women flocked to Geneva for that purpose. Anywhere else, it was illegal. I refused. He asked if I objected because of religion. I said, "No, it is not for religion. I want to keep the baby because of my personal feelings." As usual, I had chosen my heart above all options. I was confident that the Virgin Mary walked with me during my journey and that I could not be wrong no matter what. I was ready to suffer the consequences. Mr. Loi shook his head with disbelief at my stupidity. He was angry. "You give me white hair. You are like all those Vietnamese women. We offer them a glorious career and all they want is to have babies. You are like cows. 'I want babies…I want babies.' I hope that the baby will be born with blue eyes and fair hair. Otherwise, my enemies at foreign affairs in Saigon will jump at my throat. You had no idea what I went through to get you to come to Geneva and work for me."

He passed then to plan B. The second option was to give me a one-year unpaid leave of absence. I would stay away from the mission for one year. He said, "You will have to tell your family. You need their money."

An American diplomat was going to Saigon. I gave him a letter to my brother Henri, CEO of the Commercial Credit of Vietnam in Saigon, informing him of my circumstances and asking for money. Henri got my message and was furious and distraught for the shame I had brought to him and the family, but he sent the money. He informed my sisters and Maurice and Francois. He recommended that they not say one word of this to Albert and my parents. Albert had been a fierce opponent to my departure for Europe, and Henri and Albert had had a big fight about it. Henri did not want Albert to know about my current misfortune. He said, "Albert would be mad at me if he knew. He did not want her to go to Europe."

The Swiss wife of a Vietnamese friend gave me the name and address of her gynecologist, Dr. Myriam de Senarclens. By miracle, it happened that Dr. Myriam de Senarclens and her husband, Dr. Francois de Senarclens, were the best gynecologists in Geneva. Dr. Myriam looked after the pregnancies and consultations. Her husband delivered the babies. They owned an elegant private clinic. They were also humanitarians and were involved in humanitarian projects concerning single pregnant mothers. This was another blessing from the Virgin Mary. She put in my path the perfect doctors and humanitarians to help me.

Knowing that I was alone, young, single, and pregnant, they took me under their care. They suggested that I move into a building especially founded for unmarried girls expecting a baby. It would be for my security so I would not be left on my own during my pregnancy.

Most of the girls there were very young Swiss girls from poor families. They worked as salesgirls in stores. The appointed manager of our center was a young Swiss woman, Elsbeth, who had become pregnant when she went on vacation in Algeria. Her son John was now about five years old and lived with her. She was friendly. She had been in the same situation as all of us, and she was responsible and mature. Our cook was a big and fat woman; she was impressive but was not as rough as she looked. She was kindhearted.

My special privilege there was that I could take my breakfast when I wanted and I was not subject to the rules of the center. Elsbeth was instructed to call a taxi and take me to the De Senarclens Clinic when the time for my baby's delivery came.

Social Changes and Student Activism (1967-1968)

The years 1967 and 1968 were crucial years that brought changes. No one could have predicted that a war in a small country in Southeast Asia called Vietnam would become such a big tragedy for the United States, would have such an impact on the American psyche, and would change a whole generation of Americans.

As young Americans were drafted into the US Army to serve in Vietnam, most agreed to go, doing their patriotic duty; others did not. The anti-Vietnam War movement grew steadily. Many young people turned to drugs, songs, music, defiance, anti-conformism, demonstrations, and riots to voice their opposition to the Vietnam War. It was also the era of the struggle for civil rights, with Martin Luther King Jr. The 1960s shaped the destiny of the youth of America. It was the era of the Summer of Love, the hippies, and the flower children. The revolution was also led by musicians and singers, such as Bob Dylan, Joan Baez, John Lennon, and Yoko Ono.

In 1968, a student uprising in Paris called the Student Revolution spread all over Europe. It was a student rebellion against traditional organizations and systems of education. The young wanted reforms and innovations. Their new slogan was "All Power to Imagination." In 1969, around five hundred thousand young people gathered at a farm in Woodstock, New York for three days of peace and music. President Richard Nixon began to reduce the number of US ground troops in Vietnam as opposition to the Vietnam War grew stronger and stronger.

The former associations I had joined in Louvain, such as OSCO, Ad Lucem, and the Lay Auxiliaries of the Missions were abolished by this student revolution.

In 1968, in Belgium, my former alma mater, the Catholic University of Louvain, built in 1425, was decisively split after decades of turmoil and violent student fights concerning the linguistic problem. The Catholic clergy was also divided on this matter. The Flemish succeeded in kicking out the Walloon (French) students. The French-language academic world in Leuven moved then to found another university, called Louvain-La-Neuve, twenty kilometers from Brussels. A journalist, Luc Beyer de Ryke, wrote, "Louvain was the Golgotha not only of the Church but also of a united Belgium."

Sophie's Birth (January 6, 1968) and Adoption (1969)

I was very proud of myself because I had rejected a marriage proposed by Day and Gisela. Afterward I had declined offers of marriage by some Italians who liked me. A young Italian man, Giuseppe, asked me to marry him and said that the baby would be well cared for by his mother. He had already consulted his mother, and she had said she would be delighted to raise the baby.

I had rejected abortion, and I was morally right. I did not choose an easy solution to my pregnancy problem. In my mind, I was courageous and did the courageous thing. The baby was conceived by two young people who were as good as anybody else, and both of us were remarkably healthy and educated. We did not marry. So what? I could not understand or accept stupid prejudices. At that time, to be unmarried and pregnant was a shame. I defied that notion.

I was friends with Claudine Martin, a student and the daughter of Pastor Reynald Martin, the pastor of Geneva. I came to Pastor Reynald Martin for help instead of going to the Catholic clergy for help. I was full of love for the Catholic clergy men and women in Belgium. After I left Belgium and settled in Geneva for my studies, I remember one day at Foyer John Knox when I asked a Catholic priest to see me because I needed to talk about my Catholic life in Geneva. A Catholic father came. He was elderly and obese. That already was repulsive to me. He sat next to me, put his hand on my knee and wanted to show how affectionate he was. That put me off. I hated this unwanted familiarity with me, got up and terminated his visit. That was the end of my relationship with the Catholic Church in Geneva. It showed how a simple priest who was not an inspiring priest could ruin the feelings of love and faith of other people for the church.

I went to see Pastor Reynald Martin. When he learned about my pregnancy and my problems, he was absolutely wonderful. He was kind and understanding. He introduced me to his daughter Claudine, who commented to me, "If I was pregnant without being married, my father would have killed me. Look how nice he is with you!" At that time, I was a role model for girls who wanted freedom from prejudice and freedom to choose for themselves what to do with their bodies. I did not intend to be a symbol of that revolutionary idea. It was unintentional.

Claudine Martin once invited me to dinner at her student apartment near the university. I thought that the invitation was to her family home, so I went to the pastor's home. The door was open, but no one was at home. I sat at the entrance, waiting for them. The neighbors told me that they were not at home but had gone to their chalet for the weekend. I said, "Their door is open. It is not locked."

One of them replied, "The pastor's door is always open. It is never locked, in case somebody needs to get in." This shows how extraordinary Pastor Reynald Martin was. It was his Christian attitude that his home should be always left open and welcoming. Finally I realized my mistake and went to Claudine's address, where she was waiting for me. We were the same age. I found it amazing that I got along so well with her and that confirmed the saying. "The best friendships of our lives were the friendships we have had in our youth."

Most people I encountered were remarkably nice. I had lived for some months with the elderly parish priest of Coppet, his sister, and his niece. A Vietnamese friend had introduced me there. I paid nothing, and I had excellent fresh meals. At noon I went to the garden, picked up the lettuce, and whipped up a vinaigrette sauce with boiled eggs, garlic, and mustard, and it was delicious. Their niece was young, lively, and pleasant. I moved back to Geneva when I was seven months due because there was no hospital in this rural part of Coppet.

The pretty municipality of Coppet, near Nyon, was known for its historical château where lived Madame de Stael, who was famous for her writings and controversial political opinions during the French Revolution and the Napoleon Bonaparte era.

My daughter Sophie was born on January 6, 1968, on the Feast of the Epiphany, at the clinic of Dr. Francois and Myriam de Senarclens, in Geneva. She was a Capricorn—a good sign.

It was a breech birth, and it was difficult, but it went very well. I overheard the doctor talking with the nurse. "What a beautiful baby, and the mother is admirable. Those Vietnamese women are courageous." I was so proud to hear those words. I felt as if I had been vindicated for the difficult life I'd had during the past year. I looked at my baby. She was so cute with a pink peach-colored face. The doctor gave her a slap, and she uttered her first cry!

I named her Sophie from a French book I had read in my childhood, written by the countess of Segur. I quickly gave her a Vietnamese name, Le Tuyet, which means "the beauty of the snow," as I looked through the windows of my room at the clinic and was inspired by the snowflakes falling from the sky.

In January 1968, Sophie was baptized at the Church of St. Nicholas de Flue. The Church of St. Nicholas de Flue stood at the corner of the building where I had rented an apartment at 32 Avenue de Vermont, after I gave birth to Sophie.

St. Nicholas of Flue was the patron saint of Switzerland. That church was then the biggest and most modern Catholic church of Geneva. Saint Nicholas of Flue died on March 21, 1487, on his seventieth birthday. He began his life as commander-in-chief of the Swiss forces, resisting the invasions. He married and had children. Afterward, he chose to live as a hermit. After his death, he was venerated by Swiss Catholics, and in 1947, he was canonized as a saint by Pope Pius XII.

When I felt lonely, I would go to this church in the evening when there was nobody there. I bought flowers at the store around the corner of my building and deposited them at the foot of the altar. I prayed to the Virgin Mary.

The chosen godfather for Sophie was Andre Fabri, a Belgian friend working in a bank in Geneva. When I moved to Geneva in 1965, a friend I met at the University of Louvain, Anne Marie Bouvy, who lived at the Château d'Ayeneux, where I had been invited many times, introduced me to her cousin, who was Andre Fabri.

I chose Estelle as godmother. She was a French girl I had met at the center for unmarried mothers. She was an aristocrat and was expulsed from her château by her parents because of her pregnancy. Estelle lent me a baptism dress for Sophie. It had been worn by her daughter at her baptism a week before. The dress was sneaked out of the château by Estelle's mother and was a priceless heirloom worn by generations of babies in that château. Estelle soon after married a young man she had met in Geneva at La Placette, a superstore where both worked. They left Geneva to start a new life somewhere else where nobody knew them. Her role as godmother to Sophie lasted less than a month.

My choice of her as godmother was dumb. This girl and I had the same problems. I should have chosen a very rich and very cultured woman friend for that role.

I invited Dr. Myriam de Senarclens for Sophie's baptism. She came and attended the church service. My guests included Andre Fabri and his wife, Francoise, Claire de Bethune, and my Vietnamese friend Phi Anh and her little sister-in-law.

Claire came and stayed with me for some days in my tiny apartment. Claire had just given birth to her daughter Manuela six months prior. She came from Istanbul, where her husband, Dominique de Patoul, was posted at La Sabena, the Belgian Airlines. Claire lived a life of privilege. Thanks to her husband's position, she had her room already offered to her in a luxury hotel of Geneva, probably the InterContinental Hotel. She chose to stay with me, in my tiny and humble apartment. I did not even offer her a nice breakfast. I was down to my last penny. She brought a tiny gold St. Christopher medal as a gift to Sophie. When she saw me give a bottle of milk to Sophie without sterilizing it, she exclaimed, "Your daughter will die if you don't sterilize the bottles!" She rushed to buy the proper container for me to sterilize the bottles. In my ignorance regarding how to look after a baby, I did not even know about the sterilization procedure. In Vietnam, I had not seen it. Babies sucked the breasts of their mothers or of hired wet nurses, and later they ate rice soup or rice. They might pick up microbes while growing up, but they were as healthy as ever. Children in Vietnam played with dirt and acquired a strong immune system.

Claire spent her days off in Geneva to go shopping at Le Bon Genie, the most expensive women's clothing superstore of Geneva. I went with her and sat patiently for hours on a chair, waiting for her to finish trying on her clothing.

Shopping with Claire reminded me of the times in Louvain and Brussels when I accompanied her to buy her outfits and evening gowns in haute couture boutiques. She attended high society balls. I had no dancing parties to go to, and by the way, I did not know how to dance. Having elderly parents obsessed only with religion, I had not had private music and dancing lessons. I lacked the necessary education and talents to model me into a perfect, graceful society girl, able to swirl at a Viennese waltz. Therefore, I was unable to seduce a fairy tale prince.

As Claire was very tall, thin, and beautiful, she had been offered employment as a mannequin by a famous fashion designer. I forget which House it was. Dior? Helena Rubinstein? Chanel? Her parents refused the offer, claiming that it would be scandalous for their daughter to be a mannequin. Claire also took regularly a plane from Brussels to Paris to have her hair done by Alexandre, a famous hairdresser of that time.

I found her fabulous, and I always looked up to Claire. I had been always proud to have her as a friend and as a godmother. Usually women were jealous of other women when they were more beautiful and rich. In my case, I was always thrilled to be friends with women who were on top of everything, who were beautiful, intelligent and titled. I was not jealous. I admired them.

In 1967, at the Moillebeau Building, I met a Belgian-born woman, Sarah. She was the manager of the Moillebeau restaurant where we diplomats and staff from diplomatic delegations of various countries, having our offices there, went to have a coffee or lunch. The restaurant did not serve dinner. She lived with Jean Jacques Croptier, from a respectable family of Geneva. She did not need a job but she occupied herself with managing that restaurant. Jean Jacques was divorced and had a daughter, Stephane.

On my first day, during lunch at the Moillebeau restaurant, Sarah came to sit next to me. When people worked daily in the same building, they knew who was who—the regular clients and the new faces. She was aware that I was the new girl at the new permanent Mission of Vietnam, and she wanted to ask me to help her adopt a Vietnamese baby. She thought that this adoption would be easy because the country was at war and surely there were a large number of babies who were abandoned or orphaned. I informed her that our mission was not in charge of requests for the adoption of Vietnamese babies by foreigners. My ambassador was also against it. He was adamant that we should keep our babies, the future of our country, in Vietnam and not let foreigners take them away. Once out of the country, our babies would be lost forever.

One year later, in the spring of 1968, Sarah heard that I had given birth to a baby and that I was not married. I had informed a Turkish woman diplomat I knew in the Moillebeau building and told her to spread the news to Sarah. The Turkish woman said to Sarah, "This is your opportunity, Sarah. Alice is not married and has a baby. This is your chance—one that comes only once in your lifetime." Super excited, Sarah asked for my address and came to see me.

When she rang the doorbell, I was feeding Sophie with a bottle stuck in her mouth. Sarah jumped straight away on Sophie, took her in her arms, and asked me, "Tell me, Alice, what happened?" She did not really care about me and my stories. She was interested only in the baby. "I want to buy her nice clothing and healthy food. I want to take her with me and look after her. Let me be the godmother. I shall give her everything she might need."

I did go to the Church of St. Nicholas de Flue to ask if Sarah could replace Estelle as Sophie's godmother. The priest in charge was very angry with me for my stupid request, because the sacrament of baptism was unchangeable.

She asked to adopt Sophie. She advanced her case with a series of valuable arguments. She had the time to devote herself entirely to my baby and the money to give her the best education possible. She had a home in Geneva, a country property for fresh air, and a chalet in the mountains. She could not have a baby herself. All her love would be for my baby.

I saw for Sophie the opportunity to live in security and stability and to be raised by Sarah, who had only love in her heart for her, who would give her the best education that money could afford, and who would leave to my child a good inheritance. I trusted Sarah, and I was not disappointed. Sarah proved to be a loving and excellent mother. She devoted her life to Sophie. There were two other children in the family. Stephane was her stepdaughter, and Michel was adopted, but her favorite child was always Sophie. I trusted my instinct, and in the bottom of my heart, I knew that Sarah was an excellent choice for Sophie's future.

There was a great understanding between Sarah and me. Neither of us was complicated. Sarah said to me that I was like a younger sister and that if I could not care for the baby, she would raise Sophie on my behalf. The most important issue to her was the well-being of the child. Sophie would have two mothers instead of one. Whatever we decided, we did it for the happiness and the development of the child, giving her the best of life's opportunities. She was not our property.

The adoption paper was officially signed in mid-1969. After Sophie had been adopted by Sarah, some lady friends in Geneva and Belgium told me, "If I knew that you intended to put the baby up for adoption, I would have wanted to adopt her." By comparison, I still preferred Sarah to them. Sarah was not an intellectual, and she was not born in the upper class. She was an ordinary woman, married to a rich man. She prevailed because she wanted desperately to found a family with Jean Jacques, and adopting children would cement it. She loved Sophie at first sight, and it was her love and devotion to Sophie that dictated my choice.

My sisters Anna and Annie from Saigon let me know that they wished to adopt Sophie. They said they would tell our parents that Sophie was the baby of a woman friend who could not keep her baby because she had no financial means. Because of the big war going on in Saigon, I declined my sisters' offer. I did not want to send my baby to a country at war. Sarah was a better solution.

My sister-in-law Julie, Henri's wife, came to Geneva for a visit. She stayed at my place with Catherine, her eldest daughter, who had been born very crippled because the doctor, during her birth, had squeezed her head too strongly and damaged her brain. The young girl could not move, speak, or eat by herself. In Saigon, she had a nanny hired to look after her day and night. Julie came to Geneva to look for an institution to put Catherine in for better medical care than in Saigon, with the hope for a Swiss medical miracle. Julie visited several institutions but finally did not have the heart to leave her daughter behind. She brought Catherine back to Saigon.

She carried Anna and Annie's message to me: "When you return to Saigon, bring back Alice's baby. We want to adopt her."

I introduced Julie to Sarah. Julie had a favorable opinion of Sarah. Julie confided to me. "Your sisters Anna and Annie are naive. They have no experience about motherhood and raising children. It looks to me as though Sarah is a better choice."

The Tet Offensive; the Battle of Saigon (1968); Albert's Death and Funeral (March 1968)

In January 1968, the Vietcong, or South Vietnamese Communists, launched an offensive against all major cities of Vietnam during the Lunar New Year, which in Vietnamese is called Tet Mau Than. Usually, no one fought during the Lunar New Year, which was tacitly considered a holy period of the year and treated as a temporary morally agreed cease-fire. The Vietcong violated this moral understanding because they wanted to launch a surprise attack. They also expected the South Vietnamese to rise up and side with them. They expected a great and easy victory. Nothing like that happened.

The troops of the Republic of Vietnam and the Americans were caught by surprise. But they fought back with heroism and fierceness. The American soldiers had to save the military honor of the United States. The South Vietnamese soldiers fought for the survival of their nation and the lives of their family and friends. Ferocious battles erupted in all cities of South Vietnam. The most severe casualties occurred in Saigon and in Hue, the imperial capital of Central Vietnam. The Communists were very cruel everywhere and especially in Hue, where they executed and killed thousands and thousands of civilians. The ancient palaces were destroyed.

Our brother Albert, an army officer, was stationed at a military building in charge of military supplies near the hippodrome of Phu Tho. When he heard the gunshots, he got out and helped the soldiers fighting outside. Albert was hit in the head. He did not die straight away but was operated on after ten long hours lying on the floor and was released to the care of Mother, Anna, and Annie. Saigon was swamped by thousands and thousands of dead and wounded people everywhere.

Albert died in March. It was the first time that a death occurred in our family. Henri took pictures of Albert to preserve his physical memory. My parents were distraught. For years, they had tried to keep their sons safe from the war, and Albert was now dead after fighting for his country. That did not console my parents. They were bitter.

Albert Nguyen Vo My was posthumously awarded the Medal of Merit and Valour with three Palms of Honor, the highest military medal of Vietnam for officers killed in the line of duty. Although Albert's funeral was a private family event, it became grandiose, as if it were a state funeral. Our family had allies, friends, colleagues, and relatives occupying important functions in South Vietnam. A huge crowd showed up.

The prime minister and Mrs. Nguyen Van Loc bowed in front of his coffin. Mr. Loc had graduated in law with our brother Henri at the University of Montpellier in France, and they were close friends. He left after showing his respect, but his wife walked behind the hearse with our family members.

The monks and nuns followed in the footsteps of the family. The cabinet ministers, numerous high-ranking army officers, and people from the world of the finance and business in Saigon were present. Albert had been a professor at the Universities of Saigon and Can Tho, so professors and students from both universities came. Our brother Maurice Nguyen Vo Duc was an engineer, our cousin Nguyen Quoc Hung was a judge of the Supreme Court; and our cousins Nguyen Minh Chau and Tran Van Au were doctors, so their colleagues came.

The soldiers who had served under Albert's command and his students from the National Institute of Agriculture and Forestry ended the cortege with tears in their eyes. They accosted our young cousin Le Minh Quoc and told him, "Are you a member of the family? We wish to offer our condolences and tell you how much we love him."

Albert died at thirty-seven years old. He was not married, and he lived in Saigon with our parents, brothers, and sisters. They supported him. Meanwhile, he always donated the salaries he received as an army officer and as a university professor to his soldiers and his students. He had never cashed one penny out of his paychecks.

I had witnessed his generosity during the years he had lived and worked in Paris with a big salary as an agricultural engineer. He came regularly to Louvain, where I was studying, and gave me some money and some gifts bought at the Champs Élysées. He had lent money to Vietnamese friends in Paris. Many, after graduation, did not want to return to Vietnam and took jobs overseas, especially in former French colonies. They needed to pay for their travel tickets and borrowed money from Albert. No one had ever reimbursed him, and Albert did not care. He was happy to help them out and did not expect reimbursement. He was handsome, very popular, and well-liked by many Vietnamese girls, but he remained unattached because he wanted to go home and help his country and his family. It was his priority.

The offerings to the funeral were forwarded to the Association of the War Widows. Our parents inscribed on Albert's tombstone, "Like other unknown heroes, our son has paid his debt to the nation."

I was in my apartment in Geneva when Mr. Kieu, an accountant at our mission, came knocking at my door. He announced, "Do you know that your brother died?" He showed me a Vietnamese newspaper in which my parents thanked the prime minister and his wife, our armed forces, friends, and acquaintances for attending the funeral of their son Nguyen Vo My. Vietnamese newspapers were sent in the weekly diplomatic mail from Saigon.

Albert had graduated from the National Institute of Agronomy of Toulouse. He had a great career in Paris with a big salary. He returned in the spring of 1964 to serve his country, knowing that he would be drafted into the army.

His life was a life of sacrifice. Why did the gods have to take away our innocent young men? Was it worthy to die in that war? In the end, so much blood was poured for nothing.

My family was devastated. For the first time in their life, they had suffered a loss due to the war. We lived in Saigon. The war was previously going on in the countryside and in the villages but not in Saigon. Suddenly the situation changed. The war came to Saigon and big cities. Suddenly death took away our own family member.

1968 was a wake-up call in the Vietnam War. The Americans had been told that everything was going well in Vietnam. Suddenly they were seeing horrible pictures on their TV screens at home of the US soldiers desperately defending themselves and the US Embassy in Saigon almost being taken over by a group of Vietcong. During the Communist attacks in subsequent months, the South Vietnamese troops stood up against the Communists and fought bravely for their country and for their families.

On March 31, 1968, President Johnson announced that he would not seek reelection. On April 4, Reverend Dr. Martin Luther King Jr. was assassinated in Memphis. On June 5, Robert Kennedy, campaigning for the US presidency, was shot in Los Angeles.

On November 27, President Elect Richard Nixon asked Henry Kissinger to be his national security advisor.

Robert Kennedy had called the Vietnam War an unwinnable war, and Senator Mike Mansfield had commented, "We are in the wrong place and we are fighting the wrong kind of war."

My Apartment in Rome

In 1968, the apartment in Rome was in my name and had been sublet to Phuong Mai. Some of my belongings were still there. For several months, I did not receive news from her, and I got worried. I decided to return to Rome to check out the situation.

I arrived in the evening and found my apartment locked with heavy chains and surrounded by yellow tape like that used at crime scenes. As soon as he saw me, the superintendent, as instructed by the landlord, rushed to call the police, but I persuaded him to instead call the landlord. I told him that I did not know what had happened. Phuong Mai had left the apartment for London and had never been back. For several months, the rent had not been paid. I paid the arrears to the landlord, who agreed to let me retrieve my belongings. I left to him our brand-new stove and furniture. I was relieved that the story had been resolved in a smooth way.

During the time she had been sharing my apartment, Phuong Mai had an Italian boyfriend Giorgio. How did they meet? One day, Phuong Mai and I were walking along our street. Because we were foreigners, young Italians always looked at us and loudly showered us with compliments. They followed us. It was all a traditional Italian game. That day we noticed two young men who looked at us, smiled at us, and said, "Buon giorno, signorine." They were courteous and seemed well educated. One of them looked like a British student freshly enrolled at Eton College, handsome and well dressed. Phuong Mai and I smiled back to them and engaged in conversation with them. We had never done that before, but that day was fateful for Phuong Mai. It was how Phuong Mai and Giorgio got acquainted. The four of us stood socializing on the terrace of my apartment. It was a chance meeting that resulted in a genuine love story. They were very much in love with each other. We of course hid that story

142

from her parents. I was supposed to be her chaperone, but how could I be the guardian of a girl who was in every aspect more mature than me?

After my departure for Geneva, and after having taken over my apartment, Phuong Mai returned in 1967 to London, England, for vacation, and she asked her parents for authorization to marry Giorgio. Her parents refused and locked her up in her bedroom in London. She could not go out, telephone, or write letters; and she could not communicate with the external world, Giorgio, or me. That was the reason for her silence.

I wrote to her, informing her of the situation. Her parents intercepted my letter, read it, and demanded an explanation. She had to confess the truth about the apartment. The parents reimbursed me. In the end, they could not bend her will to marry Giorgio, and the young couple got married. They lived in Rome and had children, and she earned her living as a painter and artist.

Her marriage to an Italian would be beneficial for her parents and her brother after the fall of Saigon in 1975 if they chose to immigrate to Italy.

Years 1969-1971

On January 20, 1969, Richard M. Nixon was elected as the thirty-seventh US president. He was quick to declare, "The greatest honor history can bestow us is the title of peacemaker." Nixon aimed at achieving "peace with honor" and bringing back home the US troops and the US prisoners of war (POWs) detained by Hanoi. It was his promise to the American people. He was the fifth US president to cope with the Vietnam War.

On January 25, the Paris peace talks began between the delegations of the United States, South Vietnam, North Vietnam, and the Vietcong. Henry Cabot Lodge, former US ambassador to South Vietnam, was appointed senior US negotiator at the Paris peace talks. Afterward Henry Kissinger became the main negotiator for the United States.

On June 8, President Nixon and President Nguyen Van Thieu met at Midway Island. Nixon announced "the Vietnamization" of the war and a sharp withdrawal of the US troops in Vietnam. He had to appease the reticence of President Nguyen Van Thieu by promising continual support of the United States to South Vietnam should North Vietnam attack the South.

On January 31, 1969, Fr. Dominique Pire died in Louvain from cancer. He was fifty-eight years old. In 1960, he was my bridge between Saigon and Louvain, between Buddhism and Christianity, and between Earth and Eternity. He walked through my life and was part of my journey, but God had decided that he was not the purpose of my life.

On September 2, President Ho Chi Minh died at seventy-nine years old. In his last will, he urged "the North Vietnamese to fight on until the last Yankee has gone." He was embalmed by the finest embalmers of the Soviet Union. A mausoleum influenced by Soviet architecture was built to glorify his memory for generations to come and pay their respects.

In 1969, I went on vacation to Vienna, Austria, accepting the invitation of Pastor Karl Wittich, whom I had met in 1965 when I was a student at Foyer John Knox in Geneva. Pastor Wittich was the executive director of the Albert Schweitzer Student Centre in Vienna. He had stayed for several weeks at Foyer John Knox to learn about its operations. I was also friends with his wife, Dorothea, who was born as a German Swiss. Originally she was his assistant at the Albert Schweitzer Student Centre. When they started to date, they had to avoid being seen by their students so the students would not gossip about their relationship. They would meet at the Vienna cemetery, where he proposed marriage to her!

They were perfect hosts and showed me everything in Vienna that could be of interest to a tourist. They took me to a Viennese ball. On Sunday, we traveled to Mayerling, the historic location where the Archduke Rudolf and the love of his life, Vera, had committed suicide.

I went to Rome, accepting the invitation of Monsignor Remigio Musaragno, whom I had met at OSCO conferences when I was a student at Louvain. He had led a group of Italian students at the OSCO meetings. He worked at the Vatican and lived in Rome with his sister. Over the years, I frequently took the train to Rome and spent vacations with them. I remember very clearly that I was at his home in July of 1969 because it was the night of the landing on the moon by Neil Armstrong, who called that event "one giant leap for mankind." We spent the night watching the TV.

On May 1, 1970, President Richard Nixon called the antiwar students "bums blowing up campuses."

On June 1, 1971, Senator Mike Mansfield labeled the Vietnam War as "a tragic mistake."

General Nguyen Van Thieu Reelected as President of the Republic of Vietnam (1971)

In 1971, General Duong Van Minh returned from exile in Thailand. The United States wanted him and General Nguyen Cao Ky to run for elections so it looked like Vietnam enjoyed democracy. Both of them withdrew from the race, realizing that their opponent, General Nguyen Van Thieu, would do anything possible—even rigging the elections—to win the necessary votes. General Nguyen Cao Ky would later become a fierce critic of Thieu. He said, "Thieu has an excessive attachment to power." He spent his time from that day until the end of the war accusing Thieu's government of corruption, inefficiency, and despotism.

Nguyen Cao Ky complained to the Italian journalist Oriana Fallaci, "Nine out of ten of the leaders on our side are corrupt … We need a revolution … We need new laws giving power to the poor."

Fallaci responded, "This is what Ho Chi Minh said."

General Duong Van Minh was not too vocal about his plan to negotiate with the Communists, for fear of being sent back into exile. He formed an opposition party, accusing Thieu of repressive tactics.

On October 3, 1971, General Nguyen Van Thieu was reelected as president of the Republic of Vietnam. Henry Kissinger called him "a great patriot, a dauntless leader."

Geneva—Our Permanent Mission to the United Nations and Specialized Agencies (1967-1975)

In 1967, Ambassador Le Van Loi was appointed Permanent Representative of the Republic of Vietnam to the United Nations and its specialized agencies in Geneva. He rented our offices at the Moillebeau Building. There were there a number of diplomatic delegations, such as the delegations of Australia, New Zealand, Belgium, Turkey, Chile, and the Netherlands, and the Geneva International Monetary Fund (IMF) office was located there too. We shared a floor with the IMF and the delegation of Chile.

We became close friends with the IMF executives. Mr. Edgar Jones, the executive director, and Ambassador Le Van Loi played golf together. The French assistant executive director, Pierre Simonet, and his wife, Luce, became friends with me. The third executive was a young Korean, Moh, who was married to an American, Gail. They invited me often for lunches at their home. Gail was a picture of the good American girl, and she loved to cook. Mr. Loi and I were invited to all the receptions of the IMF, and I was the only woman in most of them. Wives were not invited. My IMF friends explained to the guests that I was invited as a colleague and a friend and not as a woman.

We witnessed the change of political regimes in Chile. During the presidency of Salvador Allende, Chile was socialist, so our relations with its diplomats were just polite. In 1973, during the presidency of General Augusto Pinochet, who overthrew the regime of Allende on September 11, 1973, and took the power in 1973, we became great friends with the new ambassador of Chile, Mr. Alberto Da Silva Davidson, and his staff. They shared our floor and they were newcomers, not experienced yet with Geneva and UN meetings so my ambassador, a skillful diplomat, jumped on the opportunity to be helpful to them and to nurture a great relationship with the new ambassador of Chile and staff.

In Geneva, Chile from 1973 to 1975 was among our best anticommunist supporters at the United Nations. President Pinochet explained his policy. "Everything I did, all my actions, all of the problems I had I dedicate to God and to Chile because I kept Chile from becoming Communist."

Ambassador Le Van Loi was a colleague and friend of Prince Sadruddin Aga Khan, the high commissioner for refugees. Vietnam was in a big war, with daily waves of thousands and thousands of refugees coming from across the country. One issue was the Cambodian refugees in our country. The role of the UNHCR was to assist refugees when they fled to another country and settled there. Mr. Loi had frequent business meetings with Prince Sadruddin. I joined them for lunches at the UN restaurant. During my first lunch with them, I was very intimidated. Wow…I was having lunch with a prince and a prince from the Aga Khan family! It was a dream! I was shy and speechless. Prince Sadruddin asked my ambassador. "Does the lady speak English or French?" My ambassador laughed and responded." She speaks English and French like you and me." That was not really true. I was excellent in French but not in English. The first time I met Princess Sadruddin, I was also uncomfortable but she was so warm, gentle and unsophisticated that I liked her spontaneously. Mr. Loi and I also were invited for receptions at their Château de Bellerive. I liked Prince and Princess Sadruddin Aga Khan. He was a perfect gentleman, and she was very kind and sweet to me.

At the United Nations in Geneva, I had the opportunity to see Princess Sonja of Norway, who later became queen. She came as the guest of honor, presiding at a conference organized by Prince Sadruddin. While Princess Sonja was delivering her speech at the podium, a dozen photographers from the United Nations and from some newspapers bombed her with their camera flashes. I, the little Alice, sitting next to my ambassador behind the big words "Republic of Vietnam," was the focus of continuous camera flashes from a Norwegian photographer accompanying the royal delegation. He took my pictures from different angles so many times that I became embarrassed. He had never seen a Vietnamese lady at an international conference. Furthermore, he had never before seen a Vietnamese girl!

I glanced furtively to my ambassador. As usual, Mr. Loi was imperturbable. His determination was that nothing was to disturb our dignity. We were to be cool, like stone statues. That was dignity. I looked at my international colleagues. They had fun seeing me embarrassed with that unstoppable camera zooming at me. I looked at Princess Sadruddin, who was sitting incognito in the public gallery. She sent back to me a sweet and amused smile.

At another conference, I had the opportunity to get acquainted with Mrs. Shirley Temple Black. She was posted in New York, but she arrived in Geneva as a member of the US delegation, attending a UN conference.

At the evening reception offered by the US delegation, I stood at a corner of the reception room with a friend—a tall Dutch woman with blond hair, heavy makeup, and flashy costume jewelry. Beside her, so tall and big, I looked very tiny, and I had put on my national dress, the famous Vietnamese *ao dai*. Mrs. Shirley Temple Black was all smiles and very aware of her celebrity. She walked around and shook hands with people here and there. She had been the US ambassador to Ghana and had attended some international UN conferences in New York with the US delegation. Suddenly she saw me. She crossed the room and came toward me. She extended her hand and said, "How do you do? I am Shirley Temple Black from the US delegation."

I smiled back to her and responded, "I am the delegate of Vietnam."

I was shy, and my speech was very short because of shyness. I missed the fact that I should have said, "How honored I am to meet you!" I also did not specify which Vietnam I was representing.

North Vietnam, or the Democratic Republic of Vietnam, never sent any delegation to the United Nations and its specialized agencies after the partition of Vietnam in 1954. Because Vietnam was divided into two countries, the two Vietnams did not have the status of members in the United Nations. Both Vietnams had only the status of UN observers, but we were full members of its specialized agencies, such as the World Health Organization (WHO), International Labor Organization (ILO), Conference on Trade and Development (UNCTAD), Office of the High Commissioner for Refugees (UNHCR), and many others.

North Vietnamese leaders claimed that they were the sole representatives of Vietnam from North to South. They claimed that we, the delegates of the Republic of Vietnam (South Vietnam), were not legitimate representatives. For this reason, they refused to participate in UN conferences on equal footing with us.

Mrs. Shirley Temple Black was puzzled. For a fleeting moment, she hesitated, not knowing what to say or do. She was intrigued because I did not compliment her and because I was not overwhelmed at meeting a famous actress. Perhaps she was left wondering whether I was representing the enemy and which Vietnam I stood for. She disappeared, saying, "Please excuse me. As the hostess, I must welcome other guests." She had come to greet me because she had seen my Vietnamese national dress, which was familiar to her and those in Washington.

Thanks to my ambassador, although I was young and not titled, I was invited everywhere among the dignitaries because I was in charge of most of the conferences, press, and information, and I was the hostess of our receptions and dinner parties.

Mr. Loi was married, but his French-born wife, Jacqueline, was not interested in diplomatic life. Later on, he divorced and fell in love with Tove, who was born in Denmark. Mr. Loi was very secretive about his private life, and no one really knew what was going on in it. He also never talked about any woman to another woman. He believed that women could be jealous of each other. Tove lived with him and looked after his two young children Valerie and Luc, who were from his marriage with Jacqueline. Tove stayed invisible in his official life, so I was the only woman and the only hostess of the Vietnam mission in Geneva up to the fall of Saigon in 1975.

In the summer of 1969, as a member of the Vietnamese Delegation to the International Labor Organization, I saw for the second time Pope Paul VI, who came as the guest of honor to celebrate the twentieth anniversary of the ILO. Pope Paul VI asked the Catholic delegates to gather in a special room to meet with him if they wished to. Never in the history of Vietnam had a young Vietnamese woman met with a pope not only once but twice. Here I received the second blessing on my head from Pope Paul VI.

Our mission in Geneva became the focal point of our multilateral diplomacy. Our minister of foreign affairs, Mr. Tran Van Lam, came to Geneva many times to meet with our ambassadors to Italy, England, Greece, and the Netherlands for consultations and strategic moves. I saw my former ambassador in Rome, Ambassador Nguyen Van Hieu, and Ambassador Le Ngoc Chan posted in London, England. His spouse accompanied him. After the conference with our minister Tran Van Lam, they intended to visit their daughter Phuong Mai and her husband and children in Rome.

The International Conference on Humanitarian Law, Geneva (1972-1974)

Our most decisive diplomatic battle was at the International Conference on Humanitarian Law, which lasted two years (1972-1974). The National Front for the Liberation of South Vietnam (FNL) had applied to be a member of that important and huge conference. Our government of the Republic of Vietnam did not recognize the FNL; for us the group had no legal grounds and did not exist as such. It was only a creation of North Vietnam in the South, and it was an insurgent movement—nothing else. That stirred the conference to become a political battlefield between us, the delegation of the Republic of Vietnam, and the delegation of the Democratic Republic of Vietnam, which was backed up by the Union of Soviet Socialist Republics and the People's Republic of China.

Should they be successful with their application, the Vietcong would attend the conference under the banner of Provisional Government of South Vietnam, and South Vietnam would be divided into two Vietnams. That meant that three Vietnams would be represented at this conference. The Vietcong (South Vietnamese Communists), created by North Vietnam in the South, aimed to replace us at UN international conferences and everywhere else.

We lobbied hard for the votes, and we won! All the member countries of the United Nations had the right to vote, including Mongolia, which was brought in by the Soviet Union from the Mongolian plains, and the tiny San Marino, discovered as eligible to vote by the United States. The consul of San Marino came down with the flu and declared that he was in bed. A US diplomat went to see him and brought him to the United Nations. The Republic of Vietnam won by only one vote, but we won! The consul of San Marino voted for us, and the delegate of Senegal, who should have come and vote, was noticeably absent. It was a miracle for us. Mrs. Nguyen Thi Binh, the foreign affairs minister of the so-called FNL, invited by Kurt Waldheim, the secretary general of the United Nations, to Geneva, waited outside the door of the conference room for her supposed triumphal entrance. She was defeated and had to return, empty-handed, to the jungle of South Vietnam.

Kurt Waldheim, instead of being neutral as secretary-general of the United Nations, behaved obviously against us. He turned down all of our proposals and requests. My ambassador was very frustrated. It was Kurt Waldheim who took the initiative to invite Mrs. Nguyen Thi Binh to Geneva and welcome her with great honor. Thus we were very happy to have defeated Kurt Waldheim as well.

During this international conference on humanitarian law, our chief of delegation and Ambassador Le Van Loi delivered a brilliant and passionate speech. He explained the history of the Vietnam War and why we fought the Communist North Vietnamese and the Vietcong. His speech moved the audience. The US government distributed copies of Mr. Loi's speech to US embassies around the world as a textbook explaining what the Vietnam War was about and the legitimacy of the government of the Republic of Vietnam, which was fighting for its survival with just cause.

After the votes, our victorious delegation was jubilant. In the evening, we invited the American delegates, our allies, to come to our office and celebrate with us, popping open champagne bottles that had waited two years for this moment. Mr. Le Van Loi had always been a positive fighter. He aimed for victory in spite of all odds against us.

Georges Aldrich Jr. was the head of the large US delegation, composed of thirty legal experts. He had been general attorney of the White House and chief legal advisor at the Paris negotiations in 1972–1973.

I told Georges Aldrich Jr. that I was going to immigrate to Canada. He said, "If you come to Washington, please be my guest. I and my family would like to offer a reception in your honor."

In his report to the White House, Aldrich wrote, "Our allies, the South Vietnamese delegates, led by Ambassador Le Van Loi, did an outstanding back stage lobbying."

The Mongolian delegate was a short and plump woman. The day she arrived, she saw me for the first time in the ladies' powder room. We smiled to each other, as Asian women always did. She did not know who I was, but I knew who she was. At the conference, she noticed me sitting behind the plaque for the Republic of Vietnam. She became perplexed; her eyebrows curved, and she looked at me with disapproval. She came to me and said, "I don't understand you. Why are you siding with the Americans, assassins of your people?" I smiled and brushed her off, having no time to explain to her the history of the Vietnam War. She was so brainwashed by Soviet propaganda that she would never be able to understand.

Very zealous, she approached one of the US delegates, a tall and impressive man, and yelled, "You murderers! Why do you kill innocent Vietnamese people?"

The US delegate was so annoyed that he walked away saying, "Of course, the US also created the sun and the rains."

She ran after him, screaming, "You arrogant people!"

Our Spanish driver, Antonio, was standing in the hallway, and he was well dressed, exactly like a gentleman. She mistook him for a delegate and turned to him. Antonio ran away, saying, "Me? No, no! Me? No politics!"

During this long conference, a Swedish delegate died from old age and a delegate from the Middle East died from a heart attack. The Communists were quick to spread rumors that the United States had poisoned him with cyanide in his coffee. A US delegate commented to me, "We, of course, are accused of everything happening in the world."

In 1973, King Baudouin I of Belgium and Queen Fabiola visited the United Nations in Geneva, invited by Kurt Waldheim, secretary general of the United Nations. My godfather accompanied them to Geneva but declined to attend an official dinner in the evening, saying that he had a goddaughter in Geneva and would have dinner with her.

In August 1974, Major General John E. Murray wrote, "Without proper support, the RVNAF (Republic of Vietnam Armed Forces) are going lose, may be not next week, not next month, but after the year they are going to."

A Great Love Story

The heart has its reasons of which reason knows nothing
—Blaise Pascal

Jacqueline Kennedy Onassis said that every woman on earth should experience a great love story once in her life. I had experienced the great love story of my life. It was such a magical moment for both of us when we met at a UN international conference.

One day in1969, as I took my seat behind the plaque of the Republic of Vietnam when arriving at a UN conference, my neighbor, representing the Federal Republic of Germany, stood up and advanced the seat for me. He kissed my hand in the old-fashioned way. Both of us were young and were very amused by his hand kissing, and we giggled like two schoolchildren. Jurgen was smitten by me. He was beaming, radiating from the inside out, and had a joyful smile on his face.

In the evening, we attended a reception offered by the European Communities. When I left, he followed me, wrapped me up in my coat, and said in front of everybody, "May I walk you home?" The international crowd of delegates stared at us, and we looked back at them, flashing a happy smile. We declared openly to our international colleagues that we were in love with each other. We did not hide it. We showed it off.

That was the beginning of our great love story.

We were both terribly lonely and unhappy. I was single and he was entrapped in a marriage he wanted unconsciously to escape from. We met suddenly the person we dreamed of as the love of our lives. Rainer Maria Rilke once said that love consists of this: two solitudes that meet, protect and greet each other. Jurgen was thirteen years older than me, and he had fair hair and blue eyes. He was the typical stereotype of German men. Jurgen was one of the representatives of the Federal Republic of Germany to the UN meetings. He was an expert in economics. He also represented the European Economic Committee at the United Nations. As the Federal Republic of Germany was a member of the European Communities, he often attended meetings in Brussels. He traveled the world as the representative of his country or the EC or the UN to international economic conferences.

His wife was ten years older than him. One day in 1946, she told him that he had made love to her while drunk at a Christmas party, and she obliged him to marry her, as she had become pregnant. He did not remember a thing of what had happened. He had a debt of gratitude to her because she had helped him to get a job during the hard times of postwar Germany. He did not want to marry her but he was weak and did not dare to refuse. They got married. He was eighteen years old, and she was twenty-eight. It was not a happy marriage.

Jurgen Von Branden announced to his German colleagues that he had fallen in love with me and that he wanted a divorce. He asked his wife for a divorce. She refused, not for love but because she did not want to be divorced. She thought that she would be shamed if she was divorced. She was Catholic, and he was Lutheran. She brandished her religion like a sword, calling him a sinner and saying that he would burn in hell. She would never let him go free and marry somebody else—especially a foreigner twenty-three years younger than she. She was stubborn and determined to harm him in any way possible.

Jurgen told her that she could have the home and all his money and pensions. He would leave her everything in exchange for his freedom. She refused. He told me that as soon as we got married, he would take out a huge life insurance policy so that when he died I would be financially well off.

He was weak and was no match for fighting with his wife. My German and European colleagues told me day after day to leave him. "He will not succeed in getting a divorce. He has always been weak and is afraid of his wife. Don't waste your time. You are young and beautiful. Be smart; leave him and get somebody else."

Jurgen said to me, "My colleagues, including my own brother, blame me for being weak. But I could not get a divorce over her dead body. She threatened me with her suicide. She threatened to go to the Chancellor [Helmut Kohn] and ruin my career. She told me that I was a sinner because I was a Lutheran, an adulterer, and that I abandoned her for a younger woman. What if she kills herself?"

I told him that it was only blackmail. As days and years dragged on, I convinced myself that I must leave him. I did not want to end my life like the heroine of *Back Street*, a novel published in 1930 by Fannie Hurst, who had written this: "There is not one woman in a million who has ever found happiness in the back streets of any man's life." The novel was based on a love story between a married wealthy banker and a young woman. He died unexpectedly, and she was left destitute, having sacrificed her life and career to stay with him.

In 1975, I told Jurgen in a telephone call that I had decided to leave him and had chosen Canada as my next destination. I wanted to say goodbye to the old continent and begin a new life in Canada. After a long silence, he said. "You broke my heart, but I have no right to forbid you to do what you think is best for you." I did not feel any guilt toward him. He himself had signed his own fate when, after seven years of waiting for him, he did not succeed in securing a divorce.

His own brother had met a woman at an international meeting, come home, and told his wife that he wanted a divorce. He had a strong will and got what he wanted. He criticized Jurgen for being weak. A marriage should not be a prison in perpetuity. Divorce exists to liberate people from unhappy marriages.

I did everything Jurgen asked me to do. I did not fail him. He failed me. The last method he used to get rid of his wife was to offer me a chance to elope with him for two weeks of holidays across Germany. It was his plan. I arrived in Bonn, stayed in a posh hotel overnight, and we fled Bonn at dawn. He left a letter to his wife stating that he was now living with me, he would never go back to her, and he was going to live with me no matter the consequences. He was not going to beg for a divorce anymore. He left home, and that was it.

Jurgen and I traveled across Germany. I saw cities I had not known before, such as Hamburg, Dusseldorf, Frankfurt, and Dresden. During all that time, he was worried and obsessed with the thought that "maybe she had committed suicide; maybe she is already dead." After two weeks, we returned to Geneva.

The following morning, he called me and said, "Guess what? She is here in my office. She dropped to her knees and begged for forgiveness. She pledged that she will change and be a good woman and a good wife to me. I cannot say no; it is my duty to come back to her." I was devastated and furious.

Then came a telephone call from Wolfgang, our mutual friend, who was the senior counsellor at the Permanent Mission of the Federal Republic of Germany. I had become friends with Wolfgang, who was my colleague, and I was also friends with his wife. They lived in a property on a quiet street between my apartment building and the Moillebeau building. I walked in front of their property every day of the week when going to my office.

Wolfgang told me that Jurgen had asked him to check on me because he feared that I was so distraught that maybe I would commit suicide. I was absolutely furious. Wolfgang told me, "He is a good man but too weak. He loves you but will not be able to marry you. I told you that many times. Now let us forget about him, and you must look for somebody else."

He confided that he and his wife had been lonely in Germany after the end of World War II and that they found each other through an ad in the newspaper. They married and had a home, kids, and good careers. It would not be so bad to search for somebody in ads. It would be a solution to my problem. He suggested that I should do the same look at ads or to register at an agency to find a companion. Wolfgang's conversations succeeded in distracting me, but I did not follow his advice.

What happened next was that Jurgen and I were very unhappy being apart from each other. We had been together for years, having lunches together at the UN cafeterias and driving along Lake Geneva or to the French villages at the Swiss French frontiers. We missed each other. I lacked the personal dignity to go back to him. He knew that he should be ashamed of his lack of courage to conclude successfully his love affair. He was ashamed of himself. However, we were somehow tied to each other by memories, nostalgia, love, and destiny. We were like two lost souls. We resumed our telephone calls and began seeing each other again.

I was bitter, and he was ashamed of himself. He had cut my loving heart into thousands of pieces. All that for a lack of heroism regarding getting what he wanted the most in the world. He kept repeating, "I am the most miserable man of the world."

After my departure to Canada, he wrote to me that he went to the shore of Lake Geneva, threw a bouquet of roses into the water, and watched his dream slowly disappear far away.

In the years which followed our separation, I kept in my heart this quotation from F. Scott Fitzgerald: "Suddenly she realized that what she was regretting was not the lost past but the lost future, not what had not been but what would never be."

Jurgen was born the same year as Pope Benedict XVI. They were born in the same part of Eastern Germany. When they were adolescents, they were members of the Hitler youth. It was inevitable. No one could have escaped from what was called a mandatory duty to their country. When Hitler lost the war, this region of Eastern Germany was invaded and occupied by the Soviets. The Russians shot Jurgen's father, a teacher, and they imprisoned his mother, who died in jail from cancer. Jurgen was incarcerated in a Russian concentration camp with three hundred other German youths. One day, those boys planned an escape and ran to the nearby forest. Most of them were shot dead by the Russians. Only two of them survived—Jurgen and another. They made their way through the forest to the Austrian border and were admitted into a refugee camp.

I kept Jurgen's pictures and a pile of letters he wrote to me after my departure from Geneva, from 1975 to 1978, the year I married Julian Swann in Ottawa. He narrated his life and work stories, and he always added, "How is my little flower of the Mekong? I shall always love you, Alice, until the end of my life. There will be no one else. You are the love of my life."

Jurgen was recalled to Bonn in 1977 and resumed his work at the Ministry of Economic Affairs. His years of international conferences at the United Nations, in Geneva; in Brussels, with the European Economic Committee; and around the world had ended. He told me that it would be very boring and dull for him being stuck at his office desk and at home with his wife. When they spent time at home or at a restaurant, he pretended to read a book or a newspaper and did not engage in conversation with her.

He died from leukemia in September of 1995, at age sixty-three. So he died twenty years after I left him. His son Peter telephoned me from Bonn to invite me to attend his funeral. Peter had read his father's love story about me when searching through his papers after his death. He saw pictures of me with Sophie and afterward with Christopher.

He said, "I loved my mother. But I think that she should have let him go free. When a couple does not get along, it is better to divorce … My father used to sit and read newspapers, books, all day long. I told him to get out and get a woman. He answered, 'Once, in Geneva, I met the woman of my life. She was the love of my life, and I let her go. It is the regret of my life. There will never be another woman in my life.' And now I understand that I never really knew my father."

Published French Writer (1972)

I realized one of the dreams of my childhood. In 1972, I became a published author in French. *Le Poème du Vietnam* was published by the Editions Perret-Gentil, Geneva.

I had sent my manuscript to six publishers, and Mr. Perret-Gentil called me for an appointment. His office was in the old Geneva district, along a famous sinuous, irregular paved street full of antique shops. His wife was present in his office. She was curious to see a young Vietnamese diplomat. She was much younger and she was a former theatre actress. I loved her large floral hat on her head. With his tall stature, his noble facial features, and his healthy, thick white hair, Mr. Perret-Gentil reminded me of my beloved godfather in Brussels.

Mr. Perret-Gentil was like a godfather or a godsend to young poets and writers. He published their first works to help them to get through the difficult gate to the world of published writers. He would give a chance to young authors. They were unknown at the beginning, but what if they were to become famous and had talent?

Mr. Perret-Gentil specialized in beautiful and elegant books written by historians, diplomats, and artists.

I received nice reviews in Swiss newspapers, as Mr. Perret-Gentil was well connected with journalists and authors. My ambassador said to me, "I hope that celebrity will not get to your head." A member of our embassy in Bern called me and asked, "How much did you pay the journalist from *Le Journal de Geneve* to write such a nice article about you?" This was very typical from envious Vietnamese. They suspected others must have bribed people to write nice things about them!

Robert Cornevin, president of the Association of French-Language Published Writers of France and Overseas, and member of the French

Academy, wrote to me to offer his sponsorship to become a member of his association (ADELF). He suggested that I enter *Le Poème du Vietnam* in the competition for the 1973 Literary Prize of Asia from ADELF. Every year, ADELF opened competitions for its members in different categories of books such as, for instance, the "Literary Prize of Africa". Many authors from former French colonies in Africa wrote very well in French and became well-known authors and poets. My book was a runner-up. A French woman author won the first prize with a thick book about the history of Vietnam.

Robert Cornevin became a great friend. He was devoted to promoting the French language, and he loved the French writers born in the former French colonies (Indochina and Africa). I became friends with Vo Long Te, a famous Catholic poet of Vietnam. He was also a renowned historian. Robert Cornevin, always devoted to the French culture, wrote an article in *La Gazette de Montreal* in which he praised Vo Long Te and Alice Nguyen as being among the great Catholic poets of Vietnam. In my case, I did not deserve such praise. However, Vo Long Te was truly our national treasure in matters of literature and history.

From 1972 until his sudden death two decades later from surgery in Paris, we continued a great friendship and exchanged letters. In 1979, I had the opportunity to meet him in person in Ottawa. I was then married to Julian, and we invited him for dinner in our apartment. He said that his daughter had married an English man and that he hoped I and his daughter would become great friends.

The 1973 Paris Peace
Agreement on Vietnam

The United States had initiated negotiations for peace already some years before 1973. In 1972, Henry Kissinger commented, "Peace is at hand."

The priorities for the United States were the withdrawal of their troops from Vietnam and the release of US prisoners of war (POWs).

The main people who negotiated the 1973 Paris Peace Accord were: Henry Cabot Lodge, former US ambassador to the Republic of Vietnam; Henri Kissinger; William P. Rogers; Tran Van Lam, minister of foreign affairs of the Republic of Vietnam; Mrs. Nguyen Thi Binh, minister of foreign affairs for the Vietcong or FNL (National liberation Front) or PRG (Provisional Revolutionary Government); Nguyen Duy Trinh, minister of foreign affairs of the Democratic Republic of Vietnam (or North Vietnam).

Tran Van Lam signed the accord on behalf of the Republic of Vietnam. Soon after, President Nguyen Van Thieu replaced him by Vuong Van Bac, who would take over as minister of foreign affairs. Tran Van Lam moved on to become a senator at the legislative assembly. In 1975, he was president of the Senate.

In order to pressure President Nguyen Van Thieu to sign this agreement, President Richard Nixon wrote and signed a letter of commitment to help South Vietnam should it be attacked by North Vietnam after the peace negotiations. This letter existed and was shown in public, and Henry Kissinger confirmed it. Kissinger was the man who led the Paris negotiations and later received the Nobel Peace Prize for it alongside Le Duc Tho, the representative of North Vietnam.

President Nixon had been successful in securing a peace treaty that permitted the withdrawal of US forces from Vietnam with honor and the return of US prisoners of war back home to their families. Kissinger accepted his Nobel Peace Prize, but Le Duc Tho refused it, saying that his task was not yet finished, as Vietnam was not yet reunified as one indivisible Vietnam, and thus there was not yet peace. For the world and for America, it was peace. For Hanoi, it was still war. The North Vietnamese were afraid of Nixon and his threats of retaliation should they violate the Paris accords. Hanoi was just waiting for the right time and opportunity to attack South Vietnam.

Tran Van Lam was minister for foreign affairs of the Republic of Vietnam from 1969 to 1973. He came to Geneva in 1972 and in 1973 to have meetings with some of our ambassadors posted in Europe and convened to Geneva for consultations and decisions. We also organized on his behalf big receptions and dinner parties, inviting ambassadors of allied or neutral countries accredited to the United Nations, Geneva, and the heads of UN international organizations. It was multilateral diplomacy. Our country found itself in a crucial period of the war, and we lobbied desperately for support.

In April 1973, President Richard Nixon welcomed President Nguyen Van Thieu to the United States and promised US assistance to South Vietnam in case it would be attacked by North Vietnam.

After the Watergate scandal broke out, President Nixon was depressed and perturbed by his own problems in the White House. Kissinger recalled him no longer being focused on the issues surrounding Vietnam, and President Nixon did not order retaliations against North Vietnam when North Vietnam tested his resolve by launching minor attacks against the South.

On June 24, 1973, Ambassador Graham Martin was appointed the new US ambassador to South Vietnam.

In August of 1974, President Richard Nixon announced his resignation, and Vice President Gerald Ford was sworn in as the new president of the United States.

On October 5, 1974, in an officially recorded conversation between President Gerald R. Ford and Vuong Van Bac, the new minister of foreign affairs of the Republic of Vietnam, in the presence of Henry Kissinger in the White House Oval Office, President Ford said, "I want to reassure you we will support President Thieu in every way—economically, politically, and diplomatically. Our problem is not us, but on the Hill."

Vuong Van Bac replied, "We are very grateful for your efforts, and we hope they can be kept at adequate levels."

Friendships in Geneva

I had met Fr. Ray Rocher at UN meetings. He was born in Toulouse, France, and was a missionary from the Congregation of The White Fathers. He had been in Africa as a missionary priest.

The Holy See was not a member of the UN and had the status of observer. Therefore, when our delegation attended a meeting with the status of observer, I sat next to the Holy See delegation. The first time I saw Father Rocher, he looked very austere and silent, and he acknowledged me with only a nod of his head. He was reserved and distant because I was a woman. He was always aloof and lonely, and he smoked cigarettes. He was not the ambassador; he was a member of the Holy See delegation. At the same time, the Catholic Church gave him a position as the parish priest of the parish of Pregny-Chambesy, which was a posh neighborhood adjacent to the UN headquarters. The long avenue of Pregny-Chambesy ran from one end of the United Nations along a sinuous road, passing in front of the Catholic church, of the château de Rothschild, afterward of Foyer John Knox and of Miremont, the residence of Karim Aga Khan. Father Rocher lived in the parish house, which had a small garden full of vegetables and fruit.

One day I had to go to customs to retrieve a suitcase sent from Rome. I had put a bottle of fish sauce in it, and it had broken, so the clothing inside the luggage smelled bad and I had to throw it in the garbage bin. I was sure that I smelled like fish sauce, but I had no time to go home to change my outfit, so I rushed to my meeting and ran to my seat, almost jumping over Father Rocher. I said to him, "Excuse me, Father, I smell like a rotten fish." It was so funny that I succeeded in defrosting him and making him laugh. The ascetic monk had been awakened, and he became less icy. That was how our great friendship started. We kept each other company, talking at UN meetings. When our delegations had observer status, we sat next to each other.

I spent most weekends at the parish house of Pregny-Chambesy, enjoying it and the bounty of its garden. I liked to spend some minutes in the afternoon in Father Rocher's garden and pick pears, strawberries, lettuce, carrots, and radishes for our meals. Father Rocher and I cooked and ate together. We united our solitude. He was lonely in this house. I was lonely in my small apartment. He was not happy with the Catholic Church. He had frustrations and crises.

I was very frustrated to be in love with Jurgen, a married German man, far away. Father Rocher had to bear with my whining all the time about my unfortunate situation.

I took the bus in front of my apartment building and stopped in front of a butcher shop at the village of Pregny-Chambesy, where we would buy a slice of cheap meat or a piece of liver for our weekend meals. Father Rocher and I could not afford the luxury of having a big, tender steak. The bus trip from my place at Avenue de Vermont to Pregny-Chambesy was short. Weekends there were like vacations in the countryside for me.

One day I saw a nice, juicy steak in the kitchen. I asked, "How did it come about that we have this nice steak?" Father Rocher answered that he had been shopping at the butcher's and the countess was there too. So he said loudly to the butcher, "Please, a piece of liver as usual."

The countess heard the dialogue and asked the butcher, "Is it what the father eats?" The butcher nodded. The countess then said to the butcher, "From now on, always give a nice steak to the father every week. Put it on my account."

I laughed and said to Father Rocher, "You are genial!"

One afternoon, unexpected visitors showed up. Monseigneur Paul Bouvier, head of all Geneva parishes and executive director of Caritas Geneva, came for a visit, accompanied by Isabelle Soutter, his legal advisor at Caritas.

Isabelle had a career as a judge and was a widow without children. Her late husband was a renowned sculptor. She and Monseigneur Bouvier had been friends since their childhood. She told me that he had been very shy with girls when he was a teenager. He ate alone in a corner and avoided glancing at girls. Now, having reached a venerable age, he had become very outgoing and jovial. He loved being around people because he suffered from solitude. He had celebrated her wedding and, afterward, her husband's funeral. That Sunday, he had driven her to the cemetery to lay flowers on her husband's tombstone. They decided to stop to see how Father Rocher was doing, as he was a newcomer in Geneva and had recently been appointed as the parish priest of Pregny-Chambesy.

The four of us had tea, and it was during that afternoon that a great affection developed spontaneously between Isabelle and me. Our relationship was like a love bond between mother and daughter. Isabelle was a distinguished, understanding, and always smiling lady. I needed a mother, and she needed a daughter. Our great friendship would last from that day of 1969 until 1983, the year Isabelle died.

Isabelle was born in an upper-class Catholic Swiss family. She was educated in England, where she graduated in law.

Isabelle suggested to Monseigneur Bouvier that he be my great friend too. So now we were three good friends, like a united family. I was their cherished little Alice. They had a good relationship with Father Rocher, but he was not included in our group. Monseigneur Bouvier drove Isabelle or me when we needed a ride somewhere. He was willingly our chauffeur. On Sundays, if Monseigneur Bouvier were to go to Annecy, France, only two hours by car from Geneva, to visit his aunt Celestine, he would take me with him and we would have lunch at Aunt Celestine's house. Annecy was his birthplace.

Isabelle offered her legal services to Caritas Geneva for free of charge. She told me, "Once in our lifetime, we should work free of charge for God." She was a devoted, intellectual, and very discrete Roman Catholic, conditioned by her former career as a judge. Anything I told her was sealed in secrecy. Once I told her during one of our weekly lunches that Father Rocher was so unhappy with the church that he had said to me, "Let us go to New Zealand. We could operate a sheep ranch there." Needless to say, I was not enthusiastic to encourage him to follow up with this idea. Isabelle was so amused that she had a good laugh. I assumed that she would mention it to Monseigneur Bouvier, as they were very close friends. Knowing how Monseigneur Bouvier was, I thought he too would laugh at something so amusing to hear. He was a good-humored priest who would not be scandalized but only amused.

Ten years down the road, I mentioned that story to Monseigneur Bouvier, assuming that he had already heard it from Isabelle. But no, he had not. He was naturally very amused and turned to Isabelle. "Did you know that Father Rocher wished to elope with Alice to New Zealand?" She answered.

"Yes, she told me."

I said to her. "I presumed that you would tell him, as you were very close to him."

She answered. "I was a judge. I was sworn to secrecy, so it became my second nature."

One day while I was seated at a UN conference, my neighbor, representing the Holy See, was absolutely gorgeous. He was a young priest. I said to Isabelle as a joke, "Wow …he is so handsome." The following day, the seat was vacant. I asked, "Where is he?" I was told that he had left the church to get married.

Through Father Rocher, I got acquainted with Fr. Armand Garon, a professor of theology in Ottawa, Canada. In December of 1974, Father Garon arrived in Geneva to visit Father Rocher. I cooked dinner for the three of us at Father Rocher's house. As I intended to immigrate to Canada, Father Rocher thought that Father Garon, as a Canadian, would be a useful person for me to meet. Father Garon was charming and joyful. That reinforced my vision of Canada as a land of young, handsome, and joyful men. I was determined to pursue the Canadian dream.

In January of 1975, I asked Fr. Armand Garon if he would be my sponsor, which was requisite for my Canadian immigration papers, and he did not hesitate one second before saying yes. He did not need to check my credentials. I was a dear friend of Father Rocher and of the Holy See Delegation. They were my credentials. Once again in my life, it would be a priest who was there for me when I needed help.

In January of 1975, Monseigneur Pierre Mamie, Bishop of Geneva, Lausanne, and Fribourg, came to the Church St. Nicholas de Flu to celebrate an ecumenical event. Monseigneur Paul Bouvier introduced me to him, and Monseigneur Mamie invited me for dinner at his Fribourg Episcopal palace. However, I had, to my great regret, to decline this honor, because somebody from the Canadian embassy in Bern called me to come and process my papers on the same day as the invitation date issued by

Monseigneur Mamie. I gave priority to my immigration papers, went to Bern, and cancelled the dinner with the prelate in Fribourg. He sent me a big photo of him as a bishop with his signature and his blessing.

Pierre Simonet was the assistant executive director of the International Monetary Fund, Geneva office. He was French. He was a nice man, and his wife, Luce, was a beautiful French woman with blonde hair and blue eyes. We became great friends. They introduced me to their friends Rene and Marcelly Zahles, who had been born in Luxembourg. Rene Zahles was then director of the budget of the United Nations in Geneva. I had been invited to all the residences he and his spouse Marcelly had lived in in Geneva from 1969 to 1975. In 1975, they introduced me to their daughter Marie Helene, who was eight years younger than me and lived in Ottawa. My friendship with Rene and Marcelly Zahles extended beyond my Geneva's years.

One day I saw Paul Tran Van Thinh, a Vietnamese-born Frenchman, during a UN conference. He was the chief of delegation of the European Commission (EC) – headquarters in Brussels - and also its treasurer. Having come to Geneva from Brussels, he was in charge of everything for members of his delegation. He looked after the EC policy, speeches, and negotiations, and he also organized the business travels and meals for members of his large delegation. I found him handsome and very nice, and he was also best friends with my ambassador, Le Van Loi. We became best friends too. He was as proud of me as being the delegate of Vietnam as I was proud of him for his brilliant work as the representative of the EC. As we were both Vietnamese born, of course, we were proud of our Vietnamese heritage.

I became like a member of the EC. I was inseparable from members of that delegation. In the evenings, I had dinner with them in restaurants. Tran Van Thinh often chose a Vietnamese restaurant near the station, called Vietnam, and the owner made sure that the meals were delicious. At that time, it was the only Vietnamese restaurant in Geneva. Paul Thinh and I called each other cousins.

Our Vietnamese permanent delegation had only three members going to international meetings. Each morning during the week, we met at our office and decided where each of us would go and which of us would be in charge of special conferences assigned to us. Therefore, I was everywhere and the three of us (Ambassador Loi, our colleague Pham Van Trinh, and I) interacted and visited each other's conferences to catch what was happening there, and we brought our presence and support to the other colleagues.

The genius of Paul Tran Van Thinh was that he conquered the hearts and minds of his European colleagues who respected his superior intelligence as well as the affection of their support staff and their chauffeurs. When he gave lavish receptions on behalf of the EC, he invited the drivers waiting outside to come in and enjoy the reception. His democratic manners earned him the devotion of people.

Paul Tran Van Thinh from 1960 to 1994 was a representative of the European Commission. He was Ambassador, head of the permanent delegation of the EC in Geneva in 1976. He was a negotiator for European GATT Agreements. In 1994, GATT was replaced by World Trade Organization (WTO). His celebrity as a successful economist earned him the trust of the socialist Vietnamese regime who asked him to be a special economic advisor to Vietnam. He was very much involved in this role. In 1994, he retired from his career of Ambassador and lived in a farm in France but stayed always involved in international economic issues.

Having lived in Belgium as a student and having connections with Belgian personalities, I was honored by the Belgian colleagues in Geneva. They were nice and we were like family. We often crossed the Swiss-French border at Ferney-Voltaire and had lunches in France. Small French restaurants in the villages bordering Switzerland were renowned for their food. Baron Jean Poswick was the chief of the Belgian delegation coming regularly from Brussels to attend the United Nations conferences. Later, in 1976, he would become ambassador, head of the Permanent Mission of Belgium to the United Nations. I also remember Mr. Roger Raucy, a delightful Belgian colleague.

Having resided in Italy, I considered myself Italian too and was friends with the Italian delegates.

Because I was born as a French citizen in a former French colony, I considered the French like my own people. We had the same culture. We understood the same jokes. Yves Moss was the second man of the French permanent delegation. He was divorced, so he flirted with some girls with diplomatic status. Once he asked me if I was interested in spending some vacations with him on some tropical islands. I jokingly said, "Why do not you invite a gorgeous blonde to go with you?"

He answered, "Why do you assume that I would be interested in going with a gorgeous blonde?"

We were good friends. However I did not fall in love with him because he was not my type. He was not tall, had black hair and he loved to dress with Pierre Cardin suits. I was a very naïve girl and he enjoyed my ingenuity. He was around fifty years old and we had interesting conversations about everything on earth.

German diplomats and delegates knew of my love story with one of them, and they were flattered. I belonged with the German group too.

I was friends with the Holy See ambassador and with Father Rocher, a member of that delegation. We sat next to each other when I had the status of observer in certain conferences like the GATT, a very boring conference on tariffs and trade.

When I had lunch with some young, handsome Polish delegates I met at UN international meetings, we never talked about politics. They told me about their experiences living as diplomats in Hanoi and how much they liked the Vietnamese girls over there. They said the Vietnamese girls had feelings and they looked after their men well.

Once I asked a Yugoslavian delegate, "Tell me, how it is living under a socialist regime?"

He answered, "It gave me a chance that I would not have otherwise. My father was a factory worker. The socialist regime gave me a good education, and I became a diplomat."

The only Communist delegates with whom I did not have coffee and an exchange of smiles were the Chinese delegates. They were in gray uniforms, stiff, and all buttoned up, and their faces were like impenetrable walls. They gave no smiles. They sat as a group, isolated from the rest of the world.

My ambassador once congratulated me, saying, "We are proud of you. You do your job well. You are beautiful and charismatic."

I returned the compliment: "I did nothing. You are the only one who did an outstanding job. You are handsome and brilliant."

He commented, "Each of us has his or her own job to perform. I am the one who delivered the speeches and conducted negotiations. You did your job as expected from you."

Ambassador Le Van Loi was a brilliant strategist. He was mostly active in the Asian group, in the developing countries group and at the United Nations Conference on Trade and Development (UNCTAD). He was among the top leaders and strongly raised the profile of Vietnam. That was his goal. He felt Vietnam should participate in international debates and take a leading role.

In Geneva, from the beginning of December 1974 to the end of February 1975, despite our victory at the International Conference on Humanitarian Law in 1974, I felt that after the 1973 Paris Peace Agreement, the attitude of the representatives of the countries with whom we interacted at the United Nations had changed. The nations that belonged to the group of nonaligned countries, which included countries from South America, Africa, and Asia, started to distance themselves from us. We had been considered the losers in the Vietnam War, and they began to shift their support to the North Vietnamese Communists.

I was very unhappy with my love story with Jurgen, which did not end well, and I was very frustrated with the instability of my career and my low salary. My ambassador kept repeating to me and to Susan, our American-born secretary, "Our soldiers died for us in the rice fields of Vietnam. What are you complaining about? You should be ashamed to stand in front of me asking for an increase of your salaries. War requires sacrifice and patriotism."

I had met Rhylda Knight for the first time at one of Helga Bimon's parties. Helga was a young Austrian diplomat who was my age. I continued to meet Rhylda at the United Nations because she was executive assistant to Gilbert Jaegher, a Belgian man in charge of the Southeast Asia Office of the United Nations High Commissioner for Refugees (UNHCR). Rhylda, who was older than me, and I often had coffee together at the UN cafeteria, and we invited each other for meals during weekends. She was the perfect picture of a British professional administrator. She was single and lived in an elegant apartment. When I confided to her that I was going to immigrate to Canada, she said, "Go ahead, Alice. You should go. All the British girls I knew got married as soon as they landed in Canada and Australia." She knew that I wished to get married but that it was difficult to find available men to marry in Geneva. In her office, none was free. The city was swarmed by young girls, working as support staff in innumerable UN offices. The competition was fierce, and when delegates arrived in Geneva, they were usually already married men. Of course, some had affairs, and some girls were lucky enough to be able to hook a married man, get him to secure a divorce, and marry him. Usually married men who had affairs would, at the ends of their meetings, return to their countries, wives, and stability at home.

In 1976, Rhylda retired in England after decades spent at the United Nations as an administrator. She had started as a young girl at the bottom and moved up to be the first top female administrator of the United Nations.

Delia Domingo, who was the same age as me and came from the Philippines Permanent Mission, later became ambassador of the Philippines to Switzerland, and ambassador to Germany, and she ended her career beautifully as minister of foreign affairs. She was small, thin, sweet, smart and ambitious, getting along well with everybody. She had no enemies. She rented an elegant little apartment in downtown Geneva, and I went there any time I felt lonely. She invited me to join in when she had parties and took me to the Swiss mountains, where she had friends and where she had the use of their chalet. Delia was a good friend, and we had interesting conversations. We often went to Balaxert for lunches at the MiGros. MiGros was a food superstore that offered a salad buffet with fresh salads, boiled eggs, and ham. We paid only one Swiss franc each to fill a full plate.

Because we were the same age, we discussed many topics. I remember us exchanging our views about friendship. I said that friendship should be an exchange of services—helping each other and reciprocity. Delia felt that friendship should be a responsibility.

Knowing that I was thinking of immigrating to Canada, Delia invited me to join in a dinner with two Canadian delegates from Ottawa. One was a deputy minister of urban affairs, Andre Saumier. He was very handsome, like John Kennedy, except that his hair was dark brown. He was a French Canadian and had been educated by the Jesuits. He was so smart that later on, in Canada, he resigned from his governmental position in Ottawa and moved back to Quebec to become a financial expert, and when the position of governor of the Bank of Canada was open, he was one of the candidates for this position. He did not get it, and I did not thereafter read about him anymore in the news.

I juggled the countries I could immigrate to in my head and imagination: Australia, New Zealand, the United States, and Canada. Canada emerged in my mind as the only country in this world I wanted to go to and discover. I wanted to become a Canadian citizen, have roots, and die there.

I said to Isabelle, "Definitively, I shall go to Canada. Men there are so handsome. They are tall, sportive, and in good health, and they are already ministers at a young age. You don't see that in Europe."

Isabelle, as always, was a supportive mother. "I shall miss you. But you must go to Canada. You have more chances for your future in Canada than here. You must leave Jurgen as the story does not go anywhere. You are at a dead end with him"

Immigration to Canada (1975)

I talked with Canadian colleagues about my desire to immigrate to Canada. I did not want to stay in Europe, the Old Continent. I was restless and fearless, and I wanted to discover the New World. My confidant was a young diplomat, Jean Olivier Caron. He informed me that the Canadian delegation from the Immigration Department would arrive to attend the meetings of the Executive Committee of the United Nations High Commissioner for Refugees and that I should not miss the opportunity to contact them.

I attended those UNHCR executive meetings each year as an observer for the Republic of Vietnam. I sat between the delegates of Sudan and Ethiopia, looking like a fly sitting between two tall, skinny giraffes with a long neck.

I approached the Canadian delegation and was welcomed by Kirk Bell, director at the Immigration Department. He was young and very friendly. He did not seem surprised to see me walking toward him; he had probably been briefed by Jean Olivier.

I said, "Hello, I came to you because I want to immigrate to Canada."

He smiled and asked, "Why do you want to immigrate to Canada?"

I answered, "To be frank with you, firstly we are going to lose the war. I have a diplomatic passport, and I shall need to live somewhere. My second reason is that I have a great love story with a German delegate, but he is married, and I want to put a huge ocean between us and begin a new life in Canada." That was clear enough, and that explained my situation.

Kirk Bell looked at me and commented, "Brr ...brr ... It is very cold in Canada. You cannot go with this silky dress. You will need very warm clothes."

I answered, giggling like a schoolgirl, "I have already bought a big fur coat to go to Canada." I had imagined that living in Canada, in such a freezing climate, people enveloped themselves in fur coats like bears.

He laughed and said, "The average Canadian women don't wear fur coats. If you have one, you must be rich." He added, "You will be a very nice addition to the Canadian population. However, I am not the right person for you to apply to. You must go to our Canadian immigration officer in Bern and apply to him there. I shall tell him that I have already seen you and talked with you."

I sent a letter to the Canadian embassy in Bern. I immediately received a call from somebody from the embassy, giving me an appointment in Bern. I took the train to Bern, saw the immigration officer, and completed the immigration papers.

I needed to provide the name of my sponsor in Ottawa, my chosen destination. I asked Fr. Armand Garon, a Canadian priest I had met some weeks prior at the home of Fr. Raymond Rocher. Fr. Armand Garon agreed to be my sponsor. A final formality was to go to a Swiss doctor for a medical exam. After that, all of my papers were approved for immigration.

I did not hide the fact that I was going to immigrate to Canada. Some of my friends in Geneva gave parties to send me off with their heartfelt wishes for my future. Baron Otto Von Stempel, the acting ambassador of the Federal Republic of Germany, and his spouse, gave a farewell dinner party in my honor. They had been always nice to me. Their parties were elegant, with champagne, strawberries, and vodka. The baroness was a former Russian aristocrat. She was wealthy and looked sweet, frail, and humble. Any time they invited me for a reception or a dinner party, I always asked to be the flower girl. That meant that I bought roses and decorated their dining room and table. Flowers were my gift.

The flight for Canada was scheduled for the morning of February 28, 1975, and I would be at Geneva Airport very early.

Sarah, Sophie's adoptive mother, drove me to the airport. We had a coffee while waiting for the plane to take off. Sophie was seven years old. This was an important moment because I immigrated to Canada, leaving my daughter to the care of Sarah. Although the adoption papers had been signed, Sarah said that nothing had changed and that I would always be like her younger sister and that she would raise my baby on my behalf. I hoped to take Sophie back with me in the future, but when? I flew toward an unknown continent and toward a mysterious future.

During my last weeks in Geneva, I went to see two movies: *Karamouska* and *The New World*. In the huge Boeing flying toward Canada, my new country, I was ecstatic. I was an immigrant. This word, "immigrant," sounded romantic, exhilarating, and marvelous.

I was welcomed at the Ottawa airport by Myriam De Bie Waller, with her two little daughters, Virginia and Kate. Her husband, Irvin Waller, was at work, so I saw him only in the evening.

It was only at the last minute and by chance that I got Myriam's address, without expecting it. She invited me to stay with her and her family during my first weeks in Ottawa. Myriam was one of my roommates at the Sedes Sapientiae at Louvain in 1961. Her father was my professor of sociology. In 1963, she married Irvin Waller, a graduate in law from Cambridge University and the son of a British lord. The young couple immigrated to Canada soon after the wedding.

My godfather and Pierre de Bie, her father, were both university professors, colleagues and close friends. When I was a student at Louvain, Pierre de Bie and his eldest daughter, Myriam, invited me to their home for holidays and attended my baptism.

In 1975, when the situation appeared disastrous for South Vietnam, Pierre de Bie asked my godfather about my whereabouts. My godfather sighed and said, "You know how much of a fantasist Alice is. She decided to immigrate to Canada. She is packing for the departure. I have no power to do anything, as she never listens to my advice. But I am worried, as Canada is too far away and is a risky adventure for her."

Pierre de Bie answered, "Don't worry. My daughter Myriam and her family live in Aylmer, near Ottawa. Alice can stay with them."

On the eve of my departure, I received in Geneva a letter in which my godfather gave me the address and telephone number of Myriam, who invited me to stay at her home and said she would come to pick me up at the Ottawa airport.

Fr. Armand Garon, as my sponsor, had already rented a room for me. I cancelled that and stayed with Myriam, Irvin, and the two little girls. They lived in Aylmer, in a nice, large home in a woods, with a spacious lawn and a lakeshore. At the back of the house, there were trees and trails for cross-country skiing in winter.

Irvin was then director of research at the Department of the Solicitor General of Canada. He invited some of his colleagues to come and get acquainted with me. In winter, there was a cross-country skiing party, and in the summer, he roasted a lamb on the lawn and had forty guests, mostly from his office. Professor Pierre De Bie came from Louvain to visit his daughter and me during the 1975 Christmas holidays.

After two weeks at the Wallers' home, I decided that it was time to move out. It was March of 1975. Myriam drove me to Ottawa, and I found a one-bedroom apartment near the canal in a small building at 60 McLaren Street. I took the first job available as a clerk typist in an insurance company just to earn money to pay for my apartment, food, and clothing. I did not care about a career and did not want a career. I only wished to own a restaurant or a gift shop, to get married, and to have children and a gorgeous home. My dream was to have a family, a sweet home, and roots. The little girl who wanted to have wings to fly very far away from Vietnam now had become a woman who wanted to establish roots forever in Canada.

I had the status of a landed immigrant, so I was not yet a Canadian citizen. Normally, newcomers would not land a nice professional position, as they would not yet have Canadian citizenship or Canadian experience. My knowledge of the French language was excellent, but I was not fluent in English.

As soon as I had rented my apartment and begun to live independently, I started to call some colleagues and friends I knew in Geneva who had been transferred to Ottawa as diplomats.

My first call was to the Apostolic Nuncio in Ottawa and the dean of the diplomatic corps, Monsignor Angelo Palmas. Monsignor Alberto Luoni, ambassador of the Holy See to the United Nations in Geneva, introduced me to him. Monsignor Angelo Palmas and I became great friends from the day we met until my marriage in 1978. I let him down simply by negligence on my part. He welcomed me even after I told him that I would marry a man who was divorced and who was from the Anglican Church. He still remained a dear friend, but I was busy and I focused only on marriage. Julian, my future husband, did not like the papacy. His mother did not like popes. Julian was very nervous and feared the negative interference of the Catholic Church in our plans for marriage.

We missed having dinner with Monsignor Palmas when he invited us to his residence. I forgot the right address. The Apostolic nuncio had the most beautiful diplomatic residence of Rockcliffe—number 1 Manor Avenue. In my sheer ignorance of Ottawa's map, I directed Julian to drive to Manor Park, which was an average, standard neighborhood. Julian was nervous to have to meet Monsignor Palmas because he wanted at all cost to marry me and he feared a negative influence from the Catholic Church. He was as dumb as me to get to the right address. We got lost and missed that dinner. My great friendship with Monsignor Palmas deteriorated that day. I always felt guilty about it. I felt that I had betrayed my friendship with him and my Catholic faith.

Gian Luigi Lajolo was a former colleague in Geneva who was posted in Ottawa as a minister counsellor. He responded with enthusiasm to my telephone call. He invited me for lunch, and after that first reunion, he became one of my best friends in Ottawa. He introduced me to his Italian colleagues at the embassy—including his ambassador, who was also my colleague in Geneva—and to his other Canadian and international colleagues. Gian Luigi's purpose was to introduce me to his friends in Ottawa, hoping that they might be useful for me in my hunt for jobs and that they might help to give me a happy social life. He invited me and shared with me his glamourous diplomatic life.

In 1975 and the following years, I was privileged to be part of a nice circle of friends—the cream of Ottawa society.

Fr. Armand Garon was my immigration sponsor. He did not have to help me financially. I worked and earned my living. During my first two years in Ottawa, he took me out from time to time on trips around Ottawa. After five years, we lost touch, as he felt that I did not need him anymore. He had introduced me to Sister Marie from the Catholic Immigrant Services in Ottawa. Sister Marie, elderly and sick, died soon after I met her. She was considered as a saint. I met Sister Lucienne, who was a missionary. I liked her very much, and she reciprocated my feelings. She confided to me that out of all the refugee groups she had known, the Vietnamese were her favorites. She said they were gentle and smiling, and they appreciated everything done for them. Some refugees from other countries were difficult to approach. It was like a wall. They showed no feelings, emotions, or appreciation. When Sister Lucienne returned to her posting in Africa, her successor was Sister Denise.

I did not need the help of the Catholic sisters for myself, but my brother Francois had arrived in Ottawa, and I contacted them for him. My brother Francois came to Ottawa as a boat person; he was very sick and suffering from acute schizophrenia. Francois arrived in Ottawa when I was in my last weeks of pregnancy. He had been hospitalized at the Civic Hospital and later at the General Hospital for six months. He left as an outpatient, though he would have liked to stay forever. He was happy at the hospital, and he felt safe and pampered by doctors and nurses; but of course, he could not be a permanent patient there.

Sister Marie advised me not to take Francois to live with me and my young family because it was not necessary to add more stress in my life and to be burdened by unnecessary problems. My husband and baby must be my priorities. I was surprised that she was so practical and realistic in her advice.

So was Fr. Armand Garon. He was always cheerful and gave me advice like that a normal person would give. I perceived him like my own brother talking to me and not like a priest preaching to me about duties and charity.

When I told him how much I missed Geneva and my friends in Geneva, he said to me, "Then go and spend your vacation in Geneva, visiting your friends."

I answered, "It costs money. I just arrived in Ottawa, and it is ridiculous to return to Geneva so soon."

He responded, "Money is not important. There is no amount of money more important than peace in your mind. Go, and you will return to Ottawa with peace."

I went back to Geneva in 1976 for a visit. I wanted to see again my daughter Sophie, my friend Isabelle and the man I loved, Jurgen. I stayed at the apartment of Pierre Boimond, a Swiss teacher who had been a good friend since several years. Pierre was like a brother to me. It was like returning to a foreign land. It was no more emotionally my Geneva. When I went to the bank or to the Migros (the Swiss food superstore), I was ecstatic to show off to people that I was a Canadian. I traveled with a Canadian passport for landed immigrants. It was my great pride to tell to people, "Hi, I live in Canada." I saw everybody I wanted to see. They continued their life as it was before I left them. When we left a country, we must realize that things would change, people would change and nothing will be back as you had dreamed of. People continued their life without me.

Pierre Boimond invited me to go to a trip to Greece with him and with a chartered group of Swiss people. So I had the opportunity to visit Greece, Athens, the Greek Islands.

I confided to Pierre about how unhappy I was in Ottawa. He commented."My poor Alice, you wanted to go to Canada to escape your problems. You had carried your problems with you to Geneva."

Aunt Nine, a Buddhist, pressured me to take Francois to live with me inside my home because of family and Buddhist compassion. She said, "Give him a corner of your house. Look after him. He is your brother. Be charitable." She made me feel guilty for not being a loving sister or not being charitable. I did not feel it right that I must feel guilty for problems that were not my fault. In Canada, the health care system, the social network, and the social services were very good and generous for people with illnesses.

I found accommodation for Francois in a building on Chapel Street near the Rideau Center. The renters were mostly new migrants and refugees. That suited him, and he stayed there for fifteen years. He died there.

In 1975, I called the Swiss Embassy, looking for a former Swiss colleague I knew in Geneva. The secretary at the Swiss Embassy, Erika Sibold, informed me that my friend had left for a posting in Tokyo. As I wished to be well connected with the Swiss Embassy, I sounded as if I were terribly disappointed by the news and by not seeing him. Erika became curious and asked me, "Why do you want to see him?"

I answered, "I knew him in Geneva as a colleague. I just arrived in Ottawa as an immigrant and hoped to see him."

Erika became very excited. She said, "Tonight I am going to a German Festival with my boyfriend, Joseph. We invite you to come with us. We will come to pick you up this evening." Joseph was a former refugee from Czechoslovakia, having fled the Communist regime in his former country when it was invaded in 1968 by the Warsaw Pact troops led by the Soviets.

The German Festival took place at the Civic Center. It was a huge crowd with excellent food, beer, loud music, and dancing. The crowd was mostly made of German-speaking people: Germans, Austrians, Swiss, and German-born Canadians. They enjoyed the evening with smiling faces. They assured me that Canada was the best country of the world to live in. Most of them were immigrants from the Second World War. They found here freedom, safety, happiness, and prosperity. A Swiss-born young man invited me to dance. He said that he really liked to be with me, as I was so mature in comparison with the other girls, who he said were immature. I was not interested to be his girlfriend so I told him that I was much older than him. I knew that he was twenty-six years old. I did not disclose my age to him (thirty-four). I only emphasized that there was a great difference of age between us. He did not believe me and the difference in age did not discourage him. I was truly not interested in dating young men.

Erika mobilized the staff of the Swiss embassy to become my friends, from the Swiss ambassador to the Swiss family who lived in the basement of the embassy and were the housekeepers. Switzerland was a genuinely democratic country where all human beings enjoyed equal status. I was invited to receptions and dinner parties by everybody. Erika and I had fun partying with the young Swiss couple, the janitors of the embassy, in their basement apartment. We also had fun drinking champagne with the ambassador and higher-ranking staff. Erika was a nice girl, and I learned a lot from her. She was "expensive." She always dressed "expensively," and when she was invited to dinner by a man, she ordered the most expensive items on the menu. She told me. "If you don't order expensive things, they think that you are cheap." Later on, she worked as a representative of the Swiss watch industry in New York. She lived in an expensive hotel suite and had impeccable makeup and very expensive designer outfits. Faithful to her philosophy, she looked like a million-dollar girl.

In 1975, a new ambassador of Belgium was sent to Ottawa. Ambassador Charles Kerremans was a dear friend of my godfather, Andre Molitor. They had worked together at the service of King Beaudouin I. My godfather was his principal senior private secretary, and Charles Kerremans was his chamberlain. My godfather told Kerremans that his goddaughter Alice lived in Ottawa and recommended that he look after me. It was a request from a dear friend, but at the same time it was a request from a high-ranking dignitary who had sent him to Ottawa.

Charles Kerremans, who was around sixty years old and single, was one of the best diplomats of the world because no one ever knew his real feelings. He was a charmer with women. They felt as if he genuinely loved them. He was very seductive, and his receptions were very elegant, with good food and wine. He was a perfect ambassador and extremely well liked by everybody. I had been imposing upon him, but he was always affectionate. He called me "Mon petit chou, mon petit tresor, ma petite cherie" and treated me with the utmost affection, like that of an uncle toward a favorite niece. He understood that his duty was to be a replacement for my godfather during his posting in Ottawa.

I found it amusing that one day he commented to me about my relationship with my godfather. He did not quite understand why my godfather and I had such a strong bond with each other. As he knew that our affection had begun during my university years in Louvain, he said, "It looks like the story of Abelard and Heloise." Abelard was a university professor in the twelfth century, and Heloise was his student. They fell in love with each other, and because of their great difference of age, they were condemned by society. They married, but one day Abelard was attacked and castrated. Heloise became the abbess of a convent. They continued writing love letters to each other until their death. They were buried together in the cemetery of Pere Lachaise.

This story, of course, was absolutely not mine, but I liked it because it was romantic. I wrote letters to my godfather day after day for forty-three years, from wherever I lived, and he responded from Brussels. He had huge responsibilities in his dual career as university professor and as the principal private secretary to the king, but he faithfully responded to me. He considered me a daughter given by God as one of his responsibilities.

I was his student and was twenty years of age. He was my university professor and was thirty years older than I was. So people reached their own conclusions. My godfather would never tell people why he looked after me. It was none of their business. He would never disclose "our story" to anybody. He was like a priest. Everything I told him about my daily life was sealed in secrecy. His own wife knew nothing except that a letter arrived almost daily from me to her husband. She never knew the contents of my letters unless he mentioned to her and to their daughter Anne some events happening in my life. All Mr. Kerremans knew were the words "I have a goddaughter in Ottawa. Please look well after her. She is a member of my family."

Ambassador Kerremans invited me to the same dining table as important personalities of Ottawa. I was included also for dinner with three guests who were the ambassador's permanent guests. Hamilton Southam, a millionaire and protector of the arts, the founder of the Capital National Arts Centre, was known to be among the richest men of Ottawa. His first French wife, Jacqueline, had lived as a young girl before her wedding at the Château de Ferney-Voltaire, at the border of Geneva; it was owned by her parents and ancestors. When I was living in Geneva, this château was familiar to me. That was our first bond with each other. I had met Jacqueline later during my first year in Ottawa at a literary gathering in Rockcliffe where I was invited to talk about my life. Jacqueline was a member of this circle and she was in the audience, listening to me. She came to me, offering to drive me home. I remember Ottawa being battered by a violent winter storm that day, and I recall how kind Jacqueline had been, offering help to the other ladies whose cars were stuck in the snow. She shoveled the snow for them. I found Jacqueline unpretentious and sweet, and I liked her. She had a golden heart. Mr. Hamilton Southam had divorced her and married another French woman named Marion.

Another guest at Kerremans' dining table was Mrs. Maryon Pearson, the widow of Lester Pearson, who was the fourteenth prime minister of Canada, who was sworn in during 1963 and who won a Nobel Peace Prize in 1957. He died in 1972 at age seventy-five. The third guest was Mrs. Douglas Kirkwood, who was born in Poland and had become a Canadian ambassador's widow.

Mr. Southam greeted me with "Good afternoon, good evening," and that was it. He was indifferent to me and also to others. He came only because of his friendship with Ambassador Kerremans. He was too big a personality and too busy with his own life to pay attention to people not really connected with him. Mrs. Pearson nodded a greeting to me and I overheard her asking behind my back, "Who is *that*—this girl who is always invited?" She was curious and intrigued by my presence. I found her snobbish and did not like her.

Mrs. Kirkwood and I became good friends. As a widow, she lived alone. Mr. Kerremans probably invited her because he had come to know the couple somewhere during a past posting. No one at this ambassador's dining table was interested in Mrs. Kirkwood or with me, so we became great friends with one another. She loved to invite me to her place and cook traditional Polish dishes for me.

I was invited to most of the official and private receptions and dinner parties of the ambassador. Marie Elizabeth, who followed him in all his postings as his devoted social secretary, made sure that my name was on his invitations. She also reminded the ambassador what day my birthday was, and he would have to go and buy a Hermes scarf as a birthday gift for me. He explained my presence to other guests with only these words: "She is a member of an important Belgian family." In order to incite others to invite me, he would state emphatically, "Alice is an important personality." That helped to get me invited by important Canadian and Belgian families in Ottawa who otherwise would never have invited me. Those people socialized with me because Ambassador Kerremans suggested it.

Usually diplomats' postings lasted an average of three years. So during three full years—more if they had an extension—I had fully enjoyed a glamorous diplomatic life, without being a diplomat, thanks to Ambassador Charles Kerremans, Gian Luigi Lajolo and his Italian colleagues, the Swiss diplomats and friends of friends. My social life was brilliant, and mushroomed.

I spent my days earning my salary as a secretary, and I spent my evenings being invited and going to embassy receptions and dinner parties.

When I was a small child, my father told me that I was ugly because I was not to praise myself. It was a sin for me to believe that I was beautiful. That scarred me so much that I never realized that I could be beautiful. Many men told me that they loved the way I looked. The peak of my success as a young woman was in Geneva, where I was helped by beautiful clothes and an important position.

There were ordinary men who liked me, and I never paid attention to them. The young man who changed the locks of my apartment asked me if I would be interested in going to a movie with him. One day I took a taxi coming back home from a diplomatic reception. Half an hour later, I heard a noise behind my entrance door. I opened the door and found a bouquet of roses on the floor. I ran after the delivery man and discovered that they were from my taxi driver. He said only, "I found you adorable. Welcome to Canada"

Ambassador Kerremans invited me and his secretaries to go and see the 1976 Olympics in Montreal. We had lunch there at a restaurant, and I also met the Belgian participants at the Olympics at the Ambassador's reception. One Belgian athlete said that he was single and living with his mother in Belgium, and he asked me to go out with him. I felt very embarrassed because he was not my type of man and I found that he was not good enough for me, and it was very difficult to find an excuse to reject him. I realized that I was being snobbish and that I was victim of my destiny. In Vietnam, Father always said that no man was good enough to marry my sister Annie. Now I had as a godfather the most revered Belgian dignitary of Belgium, and I was embarrassed to date an ordinary Belgian. I knew that were I to marry somebody, it would need to be an extraordinary man, because I would have to be proud to introduce him to my godfather.

Among the tenants in my building, which was an average building, was a taxi driver. He once told me that I could always have a ride in his cab free of charge. He explained, "I am a former refugee from Yugoslavia. The least I can do is give free rides to other fellow refugees." I told him the sad story of my brother Francois, who was very sick, and he replied, "Tell him that I shall drive him anywhere he needs to go, free of charge."

I could tell you many stories of former refugees who drove taxicabs and who were wonderful people with big hearts. They were educated professionals in their birth countries, but after coming here as refugees and immigrants, they drove taxicabs for a living. However, they were happy with their new lives. That was the price they paid for living in freedom.

I was friends with the manager of the building, Rita. We often walked along the canal and talked about our future. I was thirty-five years old and Rita may be was forty. We always were worried about our old age! One day, Rita died suddenly from kidney failure. I did not know that she had died. I dropped into an office on the ground floor of the building and asked, "Have you seen Rita, the manager?" The men inside, with solemn faces, showed me a notice on the wall announcing that she had died. Poor Rita! We had talked so much about our future, when we would reach the venerable age of eighty, and she had dropped dead at only forty years of age.

One day, during the time I was working at the International Development Research Centre (IDRC) on Queen Street, I was window shopping on Sparks Street during lunchtime when I met Ambassador Alberto Da Silva Davidson, whom I knew as an ambassador of Chile in Geneva. In 1976, he had been posted in Ottawa. He recognized me too. We exchanged a smile. I did not have to say anything; he knew my circumstances. Ambassador Da Silva Davidson's attitude was a model of generous and loyal friendship. He and his wife invited me to their receptions at their gorgeous residence in Rockcliffe. While I was dating Julian, we were invited together during the National Day of Chile. We invited them for our wedding. They were unable to attend but they sent two girls from the embassy with a wedding gift. Julian and I did not have money for a lavish wedding, so we rented the party room of our building at Ambleside Drive for our wedding reception. The ambassador of Chile instructed his minister counsellor, Hernan Sanchez, and his wife, Theresa, to include Julian and me in their parties and be friends with us. So Hernan and Theresa Sanchez socialized with us, we invited each other and we went out often together.

Ambassador Abeba Abeba and I met again in 1986 in Ottawa, thanks to Marie Helene Zahles. Her son Philippe and Abeba's daughter attended the same school, and that was how they got acquainted with each other. Abeba was our foe in Geneva in 1973-1974 as leader of the nonaligned group of nations at the United Nations. He had been ambassador of Algeria in Hanoi and was a great admirer of Vietnamese history and poetry. He married a Vietnamese girl, a student in Geneva named Phi Anh, whose sister had married a Norwegian ambassador. I had known this Norwegian ambassador in Geneva. He was a blond, very nice young man. Lucky girl! That was always what I was saying to myself when I saw a Vietnamese girl marrying a foreign ambassador with blond hair, blue eyes, and a ravishing smile.

When we met for the first time at a reception in Ottawa, Abeba and I did not know what to do. Would we ignore each other with nasty looks, having been enemies in Geneva, or would we become friends? Spontaneously we smiled graciously to each other and became great friends.

Phi Anh, his wife, became a great friend to me too and looked up to me as her mentor. When she was a student in Geneva, she had come to the

UN sessions, sitting in the public galleries, and she had seen me. Therefore she took me as a role model, encouraged by Abeba. Abeba told her to take lessons from me. She had invited me once to an official lunch where she had invited several wives of accredited ambassadors in Ottawa. Both of us had lunches together at restaurants during my lunch breaks. I was working for the Social Sciences and Humanities Research Centre of Canada as a fellowships officer. We went shopping together, and she had a credit card and bought expensive clothing items at Holt and Renfrew. I did not have a credit card with unlimited funds given to me by a husband, and I had never browsed at high-end luxury stores. What a nice life she had!

I, Julian, and our little son Christopher were invited to their official and family birthday parties. Abeba was an exquisite host. I was a former enemy from Geneva, but here he treated me, the vanquished enemy, with utmost consideration, as if I were an ambassador. That is the essence of great men and women. They do not curtsey only to powerful people. They honor the fallen with the same respect. That was the reason why I liked Abeba and Phi Anh so much.

Unfortunately, all that changed. One day I called the residence of the ambassador, and a man answered and informed me that they had a new ambassador and that Abeba had died. Ambassador Abeba had died suddenly in Algiers—from leukemia, the man said—and I never saw Abeba or Phi Anh again. I knew from what she had told me that her parents, who were very educated and from the upper class, lived in the United States and she had a sister married to this Norwegian ambassador and another sister married in Brussels. I presumed that she might move to live near her relatives.

Dr. Williams Jeanes was the second man of the Canadian Delegation to the World Health Organization (WHO, or in French, OMS). He was much older than me and was a colleague at WHO meetings. He specialized in tropical diseases—especially in tuberculosis. I had the privilege to have met him at the WHO general assemblies in Geneva. Our friendship died only when he died in June 2015 in Ottawa at the age of ninety-five years old. I had talked with him six months before his death and had visited him at his Rockcliffe nursing residence.

His wife had died falling down the staircase of their gorgeous residence, and he could not manage to live alone there, as he was ninety years old.

He had to sell his gorgeous mansion at Rothwell Heights and move to a retirement residence called the Rockcliffe, which was the best in Ottawa at that time. I saw him again, and despite his great age of ninety-three years, he was healthy, and he had money to pay for being a resident in that expensive home. He was surrounded by loving family members. He was well organized in life and in death. Everything was in order, and he was waiting to die. Born in Wales, he had lived a long and fruitful life as a doctor and a humanitarian.

Dr. William Jeanes was a witness of my past career in Geneva, and he kept telling everyone standing near him in Ottawa about it until his last breath. He said, "One day, a young Vietnamese girl appeared in our meetings. We were a bunch of elderly gentlemen, so she warmed us like a spring blossom. That young girl is now the lady who wrote letters published in the *Ottawa Citizen*." He read every day the *Ottawa Citizen*, so he read my letters any time they published me. He would then pick up his phone and congratulate me.

One story he loved to repeat and repeat again to his friends was that of an episode when we had a vote at a general assembly of the WHO. Usually the head of a delegation walked up to the podium and voted on behalf of his country. My minister of health, Dr. Tung, did not want to do it and left that honor to my ambassador. Mr. Loi did not want to do it, so they chose me. I walked up to the podium gracefully, floating in my silky national dress. Dr. Jeanes would say, "The conference room suddenly became silent. Hundreds of delegates stopped to talk and looked at this young and beautiful Vietnamese girl walking up to the podium …" I also remember that moment because Dr. Jeanes was standing there, as I was on my way back to my seat, with a large smile on his face. That was the beginning of our great friendship.

In 1977, I again met Dr. Jeanes in Ottawa. It was by pure coincidence. I was working as assistant coordinator at the hospitality department of the International Development Research Centre (IDRC) in Ottawa, and one day I was standing at the door of our conference boardroom, waiting for the members to get out and take a coffee break. I was the coffee girl, waiting with my trolley to serve hot coffee. People at IDRC knew me only as a Vietnamese refugee girl. That day, I noticed a delegate who kept looking at me with a large smile on his face. Dr. Jeanes had recognized me.

He was very excited. He told to people that this Vietnamese girl working as a coffee girl was the delegate of Vietnam at the United Nations in Geneva before the fall of Saigon. He even had the proof. He showed a blue book of the Geneva United Nations listing all the permanent delegations accredited there in past years, with the names of the diplomatic staff and their titles.

Dr. Jeanes and his spouse, who was a very nice person and who had accompanied him on his trips to Vietnam as a doctor training Vietnamese doctors regarding tuberculosis and contagious diseases, and who loved Vietnamese people as much as he did, invited me for dinner at their home. I was dating Julian Swann, so I took Julian with me. I remember that nice evening; he had invited some Vietnamese-born women he was friends with, such as two young women, one named Thao, who had married a Canadian diplomat who later became an ambassador to Thailand, and another one who had married a young Dutch ambassador and whose mother had married a Canadian gentleman, Dr. Jeanes's colleague at the Canadian International Development Agency (CIDA). I felt very proud of those Vietnamese women and their successful lives. They were so well educated, charming and with gracious manners.

The Fall of Saigon (April 30, 1975)

When the North Vietnamese troops at the beginning of March started openly to invade South Vietnam, streaming down from north to south along the Ho Chi Minh trail, the US Congress maintained its decision not to rescue South Vietnam, despite numerous desperate pleas from President Gerald Ford, Henry Kissinger, and the US ambassador Graham Martin, who was posted in Saigon. Those three men repeatedly begged the US Congress to save South Vietnam and to honor former president Richard Nixon's commitment to the president of Vietnam, Nguyen Van Thieu. Nixon had formally promised that the United States would intervene should North Vietnam violate the Paris Agreement.

John Gunther Dean, a US ambassador to Cambodia, wanted an evacuation from Cambodia, and Graham Martin, a US ambassador to South Vietnam, believed until the last minute that Saigon would be rescued by the United States. Henry Kissinger commented about them, "We have two nutty ambassadors. Dean wants to bug out. Martin wants a new version of the Easter Rebellion. He is supporting Thieu too strongly."

President Nguyen Van Thieu feared a coup against him and kept many troops in Saigon to ensure Saigon's security and his own safety instead of sending them to defend the provinces north of Saigon. He wanted to regroup the troops, abandon the provinces already captured by the Communists, and form a new line of resistance farther down in the South.

General Nguyen Cao Ky hated Thieu and aimed to overthrow him and take the leadership. The Americans restrained him, telling him that it was too late and that this was not the moment for such an action.

As the military situation worsened and became desperate, President Nguyen Van Thieu was forced to resign on April 21. He denounced the United States as having betrayed their alliance with South Vietnam and said bitterly, "The US has not respected its promise. It is inhumane. It is untrustworthy. It is irresponsible ... The United States did not keep its promise to help us fight for freedom ... You ran away and left us to do the job that you could not do."

He was whisked to Taiwan, his first country of exile, with the help of the CIA chief in Saigon, Tom Polgar. Their car fled to Tan Son Nhut airport in secrecy because they feared an ambush from General Nguyen Cao Ky, who would not hesitate to kill Thieu.

The vice president Tran Van Huong, seventy-two years old and half blind, assumed the presidency. Tran Van Lam, president of the Senate, persuaded President Tran Van Huong to voluntarily relinquish his position in favor of General Duong Van Minh.

As the world waited to see what the United States would do concerning the situation in South Vietnam, President Gerald Ford, in a speech at the University of Tulane, declared, "Today America can regain a sense of pride that existed before Vietnam. But it cannot be achieved by refighting a war that is finished as far as America is concerned ... These events in Indochina, tragic as they are, portend neither the end of the world nor of America's leadership in the world."

The North Vietnamese Communists said that they would negotiate only if the National Assembly elected General Duong Van Minh as president. This was done on April 28.

During the presidency of General Nguyen Van Thieu, General Duong Van Minh had been the leader of the opposition party, or third party, which advocated neutralism, negotiations, and reunification with North Vietnam. Minh was viewed as the best man to negotiate with the Communists, and his mandate was to avoid bloodshed by surrendering South Vietnam.

President Duong Van Minh nominated his new cabinet ministers. He asked our brother Henri to be his minister of economic affairs. Henri, who had always refused this position under President Nguyen Van Thieu because he preferred to remain a private banker and not be involved in politics, accepted to help out our brother Big Minh. Henri wanted to serve his country during those tragic days.

On April 28, 1975, General Duong Van Minh became the last

president of the Republic of Vietnam; and our brother Nguyen Vo Dieu, its last minister of economics affairs.

The Americans had offered to evacuate Henri, his wife, and his children to safety, but Henri had refused the offer, saying that he preferred to stay in Saigon and be useful to his country if he could.

President Minh broadcast to officers and soldiers an order to stop fighting and lay down weapons. On April 30, the Communist Company 4 of PAVN Huong Giang Tank Brigade 203 smashed through the steel gate of the Presidential Palace at 11:00 a.m. Some men climbed to the roof and raised the National Liberation Front flag. President Duong Van Minh and Prime Minister Vu Van Mau waited for them inside the palace and surrendered South Vietnam to them. Minh told the first North Vietnamese officer who entered the palace that he was ready to hand over power to them. The North Vietnamese officer responded arrogantly, "You cannot hand over what you do not have."

Chaos and Panic—People
Fled South Vietnam

Uncle Ten, Father's youngest brother, who had fought alongside the North Vietnamese Communist troops during the past thirty years, succeeded to be chosen among the first group of officers arriving by tanks and military trucks to conquer Saigon. He was eager to embrace his elderly mother, brothers, and sisters after thirty years of separation. He was nostalgic to walk again on the soil of his beloved South. Once he arrived in Saigon, his first move was to contact and see Father.

The two brothers walked along the Saigon River, and Father told Uncle Ten that he would now inherit the Mytho house. Father's heir would have been his eldest son, Rene, but Rene had settled in France and would not return. Father's other sons were not interested with that house and the heavy burden of traditions involved with it. Besides, who knew what would happen to them after the Communist takeover? The winners were now the people who had fought loyally with Ho Chi Minh. Uncle Ten was one of them.

The lawyer Trinh Dinh Thao, Rene's father-in-law, was the president or a powerful member of the Provisional Revolutionary Government (PRG), a creation of the National Liberation Front of the South (FNL). Those South Vietnamese Communists or Vietcong thought that they would be among the first "liberators" to arrive in Saigon. That never happened. All political and military power was centralized under the iron grip of the North Vietnamese.

The Vietcong flag was blue and red with a yellow star. The first tanks entered Saigon flying the Vietcong flags. Soon after, those flags disappeared, and the Vietcong (South Vietnamese Communists), their National Liberation Front, and their Provisional Government of South Vietnam would face the same fate. The North Vietnamese Communists took power and discarded the Vietcong as insignificant entity. They had used the Vietcong during the war in the South. Now the Vietcong were useless to them. The former South Vietnamese leaders of the FNL and of the PRG became disappointed and bitter. During later years, they voiced their disillusions but were simply ignored. Ironically, most of their own children fled the Communist regime as boat people.

On April 30, 1975, Radio Hanoi endlessly broadcast, "Saigon has been liberated! Saigon has been liberated!"

Bui Tin, the North Vietnamese officer in charge of receiving the capitulation of President Duong van Minh, was also a journalist for Hanoi. He declared, "Today is a happy day. All the Vietnamese are the victors. Only the American imperialists have been defeated. If you love our nation and our people, you have nothing to fear."

The Communist leaders in Hanoi embraced each other. Commander Dinh Duc Thien said, "There has been no morning more fresh, beautiful, radiant, clear, cool and sweet-scented as this morning of total victory."

President Duong Van Minh and our brother Nguyen Vo Dieu were sentenced to live under house arrest. President Minh was forced to attend political brainwashing sessions. Henri was allowed to continue to manage his bank, the Trung Nam Bank, which was now nationalized by the state. His banking expertise was needed.

The Communists requisitioned one hundred beds at the French Grall Hospital for their wounded soldiers to be treated there.

A reporter wrote, "Fear of the Vietcong had made Saigon lose its wits." During the fall of Saigon, chaos and panic were everywhere. People tried to flee.

The merchant ship *Vietnam Thuong Tin*, bought by Henri in the 1960s as an investment for the Commercial Credit of Vietnam, fled Saigon transporting about three thousand bank employees and their families. The ship reached Guam and docked there.

At Guam, there were Vietnamese people who wanted to return to Vietnam because they had left wives and children behind. Now they were nostalgic and asked to return home to their families. Vietnam wanted the *Vietnam Thuong Tin* back in Vietnam, claiming it as their property. The United States repaired the ship and sent it back to Vietnam on October 16, 1975, with 1,546 people aboard.

The ship disappeared. No one knew what happened to this ship and its passengers. After more than ten years, the truth finally emerged. The ship's captain survived and explained that once they had arrived in Vietnam, they were detained. The captain was detained for twelve years. One of the survivors wrote a book titled *The Story of the Ship* Vietnam Thuong Tin.

Cousin Juliette Mi and her husband, Mr. Giang, fled aboard their merchant ship, the *Tan Nam Viet*. They called all of their family members and friends to come on their ship and flee with them. There were more than one thousand people crammed aboard, and they reached Guam. All of them were accepted as refugees by the United States. They were the luckiest refugees, being accepted by the United States and housed on US soil. They were very well looked after, had good food and clothing, and moved on to good lives and jobs. Most of those people went to Texas and California. Most of the Vietnamese refugees coming to the US preferred to settle in California if they could, because of the warm climate and the gorgeous vegetation. Later they became good American citizens, and their children contributed greatly to the US mainstream.

During that odyssey on the ship, Mr. Giang succumbed to the charms of a young girl. He abandoned Cousin Mi for a young and fresh girl. Cousin Mi took it calmly as being something from fate she could not control. She was not his first wife and she was not the last. She settled down with her sons in California. She had ten sons with Mr. Giang. In 1989, when Mr. Giang became very ill and was dying, Cousin Mi came to visit him and remained the only woman in his life who looked after him during his last months on earth. She cooked the food he liked, and she cared for him until he passed away.

In Saigon, Duong Van Minh and our brother Henri lived under house arrest from April 30, 1975, to 1982. Most of people sent to re-education camps were imprisoned there for an average of seven or eight years. The degree of hardships and sufferings they had to endure in those camps some would call "concentration camps" rather than "re-education camps" depended on what work they had done under the former regime and "what crimes" they had committed against the population. Henri was lucky to be sentenced to manage his own former bank as he had the expertise to do so. And so was our sister Annie who was sentenced to work for her own former brick factory as a vice-director. .

Henri's wife, Julie, was frightened to live under Communist rule, and she fled Saigon in 1975 with their three children. She succeeded in leaving Saigon on a regular airplane for Paris because she had kept a Cambodian passport, having been born in Cambodia. Her parents had to flee Phnom-Penh in 1975. The Khmer Rouge led by Pol-Pot, a cruel and sadistic leader, forced the population to evacuate Phnom-Penh, capital of Cambodia. Julie's parents had to walk all the way to Saigon and succeeded in getting to France thanks to their Cambodian passports.

Julie and their children (Sylvie, Alain, and Nathalie) lived in Montpellier, France. Julie was distraught, and it was during this period of her life that she became a pious Catholic, going to church as often as possible and volunteering her services to her parish church. She lobbied with the French bankers and with the French president Valery Giscard d'Estaing, begging them to intervene with the Vietnamese Communist authorities for the release of her husband.

In Saigon, Henri lived alone with their eldest daughter, Catherine, who had been brain damaged since birth, and with the elderly nanny who looked after Catherine. He went for lunch every day at Annie's house so he could keep in touch with our parents, Annie, Anna, and Francois, all of whom were living together. Our other brother Maurice – Brother Seven - was married and he lived with his wife and two small children, Henri had a loyal secretary who relayed messages between him in Saigon and his wife, Julie, in France. Henri had been always good to friends and staff, so in his darkest days, he found help from them. No one had harmed him.

My parents, Anna, Annie, Francois, Maurice, and Maurice's young family, did not escape during the fall of Saigon. One would never escape without the rest of the family. They remained tightly united as a family. Annie had received a message from Cousin Mi offering for all members of our family to come to their ship and flee with them. Annie did not want to leave, and consequently, she did not want other members of her family to go. She did not forward Cousin Mi's message to them.

Henry Kissinger described the last hours of the Fall of Saigon in a letter addressed to the "Fall of Saigon US Marines Association":

> The last days….As Americans were being lifted from the roof of the American Embassy during the morning of April 29, 1975 (Washington time), President Ford, Defense Secretary James Schlesinger and I briefed the congressional leadership. After that, all was silence. I sat

alone in the National Security advisor's corner office in the West of the White House, enveloped by the eerie silence that sometimes attends momentous events…Neither Ford nor I could influence the outcome any longer; we had become spectators of the final act. So we sat in our offices, unable to affect the ongoing tragedy. …Ford had ordered the evacuation to continue all night so that the largest number of Vietnamese might be secured….At 4.58 am in Saigon, Ambassador Graham Martin left with the 19th helicopter…Two hours later, North Vietnamese tanks rolled into Saigon…For the sake of our long-term peace of mind, we must someday undertake an assessment of why good men on all sides found no way to avoid this disaster and why our domestic drama first paralyzed and then overwhelmed us. But, on the day the last helicopter left the roof on the embassy, only a feeling of emptiness remained…The Vietnam War…Was it worth it? Probably not for us; almost surely for Saigon, about whose survival the war had, after all, been fought.

President Gerald Ford declared that the United States would welcome the Vietnamese refugees fleeing the Communist regime. He created the Inter-Agency Task Force on Indochinese Refugee Resettlement, recognizing that they were innocent victims of war. He said, "To ignore the refugees in their hour of need would be to repudiate the values we cherish as a nation of immigrants … To welcome them in the US is the least we could do for them. We owe it to them."

The Boat People

In 1978, our brother Francois fled Vietnam when he was about to be arrested because he had been assistant professor at the University of Saigon. Henri put him in a flimsy boat owned by Chinese friends. The boat capsized. After almost drowning, he was rescued by a US destroyer and was brought to a refugee camp in Malaysia. During his escape, he had suffered from fear, isolation, and malnutrition. He was unable to look after himself, not having been taught the necessary skills at home. His mind got deeper and deeper into a big hole of helplessness and despair. Some people in his refugee camp in Malaysia knew that he was gravely mentally ill, and they helped him to process his papers for immigration to Canada to join me in Ottawa. They wrote a letter to me suggesting that as soon as he landed in Ottawa, I should take him to the hospital. They also informed me that if they had not helped him to get to me, he would have been sent to a psychiatric hospital in Sweden. Sweden specialized in helping mentally ill refugees with psychiatric care.

When Francois arrived in Ottawa by plane with a load of refugees, it was terrible. He was very sick. A young refugee boy traveling alone, out of the goodness of his heart, had helped him out. When they arrived at the refugee hostel, Francois fell, and his glasses broke and were pressed into his eyes, making them bleed profusely. The young boy called a taxi and transported him to an emergency hospital. It was at that moment that my husband Julian and I arrived at the hostel. I had been tipped off by Can Le that my brother might have arrived. Can asked me, "Do you know if he was in a concentration camp?" I found his remark strange but did not pay attention to it.

The hostel receptionist told me that Francois had had a very bad accident and had been transported to the hospital, though he did not know which hospital. I had to search frantically in the telephone book and call a series of numbers. Finally I reached the Civic Hospital, and they confirmed with me that indeed a man had been transported there and that they knew nothing about him. He had no identification, and the young boy who accompanied him did not speak French or English. When we arrived, the first thing we did was pay the taxi driver, who was waiting to be paid.

When I showed up with Julian in the operating room, there was a large gathering of doctors surrounding Francois, who was lying in a bed. Heavy with a big belly, as I was expecting a baby, I announced that I was his sister. The doctors were relieved to see me and to hear that Francois had just come from a refugee camp from Malaysia. They had no clue who he was or why he was near death. He was in a very bad shape, but he was able to smile to me and say, "I am sorry for all the troubles I give you. Say thank you to your husband." Afterward he was put under anesthesia. I signed a paper giving my authorization to the doctors to operate on his eyes. I was told that they had never done that operation before. They could not tell me with certainty whether his eyes would be saved or he would end up blind.

Julian, I, and the young boy waited together for long hours at our home. The young boy was fit, good looking, and very smart. He was all alone but was very well balanced. I wanted to adopt him to be able to look after him and help him, but he refused. He wanted to go his own way, and I knew that he was able to become successful. He was a brilliant teenager.

Finally the doctors called me and announced that the operation had been successful. Francois would not be blind but would have to wear thick glasses. Francois told me that he had been displayed in his pajamas in front of an assembly of doctors and that he was in a medical journal as the first patient to undergo that particular eye operation.

He spent six months at the hospital, where they had to treat him for all kinds of things, including malnutrition and mental illness. He remained an outpatient for years to come. Francois was admirable because he refused the doctors' offer to put him on a disability pension. He worked and graduated from the University of Ottawa in computer science. He accomplished all that despite his mental illness (schizophrenia). He never was a burden to social services because he never stopped looking for jobs and he worked.

The number of boat people—Vietnamese people who fled the

Communist regime on flimsy boats across the South China Sea—grew dramatically. Marion Dewar, the mayor of Ottawa from 1978 to 1985, founded Project 4000 in June 1979 to welcome thousands of refugees to settle in Ottawa. That set a pattern of inspiration for other cities across Canada, churches, and individual groups to sponsor refugees. Project 4000 wound down in 1984, but Canada continued to generously open its door to the flow of Vietnamese refugees. Marion Dewar was elected as a member of Parliament from 1986 to 1988. She received the Order of Canada in 2002. She died in a fall in 2008. At her funeral in 2008, the Vietnamese community called her "the best friend of the Vietnamese community in Canada."

Flora McDonald, then minister of Foreign Affairs of Canada, under the conservative federal government of Prime Minister Joe Clark, succeeded in changing the immigration quota for refugees coming from Indochina (Vietnam, Cambodia, and Laos). It was increased from eight thousand per year to fifty thousand for humanitarian reasons. The following year, it would be increased to sixty thousand. Flora McDonald received the humanitarian Nansen Medal from the UNHRC. Canada became, along with the United States, one of the most generous nations in the world by opening its doors to the Vietnamese boat people and refugees. Flora died in 2015 at eighty-nine years old.

At the beginning of the 1980s, our brother Maurice, an engineer, and his wife, Bich Van, a chemist, escaped on the *Sky Luck* with their two small children. They decided to flee because they wished for their children to have a life of freedom in the West. The *Sky Luck* arrived near Hong Kong but was denied access to Hong Kong and had to stay far away from Hong Kong Harbor. The UNHRC sent its workers to bring food and water aboard. One day, during a big storm, the boat broke and sank, and the refugees swam to Hong Kong. They were granted asylum because the Geneva Convention forbade Hong Kong to turn away people once they had landed. Hong Kong's refugee camps were known to be very harsh. After several months there, Maurice and family succeeded in immigrating to Canada. They settled in Montreal.

Henri had helped Francois—and afterward Maurice, his wife, and their two children—to flee Vietnam aboard two boats owned by Chinese friends who were former customers at his bank. Henri also helped other youths, children of his friends, to escape. Henri did not pay the Chinese in Saigon and in any way, as he did not have any money to pay them. He gave only his word of honor. The deal with the Chinese friends was that they would be reimbursed when my two brothers reached the United States or Canada and secured jobs. They would then gradually pay back the money owed to the Chinese for their passage to freedom. Once in Canada, Francois and Maurice did reimburse the Chinese. It was their number-one priority.

Our Parents; Annie; Uncle Ten; the Mytho House

After the fall of Saigon, my parents went to live with Annie. She cared for them until their deaths, and both had Buddhist funerals. Annie built two marble monuments for them in our Mytho cemetery. Mother died in 1983, and Father died in 1994 in Ho Chi Minh City.

After Mother's passing, Father went to France with Anna under the UNHRC program of reunification of families. Both of them boarded an airplane from Saigon to Paris. Father could not adjust to life in France. He hated the Western lifestyle and manners. After two years in France, he asked to return to Ho Chi Minh City, and Annie welcomed him back into her house. Anna chose to remain in Paris and became a Buddhist nun.

In 1994, on his deathbed, Father clutched in his meagre fingers the only two cherished possessions he always had kept preciously with him, which were the Medal of the Legion of Honor from France and the Medal of Merit of Vietnam, testimony of his brilliant past career. Anna flew back from Paris, and Maurice from Montreal, to say farewell to him. He had eight children, but only three were present at his deathbed.

Annie, from 1971 to 1975, owned a brick factory. The Communists nationalized her factory and let her stay there to manage it as a vice director. Her salary was very little, but at least she was not persecuted by the new regime.

When Annie was an employer, she was fair and generous to her employees. She preached justice and socialism. During the fall of Saigon, when people ran everywhere in panic, and tried to escape, she remained calm and commented, "I don't understand why people are so afraid. After all, socialism is not so bad. It brings social justice to the poor." Those words from a woman who loved to live as a notorious capitalist were surprising, but that was Annie. She had always been unique in her own ways. Father and our brothers had always criticized her for her eccentric wardrobe, her makeup, and her jewelry. But Annie did not care about what they said. She lived her life the way she liked it.

Her attitude before the takeover of the South by standing firm on her ground and praising socialism proved to be rewarding for her. Her employees never accused her of any capitalistic wrongdoing, and they loved her. She was not put on trial for capitalistic crime. The new regime offered her a tour of North Vietnam, guided by a North Vietnamese woman.

Annie always had genial business ideas. She survived under the Communist regime because she rented rooms in her large house to foreigners, cooked meals for paying guests, and organized tours. With her business skills in hotels, food, and tourism, she became very wealthy.

Having made her money through tourism and having foreign renters who became her friends, Annie had traveled to Canada, the United States, Europe, and Australia to visit relatives and friends. I found her amazing. Considering that she was always alone, courageous in her ideas, unfazed by criticism, and genial in business, and that she had reached the pinnacle of financial success under a communist regime, without support from anybody, she was admirable.

Annie had never changed. As a teenager, she loved a life of elegance. Under the Communist regime, she always dressed very well and remained extravagant. Her house was large and beautiful with flowers, plants, and elegant artifacts. She was a good and charitable person. She was a pious daughter and took care of our elderly parents until their last breath. She fought hard when the Communists wanted to nationalize our land in the countryside of Mytho for road construction and destroy our cemetery. She refused to let them do it and won her case. She became the guardian of the family's memories and tombstones.

Many businesspeople built a new economic and capitalistic reality in a socialist Vietnam. As Vietnamese families were very united, the boat people who settled in Western countries sent money back home to family members stuck in Vietnam. That money allowed many in Vietnam to open lucrative businesses and prosper.

In 1975, when Uncle Ten returned from North Vietnam, he was the only Communist of the family. He became the one who would help his family deal with Communist hardships. This was his purpose in rushing back to the South. He loved his mother, brothers, and sisters and their children. Anna escaped by boat many times and was caught and imprisoned. Uncle Ten intervened and bailed her out. A Communist wanted to marry Annie. The family strongly opposed to it because he was a Communist and, truly or falsely, found him as ugly as a frog. It was Uncle Ten who took charge and told this man, "Please, stay away from my niece."

Uncle Ten had been rewarded as director of international trade, and he lived in Ho Chi Minh City with his wife and their daughter and a stepson. Unfortunately and sadly, he died suddenly. The unsung hero of the wars against France and the United States died at the hands of his wife, a North Vietnamese health care nurse he had met in North Vietnam when he was wounded. Thus he did not enjoy long years of peace or happiness in the South. He had remained an idealistic man who had no ambitions. His wife was greedy. They had bitter arguments. One day, maybe in a fit of rage, she killed him. She covered it up and declared that he had died from illness, but one of his close friends was suspicious, investigated, and discovered that she had murdered him. She was sentenced to ten years in jail.

The fate of our Mytho house, which Father had given to Uncle Ten, remained unclear. Father had not signed any documents regarding the house. After the tragedy that struck Uncle Ten, no one really wanted to claim this house. Cousin Phuoc had lived there since 1960 with Grandmother. After Grandmother's passing, she took in an elderly man with his own children. After Cousin Phuoc's death, this man continued to live there and considered it as his own house. He looked after the house, the cult of our ancestors, and the cult of his former companion, Cousin Phuoc. In 2017, the house was returned to Cousin Ten, Cousin Phuoc's younger brother.

Albert's remains were removed from Ho Chi Minh City. Albert had died in 1968 and was buried in Saigon. In the 1980s, the Communists ordered all burial monuments in Ho Chi Minh City to be destroyed to make way for a new modern city, and the remains were to be removed. Albert was reburied in our family cemetery at Mytho, next to our parents.

Our Permanent Mission in Geneva and Staff

Our Permanent Mission of Vietnam in Geneva closed its doors at the end of June 1975. Ambassador Le Van Loi was well liked and well respected, and the Swiss government allowed him to stay in our Moillebeau offices for two additional months after the fall of Saigon. He used this time to look after the Vietnamese people stuck in Switzerland—especially the students. He helped them to process their papers, apply for refugee status, and get jobs. That was not in his mandate. We only represented Vietnam to international conferences in Geneva. It was the responsibility of the Embassy of Vietnam in Bern to look after the Vietnamese stranded in Switzerland. However, the embassy had already closed its doors on April 30, 1975.

Pham Van Trinh, my former colleague, died in Geneva from throat cancer at forty years old.

Nguyen Cong Anh Tuan had a position with us for some years and was called back to Saigon prior to 1975. He was sent to a big battle where he lost his arms and legs in an explosion, and he was thereafter confined to a wheelchair. During the fall of Saigon, he was evacuated to the United States. His first wife, whom he loved dearly, had been killed in battle. His second wife left him for an American and went to live in the United States with her American husband, taking with her the two sons she had with Tuan. His third wife was young, pretty, and educated, and I liked her, but it was not a wedding based on love. He was a trusted assistant to President Nguyen Van Thieu. The president's wife wanted him to remarry before they sent him to Geneva. One of the young couple's duties, besides those of his posting at the mission, was to look after the two Thieu children studying in Geneva. After he was recalled back to Saigon, he and his third wife had a baby daughter and divorced.

I felt sorry for his tragic life. Trinh, Tuan, and I had shared one large office room at our Geneva mission. Tuan was a handsome young man and was perfectly trilingual. He attended international meetings and receptions with us. I was extremely proud of him. He presented well and was fluent in English and French. He was also a friend and was like a brother to me. He and his wife had invited me to their home, and I had seen there the two young children of President Thieu.

In 1976, Vietnam became the Socialist Republic of Vietnam. Its flag was red with a yellow star. Saigon was renamed Ho Chi Minh City. Our former Phan Thanh Gian Avenue where we had lived from 1951 to 1957 was renamed Dien Bien Phu Avenue.

In 1977, the Socialist Republic of Vietnam became a member of the United Nations.

My former ambassador, Mr. Le Van Loi, born in North Vietnam on October 15, 1927, died in Geneva on January 17, 2016, at eighty-eight years old. He was awarded the Medal of Merit of Vietnam, First Class, in 1968 and the Vietnam National Award for Economy Service, First Class, in 1969.

After the fall of Saigon in 1975, Mr. Le Van Loi remained in Geneva, Switzerland, and had a position at the United Nations as a consultant. He kept himself deeply involved with international UN projects, humanitarian aid to Vietnam, and many more achievements in Geneva. He was proud to be among the founders of the World Trade Organization (WTO), which is based in Geneva. In January 2007, Vietnam became the 150th member of the WTO. Mr. Loi was well respected by the new socialist government of Vietnam and was on friendly terms with its permanent representative to the United Nations in Geneva. Working as a consultant for the United Nations, Mr. Loi and his second spouse, Tove, returned to Vietnam many times. Holding a UN diplomatic passport, it was safe for him to travel to Vietnam, where he experienced the joy of again seeing his relatives and getting deeply involved with humanitarian projects to help the Vietnamese population.

When Mr. Loi lost his job as ambassador of Vietnam after the fall of Saigon in 1975, his Danish-born spouse, Tove, took an administrative position with the Permanent Mission of Australia in Geneva and worked there for the next twenty years, until her retirement. She was an admirable wife to him and cared for him until his last breath.

Mr. Loi was emotional any time I returned to Geneva and visited him. Both of us were the only surviving members of our mission in Geneva. We tried to locate our former colleague, Nguyen Cong Anh Tuan, which had been evacuated in 1975 to the United States, but we did not succeed.

Re-education Camps in Vietnam

The Communists sent most of the former public servants, soldiers and officers, and professionals who had worked for the former South Vietnamese regime to re-education camps to penalize them and to teach them Communist ideology. Those camps were also called concentration camps, and the various degrees of hardships and persecution the prisoners suffered there depended on the positions they had held under the former regime.

The duration of their stay in those camps in general would be seven years. This became the fate of two sons of Uncle and Aunt Three. They had lived their younger formative years with us in Saigon, so they were like our own brothers.

Cousin Nguyen Quoc Hung, a former judge of the Supreme Court, was sentenced to be imprisoned in the harshest re-education camp of North Vietnam. After his release, he was very sick. In some pages of the memoirs he wrote later, he stated that he was ordered to clean the latrines every day, which caused him to lose his sense of smell, as the odor was so intolerable. He and another prisoner were forced to push a cart full of heavy stones up and down a hill. They starved so much that, one day, the prisoners paid one of the guards to have a dead and emaciated dog cooked in the soup. He did not participate in this and did not eat the soup. The chief commander of this camp was a young tribal woman. She told him that he and the others were being punished for having chosen the wrong side of the war.

After his release, Nguyen Quoc Hung joined his wife and daughter in Paris. He joined the Association of French jurists in Paris.

When the last emperor of Vietnam, Bao Dai, died on July 30, 1997, at eighty-three years old in Paris, he had a Buddhist funeral service in Paris and also a Catholic funeral in a Catholic church. Nguyen Quoc Hung delivered his Buddhist eulogy with respect and praise. He liked our former emperor Bao Dai, whom he described as very intelligent and a victim of tragic political circumstances. Bao Dai was buried in the cemetery of Passy. The French government sent a squadron of guards to escort his hearse to the cemetery. The pope sent an envoy with a letter to be read at the church in his honor.

Cousin Nguyen Minh Chau, a former specialist in obstetrics and, during the war, a lieutenant colonel in the army serving at the Military Hospital of Saigon, was interned in a re-education camp. He volunteered to look after the health of the prisoners of his camp. After his release, he immigrated to the United States with his wife and two daughters. They chose to live in Chicago. The two daughters studied at the University of Chicago and married very well. Cousin Minh Chau died in Chicago.

Cousin Nguyen Xuan Hue was a member of the Permanent Delegation of Vietnam to UNESCO in Paris before the fall of Saigon. He became a refugee in Paris and later died in Paris.

After seven years of imprisonment, Cousin Tran Van Au, Uncle and Aunt Six's son, a former military doctor, fled Vietnam in a flimsy boat with other people. He drowned near Singapore.

Cousin Nguyen Van Trieu, Uncle Five's youngest son, escaped as a boat person with his niece Chi, who was his eldest sister's daughter. He immigrated to Canada. Meanwhile, Chi immigrated to California, where she graduated and practiced as a doctor. She sponsored her mother to come and live with her. Trieu married a Vietnamese girl in Calgary, and they built a very successful Vietnamese restaurant business. They were blessed with four handsome and talented children.

Uncle and Aunt Nine were sponsored by their four children, who were already well settled before 1975 in France and Canada. They lived first in France and afterward moved to Canada. They died in Montreal.

There was a longevity gene in my father's family. Father died at ninety-two years old. Grandmother and Great Aunt died beyond one hundred years old. Father's three sisters—Aunt Two, Aunt Six, and Aunt Nine—died some months before or after their one-hundredth birthdays.

My Life in Ottawa

In May of 1978, I became a Canadian citizen. A new law had shortened the amount of time required for citizenship application to only three years of residency as a landed immigrant. Before that it was a mandatory five years of residency. This new law was passed in order to help out the waves of newly arrived refugees.

On June 15, 1978, I married Julian Swann in Ottawa.

I met Julian Swann during a 1977 Christmas dinner at the home of a mutual friend, Anna Casey-Stahlmer. Anna, who was German born and divorced, was a brilliant public servant and socialite. I liked her; she was very nice to me. She had the idea to invite some friends for a German Christmas dinner.

The following day, Julian invited me, Elwyn Hopkin, and John Hayes for another Christmas turkey dinner at his apartment. On the third day, Julian called and asked if I would like to go out with him. We went to Sushi Gardens for dinner. We talked about our life stories. At the end of the dinner, he proposed marriage to me and I accepted. It was a very fast romance!

We married in Ottawa on June 15, 1978, in a church that was authorized to perform weddings, and we had a marriage license from city hall. We had only our two witnesses with us—Elwyn Hopkin for Julian and Ellen Wathen for me. I had a midlength white dress and white flowers stuck in my hair. In the evening, Julian took me to a restaurant called *Town and Country* for dinner. The waitress complimented me: "You look so beautiful."

I responded, "It is my wedding day."

She went to the kitchen and told the kitchen staff. The chef decided to bake an "Alaska ice bomb" to present it to us at the end of the meal.

However, unfortunately, Julian complained that his salmon was not good, and we decided to leave the restaurant. The waitress was very disappointed and informed us that the chef had baked a nice dessert for us to celebrate our wedding.

Our wedding reception took place on Saturday June 17, in the reception room of our building at Ambleside Drive. Julian was divorced. I had met him only after his divorce proceedings, so I was not involved with what went wrong with his former marriage.

Julian did not have money because he lost almost all his money, home and baby Nikola to his former wife. The law in Ontario gave the home and the baby to the wife in a divorce. I did not have money, being a recent immigrant and taking small jobs to earn my living. We could not afford a lavish wedding party. I spent the whole night buttering small canapés and sandwiches, and we bought small cakes. The wedding cake was baked and decorated by our friends John Hayes and Anna Casey-Stalhmer. I bought white chrysanthemums (cheap price) to decorate the room, and the ambassador of Belgium, Charles Kerremans, showed up at the reception with a bouquet of fifty red roses. Anna B. Sneider, senior counsellor at the Italian embassy, bought for us some Italian Asti as champagne. Dr. William Jeanes delivered the wedding speech. As family members, we had Julian's cousins, Bob and Erna Davidson from Toronto, and on my side, I had my charming young cousins Le Minh Quoc and his sister Therese Thu Huong accompanied by her husband, Nguyen Hoang Tuyen, from Montreal.

An unexpected guest showed up—Brian Sparks, a scientist, one of my dearest friends, who had moved to Toronto. The special thing about Brian was that we were born on the same day of the same year—November 3, 1941—he in England and I in Saigon. Being both Scorpios, a sign known for being deep and mysterious, we always watched to see what happened in the other's life. Brian had girlfriends but never married. He died from cancer in his sixties. On November third, 1975, he took me out for dinner to celebrate our birthdays at the restaurant Louis Neuf. He was not my boyfriend at all, but we were like twins, sharing the same Scorpio features. That meant that we had complicated love life stories.

The wedding pictures were taken at the nearby Experimental Farm, a popular site for wedding pictures because of its gorgeous flowers in the summer. It was a lovely day. I was glad to have those wedding pictures, in which Julian and I looked young and dashing.

Our 1978 Christmas season was spent with Julian's family in England. It was the first time I visited England. During my university youth in Europe, I had not visited England, Ireland, or the Nordic countries.

His parents lived in the midlands in Staffordshire, and Julian had graduated from the University of Manchester as a mechanical engineer. He had chosen to become a patent agent or attorney. He immigrated to Canada in 1968. His father was Geoffrey Swann, a solicitor. His mother, born as Adelaide Atcheson, came from a Northern Irish family.

Her sister Margaret married a judge who became Lord Kenneth Diplock, a member of the House of Lords. Lord Diplock was famous for writing the constitution of an African country after its independence from England and riding in the royal carriage with the king of that country. Afterward, he was famous for eliminating juries from trials involving Northern Irish prisoners. He did this to protect people from juries who could be threatened by the Irish republicans. He himself, as the judge, was in great danger, and he had bodyguards with him everywhere he went.

Julian's twin sister, Brigid, was a lawyer working for the government, and her husband, John Dunn, was a published novelist. He painted beautiful artworks as a hobby, and he loved to spend his time drinking at the local pub of his village near Chichester, West Sussex. After World War II, John Dunn was among the British officers who supervised the exodus of the Jewish people to Israel and the formation of the new State of Israel.

On June 29, 1979, our son, Christopher, was born in Ottawa at the Civic Hospital.

Me and baby Christopher Swann, Ottawa, 1979.

My daughter Sophie and my son Christopher, Geneva, 2010.

Our Brother Henri and Others

Our brother Henri and former president General Duong Van Minh were freed in 1983, and both immigrated to France.

Henri joined his wife, Julie, and the children, who had already settled in France in 1975. French bankers who knew him from past times gave him a position as a director in a French bank in Paris. He retired at age sixty, which was the normal age of retirement in France, refusing to accept a prolongation of his position because he felt it was not right for him to occupy a position that should go to a French-born younger man. He chose to retire in Montpellier because the cost of living was less expensive there than in Paris and because it was the university town of his student youth. He loved Montpellier. Julie, his wife, died in Montpellier in the spring of 1996.

President General Nguyen Van Thieu died in 2001 in Boston, Massachusetts, at seventy-eight years old.

Former president General Duong Van Minh died in 2001 at age eighty-five in Pasadena, California.

General Nguyen Cao Ky died in 2011 at age eighty in Kuala Lumpur, Malaysia. He had written the books *Twenty Years and Twenty Days* (1976), *How We Lost the Vietnam War* (1976), *and Buddha's Child: My Fight to Save Vietnam* (2002).

Tran Van Lam, a former minister of foreign affairs of the Republic of Vietnam from 1969 to 1973, died in Canberra, Australia, at age eighty-eight.

Mrs. Ngo Dinh Nhu lived through an incredible family tragedy. She was sister-in-law to President Ngo Dinh Diem, who, along with her husband, Ngo Dinh Nhu, was assassinated on November 1, 1963, during the generals' coup. Mrs. Nhu was then traveling across the United States with her eldest daughter, Le Thuy. Being outside of South Vietnam during the coup saved her life. Her three youngest children were in Saigon, but the generals decided to spare their lives and to send them over to her.

Mrs. Ngo Dinh Nhu's daughter Le Thuy, as a student in Paris, died after a head-on crash with another car. Ngo Dinh Can, known for his cruelty in Central Vietnam, was executed in 1964. Two other Ngo Dinh brothers happened to be outside of Vietnam in 1963. Ngo Dinh Luyen was an ambassador of the Republic of Vietnam to London, England. Ngo Dinh Thuc was archbishop of Hue and attended the second session of the Second Vatican Council at the Vatican. Both, of course, were banned from returning to Vietnam. Later on, while in France, Ngo Dinh Thuc was involved with traditionalist Catholic movements and consecrated several bishops and priests without the authorization of the Holy See. In 2010, Pope John Paul II excommunicated him.

Mrs. Nhu had chosen Italy as her country of exile and lived as a bitter recluse. She died in 2011 in Rome at eighty-seven years old. Following her wishes, her memoirs were published in Paris only after her death.

Some months after her death, her youngest daughter, Le Quyen, died in 2011 in an accident in Rome. She rode a bicycle to work and was hit by a car. She was a humanitarian and worked for the Italian Red Cross.

My Godfather Dies in Brussels

Andre Molitor, my godfather, died in Brussels in his sleep on June 4, 2005 at the age of ninety-four. His wife had predeceased him some years before.

He had been the principal private secretary of King Baudouin I from 1961 to 1977 (seventeen years). He spent thirty-five years teaching Belgian administration at the Catholic University of Louvain. After his retirement in 1977, he was appointed to the presidency of the King Baudouin Foundation, and he served in that position until 1986. A chair of international administrative and political reforms had been created at the Catholic University of Louvain in his honor.

He had written and published books in French.

His memoirs—*Memories – A witness involved in the Belgium of the 20th century (Souvenirs – un témoin engagé dans la Belgique du 20è siècle - Éditions Duculot, Paris-Gembloux (1984)* - Personal narrations – *The Happiness of Salernes (Le Bonheur de Salernes) - 1991* and *The Four Happiness (Les Quatre Bonheurs—Éditions Racine, 1998*). In 1993 he had participated in the publishing of a museum book called *Royal Palace Brussels*. This was in addition to numerous books and articles written for historical and academic purposes, such as *The Royal Function in Belgium*.

I had kept the letters he had written to me from 1961 to 2005 as a godfather.

During the Christmas season of 2004–2005, this was his last message to me from Brussels: "I am waiting eagerly to see the Face of the Eternal. I look at your picture and am proud of the woman you have become. May God bless you and keep you always with him."

The End of the Vietnam War; the Communist Victory and Its Consequences

In 1975, the North Vietnamese were victorious because they counted on the will of the American people to end this war no matter the consequences. The United States were far more powerful than North Vietnam in the matter of military strength, and they had dropped more powerful bombs on Vietnam than all bombs dropped on Nazi Germany during World War II. The B-52s did not decimate this tough and determined enemy. The United States lost the war because the American people were tired of continuing this war. The Communists expected that to happen.

A journalist for Hanoi and one of the commanding officers who entered the presidential palace during the fall of Saigon, when asked about the impact of Jane Fonda's visit to North Vietnam in 1972, an act that had been vilified by the US soldiers as an act of treason, said, "In the USA, the people were divided. People like Jane Fonda, the main war activist, started protesting about the war. She was responsible in convincing a lot of people to go against the war. The USA, the strongest nation in the world, was brought down from the inside. While the North Vietnamese Army were having feelings of omnipotence due to public support, Jane Fonda and her followers were slowly stabbing America's will to fight. I am convinced that if only the Americans had the same will as the North Vietnamese had, America would have won the war."

General Vo Nguyen Giap confirmed that "the Vietnam War was not lost in Vietnam. It was lost at home." It exposed the power of the media to influence the heart and will of the American public.

The consequences of the defeat of the United States and the Republic of Vietnam regarding the Vietnam War resulted in a loss of prestige for the United States around the world as a world superpower and earned it the reputation of a country that did not keep its promise to its allies. It was the most crushing defeat in US military history. Almost three million Vietnamese and more than fifty-eight thousand Americans were killed.

The fall of Saigon created the greatest Vietnamese exodus in Vietnam History. People fled the horrors committed by the Communist regime, and the best way for them to escape was to jump into flimsy little boats and head out toward the high seas. Between 1975 and 1995, two millions fled Vietnam and more than one million escaped by boat. The UNHRC estimated that four hundred thousand died by drowning or being killed by pirates.

General Nguyen Cao Ky, during the fall of Saigon, initially refused to flee the country. But in the end, he changed his mind, flew his plane out of Saigon, and landed on the USS Midway. In 1976, as a refugee in the United States, he commented, "Once again, I reiterate the fact that we needed America. We could never have fought the Communists alone. But how much better it would have been if the Americans had never appeared in the picture and we Vietnamese had combined patience with American economic aid and expertise to improve the lot of the average Vietnamese family and the skills of our fighting men. We could have won the war."

Henri Kissinger wrote, "Vietnam is still with us. It has created doubts about American judgment, about American credibility, about American power, not only at home, but throughout the world. It has poisoned our domestic debate. So we paid an exorbitant price for the decision that were made in good faith and for good purpose."

President Gerald Ford blamed Congress for the loss of Vietnam. He told the American Society of newspapers Editors in April 1975, "The action of Congress did not make me proud to be an American. The United States did not carry out its commitment. If we had, this present tragic situation in South Vietnam would not have occurred."

President Richard Nixon wrote in 1985, "We fought in Vietnam because there were important strategic interests involved. But we also fought because our idealism was at stake. If not the United States, what nation would have fought for over a decade in a war half a world away at great cost to itself in order to save the people of a small country from communist enslavement?"

In 1988, President George H. W. Bush declared, "The war cleaves us still, but surely the statute of limitations has been reached. The final lesson is that no great nation can long afford to be sundered by a memory."

In 1994, thanks to President Bill Clinton, the United States lifted its thirty-year trade embargo against Vietnam. President Clinton was also the first US president to visit Vietnam since the end of the war in 1975. He received an enthusiastic welcome from the Vietnamese population.

In 1995, Vietnam and the United States restored full diplomatic relations. Vietnam also became a full member of the Association of Southeast Asian Nations (ASEAN).

Robert S. McNamara, secretary of defense for Presidents Kennedy and Johnson, was enthusiastic in the beginning to commit America into Vietnam. Disenchanted by failures, he left and became president of the World Bank. In his book *In Retrospect*, written in 1995, he described how the war had tormented Lyndon B. Johnson and had damaged his presidency. He concluded, "We of the Kennedy and Johnson administrations who participated in the decisions on Vietnam acted according to what we thought were the principles and traditions of this nation. We made our decisions in light of those values. Yet we were wrong, terribly wrong. We owe it to future generations to explain why."

Gloria Emerson, a journalist, wrote in her book *Winners and Losers*, "Each winter, walking the streets of different American cities, I used to look at the younger men in surplus army jackets, some with the patches I knew so well...For a long time, I could not bear those jackets, always suspecting they had been taken off the American corpses in Vietnam, sanitized, pressed and sold as surplus."

Tiziano Terzani, an Italian journalist, in his book *Liberation!*, wrote that he felt both "a great admiration and a subtle fear that the revolution was close to the border of Inhumanity."

In 2004, Guy Mettan, a Swiss journalist, published a book titled *Geneva, City of Peace*. He interviewed both my former ambassador, Le Van Loi, and General Vo Nguyen Giap, asking them to offer their comments about the Vietnam War.

Mr. Le Van Loi, in his interview (titled "Vietnam as a Stake in the Cold War") showcased the fact that Vietnam was a pawn in the Cold War between the United States and the Union of Soviet Socialist Republics. General Vo Nguyen Giap spoke about "Thirty years of a national liberation war."

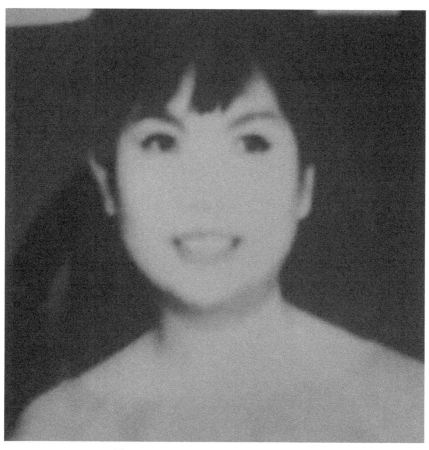

Alice Nguyen Swann, Geneva, 1973